COMMUNICATION GENIUS

COMMUNICATION
GENIUS

**40 insights
from the
science of
communicating**

TONY BUON

ABOUT THE AUTHOR

Tony Buon, Dip. Wel., BA (Psych), MA (Hons), Dip. Med., Grad Edu, CEAP, Cert. Med., MMII

Tony Buon is a psychologist, educator and author. His last book was *The Leadership Coach* (Hodder & Stoughton, 2014). Tony holds graduate and postgraduate degrees in psychology, behavioural sciences and workplace education. He is also an accredited mediator.

He specializes in workplace psychology, leadership and communication. Tony has lectured at leading universities in the UK and Australia. Among the subjects he has taught are psychology, leadership, HRM, education and criminology. He has also taught on an accredited MBA programme in Scotland.

Tony was born in Scotland and spent many years living in Australia. Today he lives in London, England. He has worked in more than 35 countries and with many of the world's leading organizations. His work has been featured in publications as diverse as *Rolling Stone* and the *Reader's Digest*. He has appeared on CNN, the BBC, Trans-World Sport and many international television and radio stations.

He is contactable through his website: www.buon.net

ACKNOWLEDGEMENTS

I would like to recognize the scientists, psychologists, philosophers, sociologists and great thinkers whose work I have examined and discussed in this book. Without their painstaking and thoughtful contributions to the science of communication, this book would have been impossible. I really do feel I have been *standing on the shoulders of giants*.

On a more personal note, I would also like to acknowledge the everlasting love and support of my wife, Caitlin. Her comments and suggestions on my early drafts were invaluable. Her support of me as a person is eternal. This book is dedicated, with much love, to her.

'This book is about the art and practice of communicating. It explores the issues and downsides of poor communications, providing both case studies and practical tips about how to communicate more effectively at work. This is a must-read for managers and others at work if you want to communicate better.'

Professor Sir Cary Cooper, Manchester Business School, University of Manchester

'*Communication Genius* is an essential read for everyone who appreciates the value of communicating more effectively. This book makes accessible to a wide readership many of the best practices and ideas of insightful thinkers and practitioners.'

Professor Ashly Pinnington, Dean of Research, The British University in Dubai

'After spending more than 30 years dealing with workplace communication issues in both the private and public sectors, along with a history of teaching that spans nearly as long, Tony Buon has effectively channelled the most applicable of workplace communication issues into one book. Tony is a communication guru and this book assembles years of experience in the area into a practical guide and resource. A valuable tool, I strongly suggest this as required reading for anyone seeking to better their communication skills in the workplace and otherwise.'

Dr Anastasia P. Rush, Clinical Psychologist, CEO HELLAS EAP (Greece)

'Tony Buon is a master of communication. His dynamic workshops and ebullient teaching style engage audiences from all sectors. His new book reflects this bold and challenging approach and he uses in-depth research to lead us through a fascinating exploration of communication strategies and methods. He calls into question accepted 'beliefs' (Maslow's hierarchy) and introduces the reader to an array of new theories from 'IQ' racism to the Obama effect. Managers at all levels will find the stimulating content immensely valuable both for themselves and their teams as they grapple with the intricacies of effective communication in a fast-changing corporate world.'

Kate Nowlan, Chief Executive, CiC Employee Assistance, Fellow Royal Society of Arts (FRSA)

'Tony has done a fantastic job in pulling together an amazing number of articles and scientific studies and making them understandable to the layperson – I certainly recommend this book!'

Andrew Kinder, Chartered Counselling & Chartered Occupational Psychologist, Employee Assistance Professionals Association (EAPA – UK) Chair

First published in Great Britain in 2015 by Hodder & Stoughton. An Hachette UK company.

First published in US in 2015 by Quercus US

British Library Cataloguing in Publication Data: a catalogue record for this title is available from the British Library.

Library of Congress Catalog Card Number: on file.

Paperback ISBN 978 1 47360 540 4

eBook ISBN 978 1 47360 546 6

1

The publisher has used its best endeavours to ensure that any website addresses referred to in this book are correct and active at the time of going to press. However, the publisher and the author have no responsibility for the websites and can make no guarantee that a site will remain live or that the content will remain relevant, decent or appropriate.

The publisher has made every effort to mark as such all words which it believes to be trademarks. The publisher should also like to make it clear that the presence of a word in the book, whether marked or unmarked, in no way affects its legal status as a trademark.

Every reasonable effort has been made by the publisher to trace the copyright holders of material in this book. Any errors or omissions should be notified in writing to the publisher, who will endeavour to rectify the situation for any reprints and future editions.

Typeset by Cenveo® Publisher Services.

Printed and bound in Great Britain by CPI Group (UK) Ltd., Croydon CR0 4YY.

John Murray Learning policy is to use papers that are natural, renewable and recyclable products and made from wood grown in sustainable forests. The logging and manufacturing processes are expected to conform to the environmental regulations of the country of origin.

Hodder & Stoughton Ltd
Carmelite House
50 Victoria Embankment
London EC4Y 0DZ
www.hodder.co.uk

CONTENTS

INTRODUCTION

Prison Captain: *You gonna get used to wearing them chains after a while, Luke. Don't you never stop listening to them clinking, 'cause they gonna remind you what I been saying for your own good.*

Luke: *I wish you'd stop being so good to me, Cap'n.*

Prison Captain: *Don't you ever talk that way to me. (Pause, then hitting him) Never! Never! (Luke rolls down hill: to other prisoners) What we've got here is... failure to communicate*
Cool Hand Luke (classic 1967 movie)

Ironically, the prison captain's famous line from the movie *Cool Hand Luke* is often misquoted as 'What we have here is a failure to communicate' rather than what is actually said: 'What we've got here is [pause] failure to communicate.'

Communication is fraught with difficulties. In particular, there are serious problems when something is said and then passed on.

In this book, I have taken 40 significant examples of research into communication. After reading thousands of journal articles, research papers, book chapters and essays, I selected 40 examples of the best that science has to offer in relation to human communication. These examples each appear as a separate chapter.

Many of the myths explored in this book are due to people reading *third* or even *tenth*-hand accounts. A classic example of this is the Mehrabian Myth that body language makes up 93 per cent of all communication (... it doesn't). This common misreporting of Albert Mehrabian's original work is covered in the first chapter and is just one of many myths we will be resolving in this book.

There is a lot of myth and hearsay about communication as well as thousands of books, many of which disagree with each other. *Communication Genius* is an attempt to present a new and different approach. This book aims to cut through the noise to bring you proven research from around the world, in a clear and easy-to-understand way.

In reading the 40 chapters, you'll get to know the scientific facts and arguments surrounding some of the most vital issues in communication. Each chapter not only describes the research but it also shows you how to make use of it in your work and life. By reading through all the chapters of this book, you will be introduced to some of the most important concepts in human communication and you will improve your own communication skills.

It is often said that authors write the books they want. This is certainly true for this book. To have access to both classic studies and the latest neurological research in one book is rare. It is even rarer to have research from diverse disciplines in one volume. In *Communication Genius* we explore research from social psychology, medicine, anthropology, philosophy, experimental psychology, neuroscience, psychotherapy and even software engineering.

The work discussed in the 40 chapters covers more than 60 years, with the earliest paper reviewed from 1951 and the latest from 2015. Each represents a compelling and significant contribution to the study of communication. Some are classic papers and others put forward cutting-edge neuro-scientific research.

STRUCTURE OF THE CHAPTERS

Each chapter is separate and you do not need to read them in any order. You can, of course, do this or you may like to read through the individual themes indicated below. Alternatively, just go to the index or the listing of research articles at the end of the book and jump to the area that most interests you.

Where one chapter relates to another, this is indicated at the end of each chapter. Each chapter has a brief introduction to the topic, followed by a description of the research and this is followed by discussion on how to apply this to your work and personal communication.

There are six themes that run throughout the book. These include common myths about communication, practical skills in communication, classic studies revisited, cultural research, neuroscientific research and social media. Of course, some chapters' crossover themes, but this classification scheme will help you navigate to the sections that most interest you.

1. Common myths about communication

The science of human communication is filled with myths. This is not surprising when you consider how complex humans are and how communication is studied across many disciplines. Further new research is often in scientific journals that are not readily available.

The myths explored involve communication issues relating to matters such as Emotional Intelligence (EI) and the efficacy of Neuro-linguistic Programming (NLP). We also look at commonly held positions on motivation, gender and brainstorming. Many of these subjects are taught by corporate trainers and/or blogged online by people who carelessly and uncritically repeat what they have read in self-help books without going to the source documents.

The following chapters explore commonly held beliefs that require rethinking:

Chapter 1: Communication is not all about body language

Chapter 2: Men and women are not from different planets

Chapter 3: Brainstorming: you may have been doing it incorrectly

Chapter 4: Does everybody lie?

Chapter 5: Can your handwriting reveal your personality?

Chapter 6: Maslow was wrong, your needs are not hierarchical

Chapter 7: The myths of emotional intelligence

Chapter 8: Subliminal communication: hidden messages

Chapter 9: Women do not talk more than men

Chapter 10: NLP and communication

Chapter 11: The placebo effect and communication

A pseudoscience is an idea or method presented as scientific when it is not; examples include astrology, clairvoyance and homoeopathy. The last chapter in this section (Chapter 11) will help explain why many myths seem believable and why many pseudosciences appear to work.

2. Practical skills in communication

It is hoped that this book will also support you in developing your communication skills. To help you achieve this goal, there are practical chapters covering areas related to skills development. Of course, the knowledge from the rest of the book will help with this, but these chapters have a particular focus on the practical development of communication skills.

The chapters with specific real-world application include:

Chapter 12: Attending skills in communication: the SOLER model

Chapter 13: Discovering active listening

Chapter 14: Restricting PowerPoint® to enhance communication

Chapter 15: Space wars: why proxemics matters

Chapter 16: Mimicry, mirroring and the chameleon effect

Chapter 17: Checking your email too often wastes time

Chapter 18: Stop judging a book by its cover

Chapter 19: Paraphrasing and listening

3. Classic studies revisited

There are many classic studies in communication and it would be impossible to cover them all in this book. However, probably the three most famous studies in psychology *are* included. These are the Asch experiments into conformity, the Milgram experiments into obedience and the Zimbardo prison experiments. While these are well-known studies, they are often wrongly reported. For example, Friend, Rafferty & Bramel examined how the Asch studies were reported in 99 psychology textbooks, and found that more than half the authors had distorted Asch's findings (1990).

As with many great ideas, a lot can be lost over time when people do not look at what was originally published. In all cases, I have attempted to go to the original publications to see what was actually said. Sometimes this was difficult as many of the older publications were out of print.

For example, Zimbardo's Stanford Prison Experiments of the 1970s was never published in a peer-reviewed journal (Haslam & Reicher, 2014). As Haslam & Reicher point out, this makes it very difficult to get a 'definitive account' of what actually happened (p 131). For this particular chapter, I reviewed several hundreds of pages from the *Philip G. Zimbardo Papers* and more than 30 published reviews of his work.

Chapter 20: We are all individuals, or are we?

Chapter 21: Obedience: the communication of compliance

Chapter 22: Communicating violence

Chapter 23: Groupthink: revisiting the theory of error

Chapter 24: The Forer Effect: gullibility in action

Chapter 25: Educational credentials and the racism of intelligence

The chapter on Irving Janis's theory of Groupthink may be less known to many readers. But the ideas are just as important. As is the Chapter on Bertram Forer's explanation of why people accept general 'personality' statements as being uniquely applicable to them.

The last chapter in this section is very different from most of the others as it is a philosophical speech. It was given by one of the greatest philosophers of the 20th century, Pierre Bourdieu. This short speech given to a UNESCO Colloquium in 1978 has changed many people's views about issues related to power, credentials, *cultural-capital* and communication.

4. Cultural research

All communication is cultural. So it was essential that this book look at the issues related to national and other types of culture. There are many different types of culture. These include occupational, organizational, age and gender. However, national culture is possibly the most persuasive.

Effective cross-cultural communication demands an understanding of the complexities of culture from structural, political, social and psychological perspectives. The five chapters in this section, along with others in this book, will increase your cultural awareness in relation to cross-cultural communication. The specific chapters about cultural issues in this book are:

Chapter 26: Measuring national culture

Chapter 27: Cultural differences in communication

Chapter 28: Silence as a form of communication

Chapter 29: Communication and facial expressions

Chapter 30: The Obama Effect: reducing stereotyping

5. Neuro-scientific and brain research

There are many myths about the brain, from the classic untruth that we use only '10 per cent of our brains' (we use the entire brain), through to the notion that people are either 'right-brained' or 'left-brained'. Brain research is also often oversold in the media and online (often as click-bait).

The research provided in this book is all from excellent journals and writers with impeccable credentials. Chapter 32 even introduces new research that demonstrates that simply having *images* of brains in an article can have a persuasive influence on the public's perception of articles (McCabe & Castel, 2008). I am proud to say, there are no such images in this book!

Chapter 31: Communication starts with the eyes

Chapter 32: Neuro-scientific communication

Chapter 33: Our brain cannot cope with too much information

Chapter 34: Reading a good book may improve your empathy

Chapter 35: Using big words doesn't make you look smarter

6. New media

Social media has become a significant way of communicating for hundreds of millions of people. Social networking tools like Twitter, Facebook, LinkedIn and the many new sites appearing every week have enabled the exchange of ideas so quickly and extensively that for many it is difficult to keep up.

Chapter 36: Turning off your smartphone can make you work smarter

Chapter 37: Social media communication

Chapter 38: Online communication: why do people troll?

Chapter 39: Selfies: a new form of communication

Chapter 40: Swearing, cursing and communication

The last chapter about swearing and cursing could have been placed elsewhere, but I wanted it to be the final chapter of this book. It also carries a warning as some of the language in this chapter could offend some people. Though the language used does have a scientific and not salacious purpose.

COMMENT ON SCIENTIFIC RESEARCH

Scientific journals often sit behind 'paywalls', making it difficult and expensive for anyone other than academics and students to access them. Often, scientific papers are difficult to read and are full of material that only interests others in a very narrow arena. Many articles published in journals are written for a minuscule and specialist audience.

Scientific journals and the publication of research is also fraught with difficulties – including 'publication bias' where only papers with a positive or significant finding are published and this can lead to misleading biases in the literature.

There is also a problem with the 'publish or perish' phenomenon, where there is severe pressure on academics to publish academic work. It has been suggested that the pressure on academics to publish can discourage bold and original work (Smith, 1990). This can mean that the focus is on what will be published rather that what should be.

Judging the quality of published materials is also a minefield. In one reported case, a once-respected Canadian medical journal was sold to new owners in 2013 and according to the *Ottawa Citizen*, they will 'print anything for a fee'. The Canadian newspaper decided to test the journal and sent them a made up 'outrageously bad manuscript' and the required CAN$1,200 fee. The article had a ridiculous title, was a plagiarized article on HIV, with the word HIV replaced with 'cardiac' and graph captions, but no graphs (Spears, 2014). The article was published.

All of this makes it very difficult for the non-academic reader to get a clear picture of any field just by reading research abstracts (available for free) – or to try to make sense of the often conflicting arguments in books and good online blogs. It doesn't help that often ill-read and lazy bloggers will just cut and paste incorrect theories from one site to another.

For example, in relation to the Mehrabian Myth (Chapter 1), I found dozens of online sites and articles quoting the '7 per cent–38 per cent–55 per cent' formula incorrectly. More worryingly, I found the formula in several 'peer-reviewed' papers, formal textbooks and even in two recently published books on communication.

A CHALLENGE TO YOU, THE READER

In this book, I have been as rigorous and cautious as I can be to check every source and reference. I have conducted extensive literature searches and sourced archival documents. I have looked at original materials, not online sources.

But no research is perfect. So in advance I apologize for any errors made and if they exist, they are all mine. If you do find any mistakes, please let me know so they can be corrected in any possible later editions.

Some of the areas I have covered in this book may also upset some people. In particular, those with a 'fundamentalist' approach to certain areas may not appreciate the criticisms of their 'gurus'. Only recently, I was explaining to a young engineer on a training course in Dubai about the Maslow hierarchy-of-needs myth. The nice fellow got infuriated with me, saying I was 'defaming one of his heroes'.

I explained to him that I thought Maslow was a great scientist who contributed much to the field of motivation and psychology, particularly with his focus on the positive in people. It was just that new research and thinking has informed the area. There is no evidence to support the contention that needs are hierarchical, as Maslow suggested. The young engineer agreed with my arguments, but he was still not happy.

I am sure that some graphologists, purveyors of subliminal tapes, those who claim to have psychic powers and even some NLP practitioners may be unhappy with some of the research provided and discussed in the next 40 chapters. That's OK with me. My aim is to encourage discussion and critical thought.

I also challenge you, the reader of this book, to read the chapters and if there is something you don't agree with, have a look at the original research. You can also see that I have provided you with extensive further reading references and weblinks to online material and YouTube™ videos. Please explore these and if you wish to contact me about anything in this book, please feel free to do so – either via my website, on LinkedIn® or by email.

As a closing thought, I was recently consulting with a large social media firm and was told by the young senior managers that if you want to know if you are *old*, take this quick test:

How do you like to communicate with friends?

By letter – *you're old*

By email – *you're old*

By text – *you're getting old*

By Facebook – *you're middle-age*d

By Twitter & BBM – *you used to be young*

By WhatsApp, Snapchat, Instagram, Viber – *you're young (for now)*

I think they were trying to tell me something, and interestingly all I got was blank looks when I asked about *faxing* or *telexes*. I hope you enjoy the book, whatever your age.

References

Friend, R., Rafferty, Y., & Bramel, D. (1990), 'A puzzling misinterpretation of the Asch "conformity" study', *European Journal of Social Psychology*, Vol. 20 Issue 1 pp 29–44

Haslam, S. A. & Reicher, S. (2012), 'Tyranny: revisiting Zimbardo's Stanford Prison Experiments' (pp 126–41). In Smith, J. R. & Haslam, S. A. (2012), *Social Psychology: Revisiting the Classic Studies*. London: Sage

McCabe, D. P. & Castel, A. D. (2008), 'Seeing is believing: The effect of brain images on judgments of scientific reasoning', *Cognition*, Vol. 107 Issue 1 pp 343–52

Philip G. Zimbardo Papers (1953-2004) [SC0750] Department of Special Collections and University Archives, Stanford University Libraries, Stanford, California

Smith, P. (1990), *Killing the Spirit: Higher Education in America*. New York: Viking

Spears, T. (2014), *Ottawa Citizen*, Published August 20, 2014. Accessed 16/4/15 from: http://ottawacitizen.com/technology/science/respected-medical-journal-turns-to-dark-side

1 COMMUNICATION IS NOT ALL ABOUT BODY LANGUAGE

*The captains of England and Australia can barely exchange
pleasantries these days without a body-language expert
immediately declaiming on the angle of their handshakes.*
Lawrence Booth, cricket writer and editor of
Wisden Cricketers' Almanack

Body language is a popular term for the process of
communicating non-verbally through conscious or unconscious
gestures and actions. This includes the subtle movements of the
face and the body. In modern usage, it can also cover vocal tone,
nuance and intonation (Morris, 1967).

It is very common to hear speakers and business trainers claim
that words account for 7 per cent of the meaning of the message,
tone of voice for 38 per cent, and body language 55 per cent.
However, few speakers and trainers seem to have bothered to
read the original research and continue to popularize the 93 per
cent myth.

In 1971, Professor Albert Mehrabian, a professor of psychology
at UCLA, wrote a book called *Silent Messages*. In this and in a
book published a year later (*Non-Verbal Communication*, 1972),
he focused on a very specific area of communication research.
This was the communication of positive or negative emotions via
single spoken words.

Mehrabian's primary assumption is that only a few basic
dimensions of human emotions are conveyed non-verbally.
He states these are: *like-dislike*, *status* and *responsiveness*

(1971). Mehrabian derived his ideas about the percentages of communication that are verbal or non-verbal from two studies he published in 1967.

In the first experiment (Mehrabian & Ferris, 1967), people listened to a recording of a woman saying the word 'maybe' in three different tones to suggest liking, neutrality and disliking. The male subjects were shown photos of women's faces demonstrating the three emotions and were asked to guess the emotions indicated by three types of communication. That is the gestures in the photos, the voices alone, and then both together. The photos received more accurate responses by a ratio of 3:2. This suggests that when we receive conflicting messages, we tend to believe what we see.

In the second experiment (Mehrabian & Wiener, 1967), subjects listened to nine recorded words: three suggesting liking ('honey', 'dear' and 'thanks'), three suggesting neutrality ('maybe', 'really' and 'oh!') and three suggesting disliking ('don't', 'brute' and 'terrible'). The words were spoken with different tones, and the subjects were asked to deduce the emotions contained in the words as spoken. The experiment found that the tone of voice had more influence on meaning.

Mehrabian then combined the two sets of data in his 1971 book (where most people seem to get the data from) to suggest the ratio of 7:38:55. In this book he asks the question, is there a systematic and coherent approach to resolving the general meaning or impact of an inconsistent message? (p 43). Mehrabian, based on his laboratory studies, suggests there is. He states that his experimental results show: Total *Liking* = 7 per cent Verbal *Liking* = 38 per cent Vocal *Liking* = 55 per cent Facial *Liking* (p 43).

So the impact of facial expression is stronger than just words. If the facial expression is inconsistent with the words, the degree of *liking* conveyed by the facial expression will dominate. Mehrabian concluded that if words and non-verbal messages are in conflict, people have confidence in the non-verbal. For example, on the telephone, if a person's vocal tone contradicts the words spoken, then the tone is what determines the total impression.

This is interesting work, but it is also very narrow and applies only to the communication of liking and attitudes. It cannot be extrapolated to communication in general. Mehrabian himself states on his website (2015) the warning:

Please note that this and other equations regarding relative importance of verbal and non-verbal messages were derived from experiments dealing with communications of feelings and attitudes (i.e., like-dislike). Unless a communicator is talking about their feelings or attitudes, these equations are not applicable (Mehrabian, 2015).

For example, can you watch a foreign film and still understand 93 per cent of what is happening. Does a book only convey 7 per cent of its meaning from the text? Can you visit a country where you do not know the language and still understand most of what you hear? Of course not.

Mehrabian never said in any publication that 93 per cent of communication is non-verbal. In fact, speech writer Max Atkinson quotes personal communication from Mehrabian to him about the myth in his 2014 book on communication. Mehrabian says:

I am obviously uncomfortable about misquotes of my work. From the very beginning I have tried to give people the correct limitations of my findings. Unfortunately the field of self-styled 'corporate image consultants' or 'leadership consultants' has numerous practitioners with very little psychological expertise (2014: p 228).

The complexity of human communication

In *New Scientist*, Caroline Williams reports that Mehrabian 'cringes every time he hears his theory applied to communication in general' (2013). In many ways, it is more interesting that the Mehrabian Myth has continued to be so resilient. Its appeal is probably linked to the fact that it is based on 'scientific research' and that it has a set of statistics that are easy to teach.

So just how important is body language and why is the 7 per cent – 38 per cent – 55 per cent formula so wrong? Body language depends on the situation entirely. Words are important and so are body gestures, vocal tone and eye movement. Any formula of how much communication is non-verbal is meaningless. It will always depend on a multiplicity of factors including context, culture and the environment (Knapp & Hall, 2005; Hostetter, 2011).

Non-verbal communication is a very complex area and requires careful analysis. Make sure it is research-based and that the research has not been conducted solely in a laboratory or just with rats. The study of non-verbal behaviour, with its strong situational, cultural and environmental influences must be researched in 'real world' settings wherever possible (Lee et al, 1992; Knapp & Hall, 2005).

Words are only part of the message, but they are a vital part. Non-verbal communication (such as tone and body gestures) supports the words spoken by conveying the speaker's feelings (McNeill, 1992). Words are vital in communication; just consider how hard it was to guess that movie title in the last game of 'charades' you played.

Non-verbal communication depends on the context. What something 'means' in one situation may be very different in another. For example, a raised voice in a negotiation can suggest anger or simply game-playing. Further, most children learn to read the facial expressions of their primary caregivers very early and can quickly read when a scolding is genuine or fake.

Most people seem to believe that when someone folds their arms they are defensive. However, this gesture can mean many different things in different situations. The person could be cold, confident, self-comforting or even vulnerable (Williams, 2013). Without culture, context and environment it is impossible to read this single gesture.

It is always better to look for clusters of gestures rather than trying to read a single gesture. For example, if a person scratches their face it does not mean they are lying (James, 2008).

However, if they scratch their face, pause, speak in a monotone and don't blink, then you may start to question what they are telling you. Of course, the above behaviours should be compared to a person's baseline (normal) behaviour.

Be aware of cultural differences in non-verbal communication. Certain gestures appear to be very similar in all people, for example, smiling and fear (Ekman, Sorenson & Friesen, 1969; Ekman, 2001). However, some body language is very specific to a particular group. Awareness of how your body language differs from others is a very useful insight and the way to improve communication.

To suggest that words make up only 7 per cent of communication is incorrect. Words are incredibly powerful. Words can hurt, and they can heal. Consider for a moment the impact of the words 'you are stupid' on a five-year-old when spoken by a teacher or parent. Consider how important the word 'sorry' is when resolving conflict or healing pain.

So what are the big takeaways here?

- **Next time you hear a body-language 'expert' tell you that words comprise only 7 per cent of the message,** be aware that they may not have read the research they are quoting.
- **The 7 per cent–38 per cent–55 per cent rule, where words make up only 7 per cent of communication, is wrong.** This formula cannot be applied to communication in general.
- **Dismiss simplistic guides to complex issues like non-verbal communication.** Human behaviour is very complex and one-dimensional explanations are often ill-informed.

Sources

Mehrabian, A. (1971), *Silent Messages*. Belmont, CA: Wadsworth

References

Atkinson, M. (2014), *Seen & Heard: Conversations and commentary on contemporary communication in politics, in the media and from around the world*. London: Sunmakers

Ekman, P. (2009), *Telling lies: Clues to Deceit in the Marketplace, Politics, and Marriage*. New York: W. W. Norton & Company

Ekman, P., Sorenson, E. R. & Friesen, W. V. (1969), 'Pan-Cultural Elements in Facial Displays of Emotion', *Science*, Vol. 164 No. 3875 pp 86–8

Hostetter, A. B. (2011), 'When do gestures communicate? A meta-analysis', *Psychological Bulletin*, Vol. 137 Issue 2 pp 297–315

James, J. (2008), *The Body Language Bible*. London: Vermilion

Knapp, M. L. & Hall, J. A. (2005), *Nonverbal Communication in Human Interaction* (6th ed.). Belmont, CA: Wadsworth

Lee, M. E., Matsumoto, D., Kobayashi, M., Krupp, D., Maniatis, E. F. & Roberts, W., 'Cultural Influences on Nonverbal Behavior in Applied Settings'. In Feldman, R. S. (Ed.) (1992), *Applications of Nonverbal Behavioural Theories and Research*. New Jersey: Lawrence Erlbaum

McNeill, D. (1992), *Hand and Mind: What Gestures Reveal About Thought*. Chicago: University of Chicago Press

Mehrabian, A. (1971), *Silent Messages*. Belmont, CA: Wadsworth

Mehrabian, A. (1972), *Non-Verbal Communication*. Chicago: Aldine-Atherton

Mehrabian, A. (2015). Professor Mehrabian's Comments on the Myth: www.kaaj.com/psych/smorder.html

Mehrabian, A. & Ferris, S. R. (1967), 'Inference of Attitudes from Nonverbal Communication in Two Channels', *Journal of Consulting Psychology*, Vol. 31 Issue 3 pp 248–52

Mehrabian, A. & Wiener, M. (1967), 'Decoding of Inconsistent Communications', *Journal of Personality and Social Psychology*, Vol. 6 Issue 1 pp 109–14

Morris, D. (1967), *The Naked Ape*. London: Cape

Williams, C. (2013), 'Lost in translation', *New Scientist*, 6 April. pp 34–7

See also

Chapter 12 – Attending skills in communication: the SOLER model

Chapter 15 – Space wars: why proxemics matters

Chapter 16 – Mimicry, mirroring and the chameleon effect

Chapter 31 – Communication starts with the eyes

Further reading

Bijlstra, G., Holland, R. W. & Wigboldus, D. H. J. (2010), 'The social face of emotion recognition: Evaluations versus stereotypes', *Journal of Experimental Social Psychology*, Vol. 46 Issue 4 pp 657–63

Darwin, C. (1872), *The Expressions of the Emotions in Man and Animals*. London: Murray

De Gelder, B. (2006), 'Towards the neurobiology of emotional body language', *Nature Reviews Neuroscience*, Vol. 7 Issue 3 pp 242–9

Ekman, P. (1993), 'Facial expression of emotion', *American Psychologist*, Vol. 48 Issue 4 pp 384–92

Ekman, P. (1994), 'Strong evidence for universals in facial expressions: A reply to Russell's mistaken critique', *Psychological Bulletin*, Vol. 115 Issue 2 pp 268–87

Fast, J. (1971), *Body Language*. London: Pan

Hauser, M. (1996), *The Evolution of Communication*. Cambridge, MA: MIT Press

Hinzman, L. & Kelly, S. D. (2013), 'Effects of emotional body language on rapid out-group judgments', *Journal of Experimental Social Psychology*, Vol. 49 pp 152–5

Krauss, R. M., Curran, N. M. & Ferleger, N. (1983), 'Expressive conventions and the cross-cultural perception of emotion', *Basic and Applied Social Psychology*, Vol. 4 pp 295–305

LaBarre, W. (1947), 'The cultural basis of emotions and gestures', *Journal of Personality*, Vol. 16 Issue 1 pp 49–68

Looser, C. E. & Wheatley, T. (2010), 'The tipping point of animacy. How, when, and where we perceive life in a face', *Psychological Science*, Vol. 21 Issue 12 pp 1854–62

Rogoff, B. (2003), *The Cultural Nature of Human Development*. New York: OUP

Russell, J. A. & Fernández-Dols, J. M. (Eds.) (1997), *The Psychology of Facial Expression*. Cambridge: Cambridge University Press

Vygotsky, L. S. (1962), *Thought and Language*. Cambridge, MA: MIT Press (Originally published 1934)

Yoon, K. L., Joormann, J. & Gotlib, I. H. (2009), 'Judging the intensity of facial expressions of emotion: depression-related biases in the processing of positive affect', *Journal of Abnormal Psychology*, Vol. 118 Issue 1 pp 223–8

Website: Professor Mehrabian's Personal Site www.kaaj.com/psych/

2 MEN AND WOMEN ARE NOT FROM DIFFERENT PLANETS

Although gender differences on average are not under dispute, the idea of consistently and inflexibly gender-typed individuals is. That is, there are not two distinct genders, but instead there are linear gradations of variables associated with sex, such as masculinity or intimacy, all of which are continuous (like most social, psychological, and individual difference variables).

Carothers and Reis (2012)

In the best-selling 1992 book, *Men Are from Mars, Women Are from Venus*, John Gray argues that there are enormous psychological differences between men and women. Central to his argument is that men and women communicate so differently that they could be from 'different planets'. But is this based on scientific fact or just based on the author's personal experiences? It would seem that the latter is true.

Gray provides no scientific evidence for his claim that men and women differ significantly in how they communicate. The myth of extreme differences between the way men and women communicate has enthralled the popular media and self-help industry. However, relatively few people have taken the time to look at the science of gender difference. In 2005, Professor Janet Hyde, from the University of Wisconsin–Madison, did so by using the scientific method of 'meta-analysis'.

Meta-analysis is a statistical technique used for combining the findings from independent studies. The name comes from the statistician Gene Glass, who stated that meta-analysis refers to the 'analysis of analyses' (Glass, 1976). In a meta-analysis, research studies are collected and interpreted using mathematical methods similar to those used in primary data analysis. The results of a successful meta-analysis are more objective than a traditional narrative review of the published literature.

In looking at the idea of psychological gender differences, Professor Hyde conducted a review of meta-analyses; if you like, a review of the review, of the review, of the literature. Her study involved a review of 46 separate meta-analyses that were conducted from 1985 to 2004. Hyde looked at meta-analyses that had explored gender differences related to cognitive abilities, communication, aggression, leadership, self-esteem, reasoning and motor behaviours (Hyde, 2005).

To understand a meta-analysis it is important to consider effect size, or the measure of any effect. In the case of gender difference, Hyde looked at the magnitude of gender differences in the 46 meta-analyses (Hyde, 2005). She applied Cohen's measurement of effect size, typically *d* (Cohen, 1988). The formula reads as follows:

$$d = \frac{M_M - M_F}{S_W}$$

So in this formula, *d* is the measure of effect size; {M_M} is the mean score for males, {M_F} is the mean score for females, and {S_W} is the average within-sex standard deviation. Hyde states:

In gender meta-analysis, the effect sizes computed from all individual studies are averaged to obtain an overall effect size reflecting the magnitude of gender differences across all studies. In the present article, I follow the convention that negative values of d mean that females scored higher on a dimension, and positive values of d indicate that males scored higher (Hyde, 2005).

Hyde is not suggesting that there are *no* differences between men and women. Her hypothesis of gender similarity claims that people are similar on most, but not all, psychological variables. In terms of statistical effect sizes, her gender similarities hypothesis states that most psychological gender differences are in the *close-to-zero* or *small* range (Hyde, 2005). The categories were:

Close-to-zero: $d \leq 0.10$
Small: $0.11 < d < 0.35$
Moderate: $0.36 < d < 0.65$
Large: d = $0.66 < d < 1.00$
Very large: $d > 1.00$

The results that Hyde found were remarkable. Thirty per cent of the effect sizes were in the close-to-zero range, and 48 per cent were in the small range. That is, 78 per cent of gender differences were small or close to zero (Hyde, 2005). The extensive evidence from the meta-analyses on gender demonstrated that males and females are alike on most, but not all, psychological variables.

Hyde also looked at the developmental course of gender differences and she found that gender differences fluctuate with age, and they are smaller or larger at different times in a person's life (Hyde, 2005). This again raises serious questions about the difference model.

There were a few notable exceptions that she found to the results of gender similarity. For example, difference was found in some 'motor behaviours' (e.g., throwing distance) and some aspects of sexuality (e.g., casual sex), and 'physical aggression'. Hyde concluded that her gender similarities hypothesis was confirmed by the research examined (Hyde).

Criticisms of meta-analysis include the possibility that they conceal valuable qualitative information and that they may not include studies that found negative or null results, as these are often unpublished and not included in the meta-analysis. A further concern is what has been described as the 'garbage-in-garbage-out' phenomenon, where a meta-analysis of poor studies will result in poor conclusions (Slavin, 1995).

Gender on a continuum

Hyde stated that gender differences seem to depend on the context in which they were measured. She cites one study that demonstrated how easy it is for setting to create apparent gender differences. In a 1999 study by Spencer, Steele & Quinn, male and female students with equal maths backgrounds were tested.

In one experiment, participants were told that the maths test had shown gender difference in the past, and in the other experiment they were told that the test had been shown to be gender neutral. When the participants had been told that the maths test was gender fair, there were no gender differences in performance. When the participants expected gender differences, women underperformed compared with men (Spencer et al, 1999).

Hyde was not the first to criticize John Gray's 'Mars and Venus' thesis. In an article published in the *Southern Communication Journal*, Professor Julia Wood argues persuasively that Gray's claims about women's and men's communication are inconsistent with the findings of credible, scientific research (2002). Professor Kathryn Dindia also found only small differences in her meta-analysis related to gender and self-disclosure (Dindia & Allen, 1992).

In a 2012 study based on the statistical analysis of 122 different characteristics involving 13,301 individuals, the researchers found that for factors such as empathy, sexuality and extroversion, men and women generally do not fall into different groups (Carothers & Reis, 2012). The researchers state: 'there are not two distinct genders, but instead there are linear gradations of variables associated with sex, such as masculinity or intimacy, all of which are continuous'.

Interestingly, this is consistent with the work of Cornell University psychologist Sandra Bem, who developed the well-known Sex-Role Inventory (1974). Bem popularized the concept of androgyny and maintained that people can combine both masculine and feminine characteristics and that this is the best of both worlds. Whether or not you support this idea, it is clear that most people seem to stereotype people in a dichotomous male/female categorization.

Carothers & Reis (2012) asked the question 'why do these categorical stereotypes of men and women persist?' They suggest as one possible answer Susan Fiske's contention that 'psychologists love dichotomies' (2010). This allows researchers and writers to simplify things rather than deal with the complexity of 'dealing with each individual as a unique case' (Carothers & Reis, 2012). Like most stereotypes, this probably speeds things up. But also, like most stereotypes, they limit communication and normally emphasize negative rather than positive characterizations.

For example, here is a quote from John Gray's book, *Men Are from Mars, Women Are from Venus*:

You see, when a Venusian is upset she not only uses generalities, and so forth, but also is asking for a particular kind of support. She doesn't directly ask for that support because on Venus everyone knew that dramatic language implied a particular request (Gray, 1992).

This quote stereotypes the way women communicate and Gray bases this on his personal observations, not the science. The science tells us women and men interact in very similar ways when it comes to this type of communication and the within-group variances would be just as large as the between-group. It's pretty ironic that the person using generalities here is John Gray.

There is a cost to the false hypothesis of male/female difference. It has an impact on the way people communicate and resolve conflict. It has an impact on schools and workplaces. It also has serious implications for communication and can be harmful in the context of relationships. People are too quick to blame communication problems on gender, without taking the time and effort to understand the complexities of human communication.

So what are the big takeaways here?

- **The extensive evidence from the meta-analyses on gender demonstrated that males and females are alike on most, but not all, psychological variables.**
- **Gender differences seem to depend on the context in which they were measured.**
- **Gender differences fluctuate with age,** and they are smaller or larger at different times in a person's life.

- **There are a few notable exceptions.** For example, differences between men and women have been found in some motor behaviours, some aspects of sexuality, and physical aggression.
- **The fundamental thesis of Mars–Venus is incorrect.** Men and women are both from the same planet – planet Earth.

Source

Hyde, J. S. (2005), 'The Gender Similarities Hypothesis', *American Psychologist*, Vol. 60 Issue 6 pp 581–92

References

Bem, S. L. (1974), 'The Measurement of Psychological Androgyny', *Journal of Consulting and Clinical Psychology*, Vol. 42 Issue 2 pp 155–62

Bem, S. L. (1981), 'Gender schema theory: A cognitive account of sex typing', *Psychological Review*, Vol. 88 Issue 4 pp 354–64

Carothers, B. J. & Reis, H. T. (2013), 'Men and women are from Earth: Examining the latent structure of gender', *Journal of Personality and Social Psychology*, Vol. 104 Issue 2 pp 385–407

Cohen, J. (1988), *Statistical power analysis for the behavioural sciences* (2nd ed.). Hillsdale, NJ: Erlbaum. Cited in Hyde, J. S. (2005), 'The Gender Similarities Hypothesis', *American Psychologist*, Vol. 60 Issue 6 pp 581–92

Dindia, K. & Allen, M. (1992), 'Sex Differences in Self-Disclosure: A Meta-Analysis', *Psychological Bulletin*, Vol. 112 Issue 1 pp 106–24

Glass, G. V. (1976), 'Primary, secondary and meta-analysis of research', *Educational Researcher*, Vol. 5 No. 10 pp 3–8

Gray, J. (1992), *Men Are from Mars, Women Are from Venus*. New York: Harper Collins

Halpern, D. F. (2012), *Sex Differences in Cognitive Abilities* (4th ed.). London: Psychology Press

Hyde, J. S. (2005), 'The Gender Similarities Hypothesis', *American Psychologist*, Vol. 60 No. 6 pp 581–2

Slavin, R. E. (1995), 'Best evidence synthesis: An intelligent alternative to meta-analysis', *Journal of Clinical Epidemiology*, Vol. 48 Issue 1 pp 9–18

Spencer, S. J., Steele, C. M. & Quinn, D. M. (1999), 'Stereotype threat and women's math performance', *Journal of Experimental Social Psychology*, Vol. 35 pp 4–28

Wood, J. (2002), 'A critical response to John Gray's Mars and Venus portrayals of men and women', *Southern Communication Journal*, Issue 67 Issue 2 pp 201–10

See also

Chapter 9 – Women do not talk more than men

Chapter 30 – The Obama Effect: reducing stereotyping

Chapter 32 – Neuro-scientific communication

Further reading

Archer, J. (2004), 'Sex differences in aggression in real-world settings: A meta-analytic review', *Review of General Psychology*, Vol. 8 Issue 4 pp 291–322

Barnett, R. & Rivers, C. (2004), *Same difference: How gender myths are hurting our relationships, our children, and our jobs.* New York: Basic Books

Cameron, D. (2007), *The Myth of Mars and Venus – Do men and women really speak different languages?.* Oxford: OUP

Eaton, W. O. & Enns, L. R. (1986), 'Sex differences in human motor activity level', *Psychological Bulletin*, Vol. 100 Issue 1 pp 19–28

Feingold, A. (1994), 'Gender differences in personality: A meta-analysis', *Psychological Bulletin*, Vol. 116 Issue 3 pp 429–56

Halpern, D. F. (2004), 'A cognitive-process taxonomy for sex differences in cognitive abilities', *Current Directions in Psychological Science*, Vol. 13 No. 4 pp 135–9

Hyde, J. S., Fennema, E. & Lamon, S. J. (1990), 'Gender differences in mathematics performance: A meta-analysis', *Psychological Bulletin*, Vol. 107 Issue 2 pp 139–55

Spencer, S. J., Steele, C. M. & Quinn, D. M. (1999), 'Stereotype threat and women's math performance', *Journal of Experimental Social Psychology*, Vol. 35 pp 4–28

Tannen, D. (1990), *You Just Don't Understand*. New York: Ballantine

Vangelisti, A. L. (1997), 'Gender differences, similarities, and interdependencies: Some problems with the different cultures perspective', *Personal Relationships*, Vol. 4 pp 243–53

Voyer, D., Voyer, S. & Bryden, M. P. (1995), 'Magnitude of sex differences in spatial abilities: A meta-analysis and consideration of critical variables', *Psychological Bulletin*, Vol. 117 Issue 2 pp 250–70

Website: Rebuttal from Uranus. An online blog that focuses on criticism of Gray's work: https://therebuttalfromuranus.wordpress.com/

Website: John Gray's corporate website: http://www.marsvenus.com/

3 BRAINSTORMING: YOU MAY HAVE BEEN DOING IT INCORRECTLY

Creativity is just connecting things. When you ask creative people how they did something, they feel a little guilty because they didn't really do it, they just saw something. It seemed obvious to them after a while. That's because they were able to connect experiences they've had and synthesize new things.

Steve Jobs, Wired, February 1996

Alex Osborn was a founding partner of the advertising firm Batten, Barton, Durstine and Osborn (BBDO). He is also the father of *brainstorming*, that ubiquitous process of ideas generation and group problem-solving. Most people know the term and have probably even been in such a session.

Some online commentators have suggested that the word 'brainstorming' may offend people with epilepsy. This myth started when a local council in the UK apparently banned the word and suggested as an alternative: 'thought showers'. The National Society for Epilepsy (now the Epilepsy Society) said it was not offensive and its spokesperson stated: 'Any implication that the word "brainstorming" is offensive to epileptics takes political correctness too far.' (Allen, 2008).

But you may have also heard that 'brainstorming doesn't work' (Lehrer, 2012) or that people working by themselves produce more ideas than when brainstorming (Taylor, Berry & Block, 1958). Others, however, have claimed that a group brainstorming will produce many more ideas than a person working alone (Osborn, 1953). Where lies the truth and what is conjecture?

Osborn states that he first used the brainstorming process in 1938 at BBDO and it was named by the participants as 'brainstorming sessions' and that it meant 'to use the brain to storm a problem' (Osborn, 1948). Brainstorming was introduced in his 1948 book and was then outlined in Chapters 12–14 of his later book, *Applied Imagination* (1953).

Osborn stated that brainstorming was about two things: creativity and ideas generation. It was not a complete process of problem-solving or decision-making. He believed that criticism, or what he incorrectly called 'negative reinforcement' (he meant negative evaluation), stifled individual creativity. Central to his thinking was the idea that if judgement were suspended, then the imagination could produce ideas.

He outlined four 'rules' for brainstorming. These were:

1. **No criticism of ideas generated**. Delayed until judgement is necessary
2. **Freewheeling**. The more crazy and wild the idea the better
3. **Quantity**. The more ideas, the more chances of useful ones
4. **Piggybacking**. Combination and improvement of ideas (p 300–1).

For Osborn, rule number one was the most important. He stated: 'No conference can be called a brainstorming session unless the deferment-of-judgement principle is strictly followed' (p 152). He was not saying you should not critically assess the ideas generated, just that this should happen later. Brainstorming was not intended to be a complete problem-solving process; it was always intended as only one stage of many.

He also suggested that the brainstorming session should have a trained leader, and the leader should outline the rules at the start and have them on permanent display throughout. He believed that people needed to be encouraged and rewarded for coming up with ideas. He stressed that all ideas, no matter how wild, should be written down, possibly on a blackboard (Osborn, 1963).

He also suggested that the session should be informal, describing the correct atmosphere as more like a 'picnic' than a formal meeting. He suggested about 12 as the ideal number for the brainstorming group and approximately 30–45 minutes as the ideal duration (Osborn, 1953). Following the process, he suggested an 'incubation' period to allow people to consider further ideas after 'sleeping on it'.

In relation to the structure of the brainstorming group, Osborn also had clear guidelines. You need a leader, associate-leader, secretary (recorder), about five 'core' members and about five 'guests'. These people should be selected because they have 'above-average facility in offering suggestions' (p 170). He also believed that you needed a few 'go-getters' to start the process but that these members needed to be monitored to make sure they don't dominate the group process (Osborn, 1953).

Osborn stated that the problem presented to the group should be simple and 'failure to narrow the problem to a single target can seriously mar the success of any brainstorm' (p 173). He also stressed that the process was not suitable for all types of problems. Using brainstorming for generating new advertising slogans for a product would qualify; deciding whether your business should move offices would not. He stated:

Group brainstorming is indicated only for problems which primarily depend on idea-finding, not for problems which depend on judgement. Nor is it indicated for any problem for which there are only two or three alternative solutions (p 158).

Are the criticisms of brainstorming fair?

We need to acknowledge that Osborn was not a social scientist; he was an advertising executive, educator, financier, author and founder of the non-profit Creative Education Foundation. Further, most of the evidence Osborn presents in *Applied Imagination* is anecdotal and case-study based. In itself, this is not necessarily a bad thing, particularly given the audience of Osborn's book.

While anecdotes provide illustrative examples, they do not constitute scientific evidence. Anecdotal evidence is of concern to social scientists as it may involve small and non-representative samples and they are hard to replicate. However, Osborn did present more empirical research in the later editions of *Applied Imagination* (1963).

The research on brainstorming has not been kind, and many of Osborn's claims for brainstorming have not been supported. For example, in what has become known as the Yale Study, Taylor et al (1958) present evidence that *individuals* using brainstorming generated more ideas than those working in *groups*. Another study, Diehl & Stroebe (1987), claims that brainstorming results in a significant waste of productivity due to the group blocking people's productions of ideas.

However, are these criticisms of brainstorming fair? A detailed examination of the literature suggests not. Much of the scientific research on brainstorming has not adequately tested the method as Osborn outlines it. For example, the Yale Study is often quoted to suggest that brainstorming doesn't work, but, in fact, this study compared individuals and groups both using brainstorming and did not actually test brainstorming.

Research by Scott Isaksen from the Creativity Research Institute reviewed 50 brainstorming studies conducted between 1958 and 1988 and found that 34/50 did not test the ground rules for brainstorming. Isaksen stated that of the 16 remaining that *did* test using the guidelines, all found support for brainstorming (Isaksen, 1998).

In 2012, *The New Yorker* magazine published an article called 'Groupthink: The brainstorming myth'. The author, Jonah Lehrer, stated: 'But there is a problem with brainstorming. It doesn't work' (2012). He then uses the misquoted Yale Study, and another paper by Professor Charlan Nemeth, published in 2003, to support this contention. Nemeth's piece is another example of a study that criticizes brainstorming but does not come even close to following Osborn's established procedure.

For example, the group studied by Nemeth (2003) comprised Californian college students, not at all similar to the brainstorm group suggested by Osborn (carefully selected idea generators). Nemeth had no leader, associate-leader, secretary, etc. Further, Nemeth had groups of five (less than half the 'optimal' size suggested by Osborn), and the groups were given 20 minutes, not the 30-45 minutes originally suggested.

Osborn advocates the need for at least half of the group to be a coherent 'core', but the students in the Californian study did not know each other. A further issue with the *New Yorker* article is that it does not clarify that in the Nemeth study the two groups who used 'basic brainstorming rules' (one with debate and another without) both actually generated more ideas than the group not given any instruction.

Beyond the procedure established by Osborn, there are several possible ways of conducting a brainstorm. Buon (2014) suggests three methods: 'popcorn', 'round-robin' and 'individual'. With **popcorn**, the panel members shout out their ideas in a random and energetic way. With **round-robin**, each person takes a turn, passing when they cannot think of any new ideas. **Individual** has people working by themselves coming up with as many ideas as possible.

Round-robin is a better approach for people who are less aggressive and more methodical. It also suits particular national cultures (less vocal and less assertive). Round-robin can also be enhanced using the Crawford Slip Method (Crawford, 1954), where slips of paper are used to record ideas silently and are then arranged on a surface into similar groups. Today, people tend to use 3M Post-it® Notes for this purpose.

Brainstorming also complements other problem-solving and decision-making processes. This includes tools such as the Nominal Group Technique (Delbecq & Van deVen, 1971), Mind Mapping (Buzan, 1974) and the Delphi Method (Dalkey & Helmer, 1963). Brainstorming is an excellent tool, but it needs to be used correctly and when appropriate.

So what are the big takeaways here?

- The problem addressed in the brainstorm should be simple and have a single target.
- Appoint a trained leader, associate-leader, secretary (recorder), about five 'core' members and about five 'guests'.
- Use it only with groups where at least approximately half the group know each other well.
- Keep things informal and create a comfortable environment (think 'picnic').
- The ideal length is approximately 30-45 minutes.
- Put up a poster or slide with the four rules visible to all:

  1. *No criticism of others' ideas*
  2. *Allow for freewheeling – the wilder the idea the better*
  3. *Aim for quantity, not quality*
  4. *Facilitate piggybacking (combining and improving on ideas)*

- All ideas, no matter how bizarre, should be written down.
- One person speaks at a time, with no interruption.
- After the brainstorm and incubation period, a list of all ideas generated is prepared, edited, classified and then evaluated critically (by the group, outsiders or a mix).

Source

Osborn, A. F. (1953), *Applied Imagination: Principles and Procedures of Creative Thinking*. New York: Charles Scribner's Sons

References

Allen, N. (2008), 'Council bans brainstorming', *The Telegraph*, 20 June 2008

Buon, T. (2014), *The Leadership Coach*. London: Hodder & Stoughton

Buzan, T. (1974), *Use Your Head*. London: BBC Books

Crawford, R. P. (1954), *The Techniques of Creative Thinking*. New York: Hawthorn Books

Dalkey, N. C. & Helmer, O. (1963), 'An experimental application of the Delphi Method to the use of experts', *Management Science*, Vol. 9 No. 3 pp 458–67

Delbecq A. L. & Van de Ven A. H. (1971), 'A Group Process Model for Problem Identification and Program Planning', *The Journal of Applied Behavioral Science*, Vol. 7 No. 3 pp 466–92

Diehl, M. & Stroebe, W. (1987), 'Productivity loss in brainstorming groups: Toward the solution of a riddle', *Journal of Personality and Social Psychology*, Vol. 53 No. 3 pp 497–509

Isaksen, S. G. (1998), 'A review of brainstorming research: Six critical issues for inquiry', Creativity Research Unit, Creative Problem Solving Group-Buffalo, Buffalo, New York

Lehrer, J. (2012), 'Groupthink: The brainstorming myth', *The New Yorker*, 30 January: http://www.newyorker.com/magazine/2012/01/30/groupthink

Nemeth, C. J. & Nemeth-Brown, B. (2001), 'Better than Individuals? The potential benefits of dissent and diversity for group creativity'. In Paulus, P. B. & Nijstad, B. A. (Eds.) (2003), *Group Creativity*. Oxford: OUP

Osborn, A. F. (1948), *Your creative power: How to use imagination*. New York: Charles Scribner's Sons

Osborn, A. F. (1953), *Applied Imagination: Principles and procedures of creative thinking*. New York: Charles Scribner's Sons

Osborn, A. F. (1957), *Applied Imagination: Principles and procedures of creative thinking* (2nd rev. ed.). New York: Charles Scribner's Sons

Osborn, A. F. (1963), *Applied Imagination: Principles and procedures of creative problem solving* (3rd rev. ed.). New York: Charles Scribner's Sons

Taylor, D. W., Berry, P. C. & Block, C. H. (1958), 'Does group participation when using brainstorming facilitate or inhibit creative thinking?', *Administrative Science Quarterly*, Vol. 6 pp 22–47

Wolf, G. (1996), 'Steve Jobs: The Next Insanely Great Thing', *Wired*, February: http://archive.wired.com/wired/archive/4.02/jobs_pr.html

See also

Chapter 20 – We are all individuals, or are we?

Chapter 23 – Groupthink: revisiting the theory of error

Chapter 33 – Our brain cannot cope with too much information

Further reading

Bouchard, T. J., Barsaloux, J. & Drauden, G. (1974), 'Brainstorming procedure, group size, and sex as determinants of the problem-solving effectiveness of groups and individuals', *Journal of Applied Psychology*, Vol. 59 Issue 2 pp 135–8

Gallupe, R. B. & Cooper, W. H. (1993), 'Brainstorming Electronically', *Sloan Management Review*, Vol. 35 pp 27–36

Janis, I. L. (1982), *Groupthink* (2nd ed.). Boston: Houghton Mifflin

Nemeth, C. J. (2002), 'Minority dissent and its "hidden" benefits', *New Review of Social Psychology*, Vol. 2 pp 21–8

Osborn, A. F. (1921), *A Short Course in Advertising*. New York: Charles Scribner's Sons

Wilson, C. (2013), *Brainstorming and Beyond: A User-Centered Design Method*. Massachusetts: Morgan Kaufmann

4 DOES EVERYBODY LIE?

Col. Jessep: *You want answers?*
Kaffee: *I think I'm entitled to!*
Col. Jessep: *You want answers!?*
Kaffee: *I want the truth!*
Col. Jessep: *You can't handle the truth!*
A Few Good Men *(1992 movie, Columbia Pictures)*

It is widely quoted that 'everybody lies' (Vrij, 2000). Moreover, if this is true then lying is an essential component of human communication. You may even benefit from learning how to do it better.

However, is this conjecture correct? Does everybody lie? One of the most cited research studies that seems to support the idea that everyone lies is the work by Bella DePaulo and her colleagues published in the *Journal of Personality and Social Psychology* (1996). This research, based on diaries kept by 77 US college students, suggested that people tell on average two lies each day. The authors concluded: 'As we expected, lying is a fact of daily life.' (DePaulo et al, 1996).

So what exactly constitutes lying? Researchers from the Department of Communication, at Michigan State University, have defined it as follows:

In order to study the prevalence of lying, it is necessary to consider what constitutes a lie. Simply and broadly put, lying occurs when a communicator seeks knowingly and intentionally to mislead others (Serota et al, 2010).

The claim that everybody lies is challenged in the literature. One thousand US adults were asked to report the number of lies told in a 24-hour period (Serota et al, 2010). The results were similar to those of DePaulo, and the average number of lies told was 1.65. However, 60 per cent of the subjects reported telling no lies at all, and almost half of all lies were told by only 5 per cent of subjects. A few prolific liars told most lies, and this heavily skewed the results.

To test the idea 'does everybody lie?', researchers from the University of Amsterdam in the Netherlands and the Ben-Gurion University of the Negev in Israel conducted two studies to question whether lying is normative and common among most people or are most people honest and it is only a small minority that frequently lies (Halevy et al, 2014).

In the first study, the researchers administered a questionnaire to all first-year students at the University of Amsterdam. Attempting to replicate the results of Serota et al, it was a Dutch translation of the same questionnaire used in the US study.

In the Dutch study, 527 first-year psychology students completed a questionnaire and in addition completed two additional personality inventories to measure traits of psychopathic personality. The results of this first study found an average of 2.04 lies per day. However, 41 per cent of the students reported telling no lies, 51 per cent told 1 to 5 lies, and 8 per cent told more than 6 lies. Overall, 5 per cent of the subjects told 40 per cent of all reported lies. Results further showed the expected positive correlation between lying frequency and psychopathic tendencies (Serota et al, 2010).

In the second study, 31 of the original subjects, and an additional 20 subjects, were brought into the psychology lab for more detailed analysis. The subjects were given a test to assess moral development ('DIT-2') (Rest et al, 1999) and a test to determine attitude towards deception ('Feeling Thermometer') (Jung & Lee, 2009).

Two practical tasks were also given in which subjects had the opportunity to cheat privately for financial profit. The 'Die Under Cup' task (Fischbacher & Heusi, 2008) saw participants receive a regular die inside a paper cup with a small hole, enabling them to privately roll the die under the cup and see the outcome.

A second cheating task, the 'Words' task (Wiltermuth, 2011), was also used. In this task, subjects were asked to solve word jumbles in the order in which they were presented and were paid according to their self-reported success.

Overall, the results from the two studies replicated the skewed distribution of lying frequency described by Serota et al and showed that people reporting a high lying rate are also more likely to cheat for personal profit. Finally, the results showed a correlation between lying frequency and 'psychopathic tendencies' (Halevy et al, 2014).

Most people tell the truth

So do most people lie? Well, the answer appears to be no. Most people tell the truth, but some people do lie. It is not difficult to understand why many people believe lying is common in human communication; personal experience, anecdotal evidence and misinterpreted reading of research encourage this conviction. However, it is nevertheless wrong.

Most people lie on occasion and some people lie a lot. People do not lie twice a day on average and are generally honest in their communications. As Serota et al stated:

The inference of pervasive daily lying, drawn from the statistical average of one to two lies per day, and reinforced by media coverage of corporate deception and political malfeasance, as well as pop culture portrayals of deception detectors, belies the basic honesty present in most people's everyday communication (p 22–3).

It is also worth noting that most of the studies into lying frequency have been conducted with students (commonly, American) and in controlled laboratory settings. It is, therefore, very difficult to accurately extrapolate these research findings to everyone. Unfortunately, it is all too common for journalists and bloggers to take good scientific research and corrupt what the researchers found, all for a good headline, an attention-grabbing statistic or click-bait.

As is the case with most psychological research, there is very limited data in relation to cultures other than Western ones. Good research on race and lying is almost non-existent. There is also little proper research in relation to gender or age with regard to lying behaviour.

The study by Halevy et al (2014) shows that individual differences play a role in deceptive communication and may even help us to distinguish frequent liars from the rest of the population. The profile emerging from the Dutch study suggests that a frequent liar is someone who has higher scores on psychopathic traits measures and is more prone to cheating. This person also seems to have limited moral concerns about their lying (Halevy et al, 2014).

In human communication, there appears to be a necessary belief that we are not being lied to by others. This is essential. Otherwise, we would always be checking out and questioning what we are told or read. This would inhibit communication flow and simply take too long. So it would appear that like many typical and unconscious communication behaviours, we have got it right. We can trust most people, most of the time.

While there are some people who lie a lot there are some who are even 'pathological liars', people who demonstrate the behaviour of habitual or compulsive lying. These people represent a small minority, and their existence should not stop us from trusting what people communicate to us on a day-to-day basis. A further benefit of trusting what others say is that it improves our two-way communication and saves us much time. Moreover, the research backs it up.

So what are the big takeaways here?

- Most people do not lie and are generally honest in their communications.
- People do not lie twice a day on average.
- Most people probably occasionally lie. However, some people lie a lot.
- Trust what people say unless they give you a strong reason not to.

Source

Halevy, R., Shalvi, S. & Verschuere, B. (2014), 'Being Honest About Dishonesty: Correlating Self-Reports and Actual Lying', *Human Communication Research*, Vol. 40 Issue 1 pp 54–72

References

Ariely, D. (2012), *The Honest Truth About Dishonesty: How we lie to everyone – especially ourselves*. New York: HarperCollins

DePaulo, B. M., Kirkendol, S. E., Kashy, D. A., Wyer, M. M. & Epstein, J. A. (1996), 'Lying in everyday life', *Journal of Personality and Social Psychology*, Vol. 70 Issue 5 pp 979–95

DePaulo, B. M., 'The many faces of lies'. In Miller, A. G. (Ed.) (2004), *The Social Psychology of Good and Evil*. New York: Guilford Press

Fischbacher, U. & Heusi, F. (2008), 'Lies in disguise: an experimental study on cheating', Working Paper Series No. 40. Thurgau Institute of Economics, University of Konstanz

Halevy, R., Shalvi, S. & Verschuere, B. (2014), 'Being Honest About Dishonesty: Correlating Self-Reports and Actual Lying', *Human Communication Research*, Vol. 40 Issue 1 pp 54–72

Jung, K. H. & Lee, J.-H. (2009), 'Implicit and explicit attitude dissociation in spontaneous deceptive behavior', *Acta Psychologica*, Vol. 132 Issue 1 pp 62–7

Rest, R. J., Narvaez, D., Thoma, S. J. & Bebeau, M. J. (1999), 'DIT2: Devising and testing a revised instrument of moral judgment', *Journal of Educational Psychology*, Vol. 91 Issue 4 pp 644–59

Serota, K. B., Levine, T. R. & Boster, F. J. (2010), 'The Prevalence of Lying in America: Three Studies of Self-Reported Lies', *Human Communication Research*, Vol. 36 pp 2–25

Shalvi, S. (2012), 'Dishonestly increasing the likelihood of winning', *Judgment and Decision Making*, Vol. 7 Issue 3 pp 292–303

Wiltermuth, S. S. (2011), 'Cheating more when the spoils are split', *Organizational Behavior and Human Decision Processes*, Vol. 115 Issue 2 pp 157–68

See also

Chapter 24 – The Forer Effect: gullibility in action

Chapter 29 – Communication and facial expressions

Chapter 39 – Selfies: a new form of communication

Further reading

Aoki, K., Akai, K. & Onoshiro, K. (2010), 'Deception and confession: Experimental evidence from a deception game in Japan', Osaka University Discussion Paper No. 786

Bok, S. (1999), *Lying: Moral Choice in Public and Private Life*. New York: Vintage

Cappelen, A. W., Sørensen, E. O. & Tungodden, B. (2013), 'When do we lie?', *Journal of Economic Behavior & Organization*, Vol. 93 pp 258–65

Christie, R. & Geis, F. L. (1970), *Studies in Machiavellianism*. New York: Academic Press

Ekman, P. (2001), *Telling Lies. Clues to Deceit in the Marketplace, Politics, and Marriage*. New York: W. W. Norton & Company

Erat, S. & Gneezy, U. (2012), 'White lies', *Management Science*, Vol. 58 Issue 4 pp 723–33

Gibson, R., Tanner, C. & Wagner, A. F. (2013), 'Preferences for Truthfulness: Heterogeneity Among and Within Individuals', *American Economic Review*, Vol. 103 Issue 1 pp 532–48

Patterson, J. & Kim, P. (1991), *The Day America Told the Truth*. New York: Prentice-Hall

Sutter, M. (2009), 'Deception through telling the truth?! Experimental Evidence From Individuals and Teams', *The Economic Journal*, Vol. 119 Issue 534 pp 47–60

Vrij, A. (2000), *Detecting Lies and Deceit*. Chichester: Wiley

5 CAN YOUR HANDWRITING REVEAL YOUR PERSONALITY?

There exists in society a very special class of persons that I have always referred to as the Believers. These are folks who have chosen to accept a certain religion, philosophy, theory, idea or notion and cling to that belief regardless of any evidence that might, for anyone else, bring it into doubt. They are the ones who encourage and support the fanatics and the frauds of any given age. No amount of evidence, no matter how strong, will bring them any enlightenment.
James Randi – magician and sceptic (1990)

Graphology claims to interpret your psychological makeup and analyse your character. In Europe (particularly France), Israel and the United States it is often used for job selection by HR practitioners (Neter & Ben-Shakhar, 1989).

According to The Association of Qualified Graphologists (AQG), graphology can be used for recruitment, career guidance, negotiations, compatibility, security checks, forensic examination, promotional events and genealogy. It states that graphology is:

The study of personality through an analysis of handwriting. (Writing is frozen body language). From handwriting a graphologist can determine a range of characteristics such as energy, expressiveness, dominance, impulsiveness, intelligence, and levels of anxiety (AQG, 2014).

In the book *50 Great Myths of Popular Psychology*, the authors suggest graphology is a pseudoscience along the lines of phrenology (reading bumps on the head), tasseography (tea-leaf reading) and palmistry (reading lines on hands) (Lilienfeld et al, 2010).

At the outset it is important not to confuse graphology with the well-regarded scientific study of handwriting. Typically referred to as 'forensic handwriting analysis' (though confusingly some graphologists use this description), this method assesses documents for law enforcement and courts in relation to areas such as whether two documents were written by the same person or to test the validity of a signature or autograph. There is no attempt to assess personality.

Graphology uses a variety of techniques to support its claims, and these include the analysis of handwritten characters such as crossed t's and dotted i's and the slope of a person's handwriting. Some graphologists prefer to analyse the use of space between characters, words and sentences; others take a more 'holistic' approach and look at the entire piece of writing.

Numerous studies over the past seven decades have consistently shown that graphology lacks both reliability and validity (Eysenck, 1945; Gardner, 1957; Fluckiger, Tripp & Weinberg, 1961; Lemke & Kirchner, 1971; Furnham & Gunter, 1987; Dean, 1992; King & Koehler, 2000; and Gawda, 2014). However, there have also been studies that have claimed to find a connection between handwriting and personality (Van Rooij & Hazelzet, 1997; Wellingham-Jones, 1989). So how do we decide whether graphology works?

Well, the best that science has to offer is the meta-analysis. Meta-analysis is a statistical technique for combining the findings from independent studies (Glass, 1976). In the sciences, it is common to find that many studies have attempted to answer similar questions about the reliability and validity of something. By combining the results of the individual studies and then applying meta-analytic techniques a detailed collective assessment of the effectiveness of the area can often be revealed.

In 1989, two researchers from the Hebrew University of Jerusalem in Israel conducted a meta-analysis of graphology as a device for personnel selection (Neter & Ben-Shakhar, 1989). The researchers utilized 17 studies dealing with graphology and personnel selection. Their dataset included 63 graphologists and 51 non-graphologists who evaluated 1,223 samples of handwriting.

Efrat Neter and Gershon Ben-Shakhar applied meta-analytic techniques to estimate the validity of predictions for future job performance based on handwriting analysis. Of the 17 studies, 11 were published papers and 6 unpublished papers (all the unpublished data was from Israel). They then conducted a meta-analysis for each type of assessor (graphologist, psychologist and layperson) and found no evidence whatsoever that the graphologists could predict the future work performance of subjects from their handwriting samples.

The researchers were also surprised to find that when the different assessors were compared, the graphologists were less successful in predicting future behaviour from handwriting analysis than psychologists in almost all the dimensions. The researchers reported that the results of their meta-analysis demonstrated that graphologists are no better than non-graphologists in predicting future performance on the basis of handwritten scripts; in fact, they are often worse.

They also found that the graphologists' results were better when they analysed content-laden material than when they used neutral samples of handwriting, but there was limited data to explore the second deduction entirely. They conclude by discouraging the use of graphology as a predictive tool for job selection.

Irrational beliefs about pseudosciences

The meta-analysis from Neter & Ben-Shakhar – plus all of the other research conducted over the past 70 years – clearly demonstrates that we should not use graphology as a basis for job selection.

So why do people seem so willing to accept the claims of graphology, given the evidence against it? The answer to this may lie in three possible explanations. Moreover, each explanation may also provide us with a framework to explore irrational beliefs of other pseudosciences.

The Barnum Effect

This refers to the tendency for people to accept as true to themselves a statement that could be applied to anyone.

Phineas Taylor Barnum was the American showman who is said to have claimed for his circus: 'We have something for everybody.' The Barnum Effect shows that people will give high accuracy ratings to descriptions of their personality that seem to be tailored specifically for them, but are, in fact, general enough to apply to a broad range of people. It is also known as the *Forer Effect*.

In one study, subjects read personality statements by a certified graphologist and a number of 'Barnum statements' written to be applicable to almost everyone. The subjects rated the graphologist's descriptions of strangers as being just as accurate descriptors of themselves as the intentionally vague Barnum statements (Karnes, 1992).

The term 'Barnum Effect' was based on the work of Professor D. Paterson and was not coined by Meehl as is often claimed (*see* Meehl, 1956 p 266)

The Simplicity Hypothesis

This is the suggestion that people prefer simple rather than complex answers to problems.

With graphology, you do not have to deal with the fact that people are complex beings and that their personalities are equally complex and elusive. You don't have to conduct a costly and time-consuming job analysis, and then go through difficult interview processes and even assessment centres. You don't have to concern yourself with complex ideas such as 'validity' and 'reliability' of selection methods.

Dr Karen Stollznow, the sceptic researcher, when investigating graphology, reported:

As part of my investigation I road-tested a graphologist who gave me a 'romance reading'. The graphologist analysed handwriting examples from myself, and my boyfriend. She made some vague references to personality traits, then determined that we were a happy couple and would marry one day, provided we sort out a few minor relationships problems. Mostly, we were compatible. This was fortunate, because both examples were of my own handwriting (Stollznow, 2014).

Seeing numbers that aren't there

Scientists call this seeing 'illusory correlations'.

Chapman & Chapman (1969) described 'illusory correlation' as seeing a relationship between variables even when no such relationship exists. People seem to overestimate relationships between two groups when distinctive and unusual information is presented. This is related to stereotyping, superstition, confirmation bias and selective attention.

In relation to graphology, King & Koehler (2000) had participants judge the connection between handwriting features and personality. Participants were then given random (zero correlation) pairings of handwriting samples and brief personality profiles. The participants found a significant correlation of 0.65, where there was none.

People are very quick to assume things are correlated when they are not. When we make this error, we will believe the correlation or we will find ways to 'prove' it. This explains, at least in part, why graphology still has firm believers who continue to claim its 'scientific accuracy' in spite of any evidence to the contrary.

So what are the big takeaways here?

- The truth about graphology is very evident. It doesn't work.
- There is no scientific evidence for the assessment of personality traits using handwriting analysis and no evidence for other spurious claims such as health diagnosis or the use of graphology as a type of psychotherapy.
- The use of graphology for job selection is ineffective, and research has found no evidence that graphologists can predict the future work performance of people from their handwriting samples.

Source

Neter, E. & Ben-Shakhar, G. (1989), 'The Predictive Validity of Graphological Influences: A Meta-Analytic Approach', *Personality and Individual Differences*, Vol. 10 Issue 7 pp 737–45

References

The Association of Qualified Graphologists (AQG) www.aqg.org.uk/index.html

Chapman, L. J. & Chapman, J. P. (1969), 'Illusory correlation as an obstacle to the use of valid psychodiagnostic signs', *Journal of Abnormal Psychology*, Vol. 74 Issue 3 pp 271–80

Dean, G. A. (1992), 'The Bottom Line: Effect Size'. In Beyerstein, B. L. & Beyerstein, D. F. (1992), *The Write Stuff: Evaluation of Graphology – The Study of Handwriting Analysis*. Amherst: Prometheus Books

Eysenck, H. J. (1945), 'Graphological analysis and psychiatry: an experimental study', *British Journal of Psychology*, Vol. 35 Issue 3 pp 70–81

Fluckiger F. A., Tripp, C. A. & Weinberg, G. H. (1961), 'A review of experimental research in graphology, 1933–1960', *Perceptual & Motor Skills*, Vol. 12 pp 67–90

Forer, B. R. (1949), 'The Fallacy of Personal Validation: A Classroom Demonstration of Gullibility', *The Journal of Abnormal and Social Psychology*, Vol. 44 Issue 1 pp 118–23

Furnham, A. & Gunter, B. (1987), 'Graphology and Personality: Another Failure to Validate Graphological Analysis', *Personality and Individual Differences*, Vol. 8 Issue 3 pp 433–5

Gardner, M. (1957), *Fads and Fallacies in the Name of Science* (2nd ed.). New York: Dover Publications

Gawda, B. (2014), 'Lack of evidence for the assessment of personality traits using handwriting analysis', *Polish Psychological Bulletin*, Vol. 45 Issue 1 pp 73–9

Glass, G. V. (1976), 'Primary, Secondary, and Meta-Analysis of Research', *Educational Researcher*, Vol. 5 No. 10 pp 3–8

Hofsommer W., Holdsworth R. & Seifert T. (1965), 'Zur Reliabilitätsfragen in der Graphologie', *Psychologie und Praxis*, Vol. 9 pp 14–24

Karnes E. & Leonard S. D., 'Graphoanalytic and psychometric personality profiles: Validity and Barnum effects'. In Beyerstein, B. L. & Beyerstein, D. F. (1992), *The Write Stuff: Evaluation of Graphology – The Study of Handwriting Analysis*. Amherst: Prometheus Books

King, R. N. & Koehler, D. J. (2000), 'Illusory Correlations in Graphological Inference', *Journal of Experimental Psychology: Applied*, Vol. 6 Issue 4 pp 336–48

Lemke E. A. & Kirchner J. H. (1971), 'A multivariate study of handwriting, intelligence, and personality correlates', *Journal of Personality Assessment*, Vol. 35 pp 584–92

Lilienfeld, S. O., Lynn, S. J., Ruscio, J. & Beyerstein, B. L. (2010), *50 great myths of popular psychology: Shattering widespread misconceptions about human behavior*. New York: Wiley-Blackwell

Meehl, P. E. (1986), 'Causes and Effects of My Disturbing Little Book', *Journal of Personality Assessment*, Vol. 50 pp 370–5

Neter, E. & Ben-Shakhar, G. (1989), 'The Predictive Validity of Graphological Inferences: A Meta-Analytic Approach', *Personality and Individual Differences*, Vol. 10 Issue 7 pp 737–45

Randi, J. (1990), *The Mask of Nostradamus: The Prophecies of the World's Most Famous Seer*. New York: Scribner

Stollznow, K. (2014), 'Graphology: Write but Wrong': http://archive.randi.org/site/index.php/swift-blog/551-graphology-write-but-wrong.html

Van Rooij, J. J. & Hazelzet A. M. (1997), 'Graphologists' assessment of extraversion', *Perceptual & Motor Skills*, Vol. 85 pp 919–1009

Wellingham-Jones, P. (1989), 'Evaluation of the Handwriting of Successful Women through the Roman-Staempfli Psychogram', *Perceptual & Motor Skills*, Vol. 69 pp 999–1010

See also

Chapter 8 – Subliminal communication: hidden messages

Chapter 10 – NLP and communication

Chapter 11 – The placebo effect and communication

Chapter 24 – The Forer Effect: gullibility in action

Further reading

Bangerter, A., König, C. J., Blatti, S. & Salvisberg, A. (2009), 'How Widespread is Graphology in Personnel Selection Practice? A case study of a job market myth', *International Journal of Selection and Assessment*, Vol. 17 Issue 2 pp 219–30

Tett, R. P. & Palmer, C. A. (1997), 'The validity of handwriting elements in relation to self-report personality trait measures', *Personality and Individual Differences*, Vol. 22 pp 11–18

Zdep, S. M. & Weaver, H. B. (1967), 'The graphoanalytic approach to selecting life insurance salesmen', *Journal of Applied Psychology*, Vol. 51 Issue 3 pp 295–9

Website: Video of James Randi and a graphologist: https://www.youtube.com/watch?v=NeYkOHQ683k

6 MASLOW WAS WRONG; YOUR NEEDS ARE NOT HIERARCHICAL

Kids, you tried your best, and you failed miserably.
The lesson is, never try.
Homer Simpson *(1994),* **The Simpsons**

There is a great variety of approaches to understanding motivation and a great deal of research that has been carried out in the area. There is also an apparent lack of agreement between the major theorists, which results in the absence of a neat, workable theory. In some ways, this is not surprising as people are complex beings with a variety of changing, often conflicting needs, which they try to satisfy in a variety of ways.

Motivation tries to explain people's behaviour. There have been many attempts to define motivation, and not all have been successful. In simple terms, motivation is what drives or stimulates people to take certain actions or, indeed, not to act.

So did you get up this morning and exercise? If you did, why? If you did not, again, why not? The answer to this lies in understanding what motivates or drives you to do something or not. And, of course, to keep doing it.

Possibly one of the most famous motivation theories is that of Abraham Maslow. Maslow was born in Brooklyn, New York in 1908 and died in 1970. His parents were Russian Jews – and he faced anti-Semitism throughout his life. His work had great influence on industry and business leaders, psychotherapy and even the New Age movement.

During the 1950s Maslow was the founder of a branch of psychology known as 'humanistic psychology'. This humanistic psychology emphasized the study of the whole person and can be seen as rebellion against behaviourist psychology (e.g. B. F. Skinner) and psychodynamic psychology (e.g. Sigmund Freud). This eventually led to many of the ideas still evident in the professional practice of psychotherapy and the modern self-help industry.

Maslow introduced his theory of motivation in his 1943 paper, *A Theory of Human Motivation*. At the time, psychology was mainly focused on the negative or troubled side of the human mind, and Maslow was attempting to produce a positive (humanistic) theory of motivation. Maslow's theory was an important shift in psychology: rather than focusing on abnormal behaviour, Maslow's humanistic psychology was focused on the development of healthy individuals.

Maslow theorized that there is a natural process whereby individuals fulfilled needs in ascending order from most immature to most mature. His 'hierarchy of needs' theory is most often displayed as a pyramid, as can be seen in the next illustration. Maslow himself never used the pyramid figure and this came from later writers.

Maslow's Hierarchy of Needs

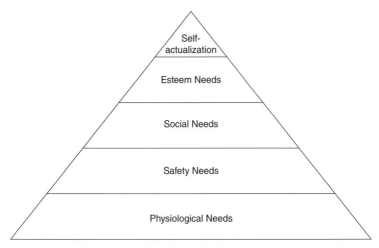

Figure 6.1   Maslow's Hierarchy of Needs (Source: Maslow, 1943; 1954)

1. **Self-actualization:** growth, achieving one's potential and self-fulfilment
2. **Esteem:** self-respect, autonomy, achievement, status and recognition
3. **Social (Love):** belongingness, acceptance and friendship
4. **Safety:** security and protection from physical and emotional harm
5. **Physiological:** hunger, thirst, shelter, sex and other bodily needs

According to Maslow, progression through the need hierarchy is seen as a sequence where the individual must have satisfied the lower level before advancing to a higher level need. The awareness of the need higher up is a function of having fulfilled the preceding need. Only satisfactory fulfilment of this need will allow the person to deal with the new need (Maslow, 1970).

According to Maslow, no need is ever completely satisfied; rather, there must be at least partial fulfilment before an individual can become aware of the higher-order need and be able to pursue it (p 373). For Maslow, only unsatisfied needs are a source of motivation (Maslow, 1954).

Questioning the needs hierarchy

Maslow's need hierarchy theory is well known, particularly among managers and corporate trainers. However, most research has not been able to substantiate the idea of a needs hierarchy. Maslow himself provided no empirical substantiation for his theory and several studies that sought to validate his theory failed to do so (Lawler & Suttle, 1972; Wahba & Bridwell, 1976).

Maslow's research on *self-actualization* was based on a tiny sample, including people he knew personally and on the written biographies of famous individuals that Maslow himself believed to be self-actualized (e.g. Albert Einstein). He had great difficulty even writing a precise definition of self-actualization.

He did not display the level of academic rigour in his work as would be required today. This was evident in the lack of standard definitions of concepts or keywords used ('needs', 'self-actualization', etc.). Maslow was not interested in the ideas of 'empirical verification' of theory and believed in a more 'humanistic' approach to research.

There is little scientific evidence for Maslow's ranking of needs and even less evidence that these needs are organized in a hierarchical order (Miner & Daehler, 1973; Wofford, 1971). Mahmoud Wahba and Lawrence Bridwell were researchers from The City University of New York who in 1976 were concerned about 'the uncritical acceptance of Maslow's need hierarchy theory despite the lack of empirical evidence'. They set out to test his theories – in particular, how they hold up in a work setting.

They found little support for Maslow's theories and even question whether self-actualization is a basic need, suggesting that it may be better described as a wish to be something, rather than a need to be something. The researchers also point out that Maslow was not even clear about what he meant by the concept of need. They concluded:

This literature review shows that Maslow's Need Hierarchy Theory has received little clear or consistent support from the available research findings. Some of Maslow's propositions are totally rejected, while others receive mixed and questionable support at best. The validity of Maslow's Need Classification scheme is not established, although deficiency and growth needs may form some kind of hierarchy (p 233).

Consider a person who is living in a refugee camp, this person has limited food and shelter (physiological needs not met), is in constant danger of attack or harm (no safety needs met) and may have lost all their family and friends when escaping persecution (social needs not met). Do you think it is possible for this person to have self-respect (esteem needs) or spiritual calm (self-actualization)? Of course they can – needs are not hierarchical, life is simply more complicated than that.

Also, what about the mountain climber who ignores his or her need for safety in pursuit of the summit? Or the two French BASE jumpers (parachuting from a fixed structure or cliff) who climbed the 828-m (2,716-ft) Burj Khalifa tower in Dubai and jumped? There are many other human examples that all question Maslow's theory (starving artist, spiritual hermit, etc.).

Unfortunately, Maslow's work is all too often put forward as fact, not unsupported theory. His work had major historical significance, but it is often used for inappropriate justification of strategy and decisions, ranging from third-world development to corporate reward systems. If we believe that needs are hierarchical, then we may make serious miscalculations and poor decisions.

Self-actualization is also a vague and undefined concept. The pyramid suggests an ascension up the hierarchy towards self-actualization. However, not everyone wants, needs or is able to be self-actualizing. Not everyone wishes to be a leader or to 'reach the top', and the Maslow need hierarchy suggests this is the ultimate goal of humankind. This is a particularly 'Western' view of life and has serious limitations, both in practice and theory.

As Indian business professor Anil Gupta in a TED Talk (2009) said:

There could be nothing more wrong than the Maslowian model of hierarchy of needs. … Please do not ever think that only after meeting your physiological needs and other needs can you be thinking about your spiritual needs or your enlightenment (Gupta, 2009).

Regardless of these criticisms, Maslow's theory was a ground-breaking study at the time. He moved people away from the negative side of human motivation and thought towards a positive view of people. While he never operationally defined 'self-actualization', the focus on this positive construct was necessary at the time and remains so today.

So what are the big takeaways here?

- **Maslow's Need Hierarchy Theory has little clear or consistent support in the psychological literature.**
- **Some of Maslow's propositions, such as the hierarchy of needs, can be rejected,** while others have very limited support at best.

- **If you see someone using the famous Maslow pyramid in a training course or to argue a position on human motivation, question them.**
    Have they read his original work? Do they understand the limitations of his work and the lack of empirical support for the fundamental ideas? Are they quoting Maslow as a theory or fact?
- **Maslow's theory was a ground-breaking study at the time.** He moved people away from the negative side of human motivation and thought towards a positive view of people.

Source

Maslow, A. H. (1943), 'A Theory of Human Motivation', *Psychological Review*, Vol. 50 Issue 4 pp 370–96

References

Gupta, A. (2009), TED Talks: 'India's hidden hotbeds of invention'. Filmed Nov 2009, posted May 2010, TEDIndia. www.ted.com/talks/anil_gupta_india_s_hidden_hotbeds_of_invention.html

Lawler, E. E. & Suttle, J. L. (1972), 'A causal correlational test of the need hierarchy concept', *Organizational Behavior and Human Performance*, Vol. 7 pp 265–87

Maslow, A. H. (1943), 'A Theory of Human Motivation', *Psychological Review*, Vol. 50 Issue 4 pp 370–96

Maslow, A. H. (1954), *Motivation and Personality*. New York: Harper & Row

Maslow, A. H. (1968), *Toward a Psychology of Being* (2nd ed.). New York: D. Van Nostrand

Maslow, A. H. (1970), *Motivation and Personality* (2nd ed.). New York: Harper & Row

Miner, J. B. & Dachler, H. P. (1973), 'Personal attitudes and motivation', *Annual Review of Psychology*, Vol. 24 pp 379–402

Wahba, M. A. & Bridwell, L. G. (1976), 'Maslow Reconsidered: A Review of Research on the Need Hierarchy Theory', *Organizational Behavior and Human Performance*, Vol. 15 pp 212–40

Wofford, J. C. (1971), 'The motivational bases of job satisfaction and job performance', *Personnel Psychology*, Vol. 24 Issue 3 pp 501–18

See also

Chapter 7 – The myths of emotional intelligence

Chapter 25 – Educational credentials and the racism of intelligence

Chapter 27– Cultural differences in communication

Further reading

Daniels, M. (1988), 'The Myth of Self-Actualization', *Journal of Humanistic Psychology*, Vol. 28 Issue 1 pp 7–38

Geller, L. (1982), 'The Failure of Self-Actualization Theory', *Journal of Humanistic Psychology*, Vol. 22 Issue 2 pp 56–73

Goodman, R. A. (1968), 'On the operationality of the Maslow Need Hierarchy', *British Journal of Industrial Relations*, Vol. 6 Issue 1 pp 51–7

Graham, W. & Balloun, J. (1973), 'An empirical test of Maslow's need hierarchy', *Journal of Humanistic Psychology*, Vol. 13 Issue 1 pp 97–108

Hall, D. T. & Nougaim, K. E. (1968), 'An examination of Maslow's need hierarchy in an organizational setting', *Organizational Behaviour and Human Performance*, Vol. 3 pp 12–35

Maslow, A. H. (1970), *Motivation and Personality* (2nd ed.). New York: Harper & Row

Neher, A. (1991), 'Maslow's Theory of Motivation: A Critique', *Journal of Humanistic Psychology*, Vol. 31 No. 3 pp 89–112

Payne, R. (1970), 'Factor analysis of a Maslow-type need satisfaction questionnaire', *Personnel Psychology*, Vol. 23 Issue 2 pp 251–68

Roberts, K. H., Walter, G. A. & Miles, R. E. (1971), 'A factor analytic study of job satisfaction items designed to measure Maslow need categories', *Personnel Psychology*, Vol. 24 Issue 2 pp 205–20

Vroom, V. H. (1964), *Work and Motivation*. New York: Wiley

Waters, L. K. & Roach, D. A. (1973), 'A Factor Analysis of Need Fulfilment Items Designed to Measure Maslow Need Categories', *Personnel Psychology*, Vol. 26 pp 185–90

Wuthnow, R. (1978), 'An empirical test of Maslow's theory of motivation', *Journal of Humanistic Psychology*, Vol. 18 Issue 3 pp 75–7

7 THE MYTHS OF EMOTIONAL INTELLIGENCE

If the person you are talking to doesn't appear to be listening,
be patient. It may simply be that he has a small piece
of fluff in his ear.
Pooh's Little Instruction Book (1996).
Inspired by A. A. Milne

Emotional Intelligence (EI) has been widely promoted and discussed in the popular press, trade journals and scientific literature. Most people have heard the claims by writers such as Daniel Goleman, who stated 'it matters twice as much as IQ' (Goleman, 1998) or that EI and good communication skills are 'positively related' (Erigüç & Köse, 2013). It has also been strongly argued that EI can predict leadership effectiveness (Prati et al, 2003).

However, others have claimed that many of the ideas presented by those promoting EI are not supported by the peer-reviewed scientific literature (Antonakis, 2004; Matthews, Roberts & Zeidner, 2004; Murphy, 2006). Others have argued that EI has too many confusing definitions (Waterhouse, 2006) and that EI is not predictive of outcomes in real-world settings (Matthews et al, 2004).

In a 2004 paper published in the journal *Psychological Inquiry*, Gerald Matthews, Richard Roberts and Moshe Zeidner set out not to dismiss EI but to outline the limitations of EI as a construct. They described seven myths about EI, by which they meant 'strong, widely believed claims that purportedly give the concept of EI scientific credibility'. The authors acknowledged that each of the seven could eventually be accepted as scientific fact, and they evaluated the likelihood that the myth may be substantiated by future research.

The seven myths were:

Myth 1: Definitions of EI are conceptually coherent
Myth 2: Measures of EI meet standard psychometric criteria
Myth 3: Self-report EI is distinct from existing personality constructs
Myth 4: Ability tests for EI meet criteria for a cognitive intelligence
Myth 5: EI relates to emotion as IQ relates to cognition
Myth 6: EI predicts adaptive coping
Myth 7: EI is critical for real world success.

Myth 1. Definitions (prospects for future progress: *fair*)

It is almost impossible to get an agreed upon definition of EI. This is due in part to the clash between the popular concepts of EI (Gibbs, 1995; Goleman, 1998; Bradberry & Greaves, 2009) and the 'scientific' (Mayer & Salovey, 1997; Bar-On, 1997; Antonakis, 2004). This had led to much confusion and contradiction.

There are also conceptual difficulties with what EI actually is. For example, various writers use terms such as 'competencies' (Goleman, 1998), 'skills' (Mayer et al, 2003), 'qualities' (Bar-On, 1997) and 'abilities' (Van Rooy & Viswesvaran, 2004) to describe what makes up EI.

Myth 2. Measures (prospects: *good*)

The authors claim there are serious problems with how people have attempted to test EI and often the standards do not meet the criteria set for established psychometric testing. For example, the ECI-360 developed by Goleman and the Bar-On EQ-i test have been dismissed as not valid tests of EI (Matthews, Zeidner & Roberts, 2002). Matthews, Roberts & Zeidner (2004) do suggest that some progress has been made with the MSCEIT developed by Mayer and his colleagues.

Myth 3. Self-reports (prospects: *poor*)

Matthews, Roberts & Zeidner (2004) state that the self-reported scales used to test for EI have significant overlap with both the Big Five personality concepts and other concepts such as empathy, self-esteem and optimism. The authors conclude that self-reported EI gained from questionnaires is not different from the existing personality theories.

Myth 4. Ability tests (prospects: *fair*)

The authors state that EI does not meet the criteria required for a traditional, cognitive test of intelligence. They criticize the existing tests as not establishing 'veridical criteria', that is, if EI is a new intelligence then in its entirety it ought to be assessed through items that can be responded to correctly or incorrectly. That is not the case with existing EI tests.

Myth 5. Relates to cognition (prospects: *poor*)

The authors point out that the argument for separate emotional and rational minds is not consistent with current cognitive models. They go on to state that the idea that EI can be directly attributed to particular brain systems (e.g. the amygdala and frontal cortex) is not supported by the existing literature.

Myth 6. Predicts adaptive coping (prospects: *good*)

EI proponents claim that effective handling of stressful encounters is central to EI (Goleman, 1998; Bar-On, 2010). The authors state:

EI tests may correlate with coping scales and outcome measures, sometimes. However, it is simplistic to suppose such findings support a single continuum of individual differences in adaptation (p 193).

Myth 7. Critical for real world success (prospects: *fair*)

The authors state that existing studies do not support the claims that EI is strongly predictive of results in real-world settings or that methods used to increase EI (e.g. training) are cost-effective.

The real-world application of EI

The work of Matthews, Roberts & Zeidner has illustrated problems in seven critical areas of EI. Definitional problems are particularly difficult for the casual reader, since what exactly 'EI' is may change depending on which book you pick up.

Although ideas related and similar to EI can be traced back 50 years (Beldoch, 1964), modern interest in EI began with Salovey & Mayer's (1990) article defining it. Mayer et al (2003) conceptualized three main models of EI: the Ability Model, the Mixed Model and the Trait Model.

The **Ability Model** states that EI is a new type of intelligence and can best be illustrated by Mayer & Salovey's four-branch model (1997). This model 'focuses on emotions themselves and their interactions with thought' (Mayer et al, 2003: p 403).

The **Mixed Model** is very different to the Ability Model and focuses on EI as a broad set of competencies and skills (Goleman, 1998). The **Trait Model** is related to the Mixed Model and sees EI as a personality trait made up of a collection of non-cognitive capabilities, competencies and skills (Bar-On, 1997). However, most EI writers would possibly agree with the idea that EI is about being aware of emotions in yourself and others, and being able to manage those emotions.

There are also serious issues around measurement and self-reporting. Existing tests for EI seem to lack both validity and reliability. To be valid, a test must measure what it claims to measure; to be reliable, the measurement tool must be consistent, giving similar results each time it is used. For now, the MSCEIT appears to be the most valid and reliable of all the EI tests.

While the term intelligence is used differently by different writers, it has an accepted meaning in the sciences. Intelligence is usually described in relation to problem-solving ability, spatial manipulation and language acquisition. Howard Gardner described multiple intelligences: linguistic, logical-mathematical, musical, bodily-kinesthetic, spatial, interpersonal, intrapersonal, and naturalist (Gardner, 1999).

Whether EI is a type of intelligence or not may seem to be dabbling in semantics to the casual reader. However, there is a number of serious issues at the root of this question, including whether EI changes developmentally and how it aligns with personality and abilities. Currently, the strongest arguments are for EI being a skill and not an intelligence.

In relation to EI and success, Matthews, Roberts & Zeidner were cautious as they believed the EI field offered little to the practitioner, given the existence of much better validated personality and ability measures. The question of whether EI can predict effective leadership or general success is central to the whole construct of EI.

Since the publication of the article in 2004 there have been a number of studies that have supported the predictive ability of EI in relation to areas such as leadership effectiveness (Rosete & Ciarrochi, 2005) and employee engagement (Palmer & Gignac, 2012). However, much of the research done in the EI area is still often reported in business publications and unpublished theses and not in peer-reviewed journals.

A 2010 meta-analysis found that EI has an unclear impact on job performance: 'EI positively predicts performance for high emotional labor jobs and negatively predicts performance for low emotional labor jobs' (Joseph & Newman, 2010). A different meta-analysis, also published in 2010, found a positive and significant correlation with job performance (O'Boyle et al, 2010).

Overall, recent research has added support to the real-world application of EI. However, the claims often exceed the evidence found in the peer-reviewed research. Research has found that EI measurements provide very little additional information over general intelligence and personality tests. Further, there is still confusion over whether EI is a skill, a competency or a type of intelligence.

So what are the big takeaways here?

- **There are many different and contradictory definitions of EI.**
- **However, most definitions agree that EI is about being aware of emotions in yourself and others,** and being able to manage those emotions.
- **It remains unclear whether EI is a skill, a competency or an intelligence.** At the moment, the case for it being a skill may be the strongest.

- **EI may predict certain outcomes such as work-performance or leadership ability.** However, the claims by EI proponents often exceed the scientific evidence.

Source

Matthews, G., Roberts, R. D. & Zeidner, M. (2004), 'Seven myths about emotional intelligence', *Psychological Inquiry*, Vol. 15 No. 3 pp 179–96

References

Antonakis, J. (2004), 'On why "Emotional Intelligence" will not predict leadership effectiveness beyond IQ or the "Big Five": an extension and rejoinder', *Organizational Analysis*, Vol. 12 Issue 2 pp 171–82

Bar-On, R. (1997), 'The Emotional Intelligence Inventory (EQ-i)': Technical manual. Toronto, Canada: Multi-Health Systems

Bar-On, R. (2010), 'Emotional intelligence: An integral part of positive psychology', *South African Journal of Psychology*, Vol. 40 Issue 1 pp 54–62

Beldoch, M., 'Sensitivity to expression of emotional meaning in three modes of communication'. In Davitz, J. R. (Ed.) (1964), *The Communication of Emotional Meaning.* New York: McGraw-Hill

Bradberry, T. & Greaves, J. (2009), *Emotional Intelligence 2.0.* San Diego: TalentSmart

Erigüç, G. & Köse, S. D. (2013), 'Evaluation of Emotional Intelligence and Communication Skills of Health Care Manager Candidates: A Structural Equation Modeling', *International Journal of Business and Social Science*, Vol. 4 Issue 13 pp 115–23

Gardner, H. E. (1999), *Intelligence Reframed: Multiple Intelligences for the 21st Century.* New York: Basic Books

Gibbs, N. (1995), 'THE EQ FACTOR', *Time*, October 2 pp 60–8

Goleman, D. (1998), *Working with Emotional Intelligence*. New York: Bantam

Joseph, D. L. & Newman, D. A. (2010), 'Emotional intelligence: An integrative meta-analysis and cascading model', *Journal of Applied Psychology*, Vol. 95 Issue 1 pp 54–78

McCabe, D. P. & Castel, A. D. (2008), 'Seeing is believing: The effect of brain images on judgments of scientific reasoning', *Cognition*, Vol. 107 Issue 1 pp 343–52

Matthews, G., Zeidner, M. & Roberts, R. D. (2002), *Emotional Intelligence: Science and Myth*. Cambridge, MA: MIT Press

Matthews, G., Roberts, R. D. & Zeidner, M. (2004), 'Seven myths about emotional intelligence', *Psychological Inquiry*, Vol. 15 No. 3 pp 179–96

Mayer, J. D. & Salovey, P., 'What is emotional intelligence?'. In Salovey, P. (Ed.) (1997), *Emotional Development and Emotional Intelligence*. New York: Basic Books

Mayer, J. D., Salovey, P., Caruso, D. R. & Sitarenios, G. (2003), 'Measuring emotional intelligence with the MSCEIT V2.0', *Emotion*, Vol. 3 Issue 1 pp 97–105

Murphy, K. R. (Ed.) (2006), *A Critique of emotional intelligence: What are the problems and how can they be fixed?*. Mahwah, NJ: Lawrence Erlbaum

O'Boyle, E. H., Humphrey, R. H., Pollack, J. M., Hawver, T. H. & Story, P. A. (2010), 'The relation between emotional intelligence and job performance: A meta-analysis', *Journal of Organizational Behavior*, Vol. 32 Issue 5 pp 788–818

Palmer, B. R. & Gignac, G. E. (2012), 'The impact of emotionally intelligent leadership on talent retention, discretionary effort and employment brand', *Industrial and Commercial Training*, Vol. 44 Issue 1 pp 9–18

Prati, L. M., Douglas, C., Ferris, G. R., Ammeter, A. P. & Buckley, M. R. (2003), 'Emotional intelligence, leadership effectiveness, and team outcomes', *The International Journal of Organizational Analysis*, Vol. 11 pp 21–40

Rosete, D. & Ciarrochi, J. (2005), 'Emotional intelligence and its relationship to workplace performance outcomes of leadership effectiveness', *Leadership and Organization Development Journal*, Vol. 26 pp 388–99

Salovey, P. & Mayer, J. D. (1990), 'Emotional intelligence', *Imagination, Cognition and Personality*, Vol. 9 pp 185–211

Van Rooy, D. L. & Viswesvaran, C. (2004), 'Emotional intelligence: A meta-analytic investigation of predictive validity and nomological net', *Journal of Vocational Behavior*, Vol. 65 Issue 1 pp 71–95

Waterhouse, L. (2006), 'Multiple intelligences, the Mozart effect, and Emotional Intelligence: A critical review', *Educational Psychologist*, Vol. 41 Issue 4 pp 207–25

See also

Further reading

Ashkanasy, N. M. & Daus, C. S. (2005), 'Rumors of the death of emotional intelligence in organizational behavior are vastly exaggerated', *Journal of Organizational Behavior*, Vol. 26 Issue 4 pp 441–52

Fineman, S. (2004), 'Getting the Measure of Emotion – And the Cautionary Tale of Emotional Intelligence', *Human Relations*, Vol. 57 Issue 6 pp 719–40

Herrnstein, R. J. & Murray, C. A. (1994), *The Bell Curve: Intelligence and Class Structure in American Life*. New York: The Free Press

Schmidt, F. L. & Hunter, J. E. (1998), 'The validity and utility of selection methods in personnel psychology: Practical and theoretical implications of 85 years of research findings', *Psychological Bulletin*, Vol. 124 pp 262–74

Walter, F., Cole, M. S. & Humphrey, R. H. (2011), 'Emotional Intelligence: Sine Qua Non of Leadership or Folderol?', *The Academy of Management Perspectives*, Vol. 25 Issue 1 pp 45–59

Zeidner, M., Matthews, G. & Roberts, R. D. (2004), 'Emotional Intelligence in the Workplace: A Critical Review', *Applied Psychology: An International Review*, Vol. 53 Issue 3 pp 371–99

SUBLIMINAL COMMUNICATION: HIDDEN MESSAGES

Don't lose out because you don't have the confidence! Lose that lack of self-confidence with this Mobile Application. Learn tips and techniques to approach situations in your job, relationships and school with more confidence then you ever dreamed of...

Description of a paid subliminal app on Google Play™, October 2014: Price: £6.03

The word 'subliminal' describes something that is below the threshold of consciousness, but that still produces a response. There is a multimillion-dollar industry of self-help tapes, DVDs and apps that claim to help with self-confidence, weight loss, health, fitness, sleep problems, giving up smoking, improving memory and relationships, and even becoming successful.

Subliminal techniques use images or words so fleetingly that the person receiving the message does not consciously see or hear them. There has also been much controversy about the use of subliminal messages in advertising, TV and film.

Does it work? Do subliminal messages change our behaviour and emotions? Can we be 'forced' to purchase something, we didn't intend to? Let's allow scientific research to answer that question.

In 1991, a team of US psychologists published a research report in the flagship journal of the Association for Psychological Science (previously the American Psychological Society) on a study into subliminal self-help tapes (Greenwald, Spangenberg, Pratkanis & Eskenazi, 1991).

These tapes claim, among other things, to help you to:

- improve your memory
- stop smoking
- improve your self-confidence
- reduce stress
- get fit
- get rich
- be happy
- become attractive
- improve your learning ability
- learn foreign languages
- lose weight
- attract wealth
- develop a healthy lifestyle
- and much more....

The researchers in the 1991 study focused on just two of these claims. Anthony Greenwald and his colleagues conducted a test of commercially available subliminal audiotapes that claimed to enhance memory or self-esteem (Greenwald et al, 1991). The study utilized a four-part procedure as follows:

1. A double-blind method was used to remove any possible placebo effect. In the double-blind approach, both the researchers and the subjects do not know who is getting which particular treatment.
2. They carefully set up the experiment to make sure that the conditions closely met the ordinary use of such subliminal tapes.
3. The chosen subjects were motivated to achieve the goals promised by the tapes. This was because they felt that such motivation was plausibly a precondition in the subliminal marketplace.
4. Both pre-test and post-test measures of self-esteem and memory were used to allow for appropriate statistical testing of any outcomes.

Subjects were recruited from both student and adult populations at a US university. Of the 288 volunteers, 237 people returned to conduct the post-tests (149 women, 88 men). Subliminal tapes from three different manufacturers were used, and they contained relaxing music or nature sounds and the subliminal messages of either 'memory improvement' or 'increased self-esteem'.

Half the subjects were told they were being given memory-improving tapes, the other half the self-esteem improving tapes. In an interesting twist, the researchers gave half the tapes the wrong label. Therefore, some of the subjects who believed they were using memory tapes were really using self-esteem tapes and vice-versa.

This label switch put in place the placebo effect, that is, the measurable and observable change in behaviour or health not attributable to the treatment that was administered. So the subjects who received the self-esteem tapes labelled as memory tapes were both a treatment group and a control group for the placebo effect – and the same was true for those who had the wrongly labelled memory tapes.

The researchers used three well-recognized tests of self-esteem and memory before and after subjects used the tapes daily for a month. After a month of using the subliminal tapes, neither the memory tapes nor the self-esteem tapes had produced their claimed effects.

The researchers did find a non-specific placebo effect where self-esteem and memory increased independently of assignment. This may have been a 'true' placebo effect or may have been only due to practice improving people's scores between the pre-and post-test. It was not attributable to the tapes.

However, more than a third of subjects had the *illusion* of improvement, and this corresponded to the switched label on the tape, not the actual contents of the tape. Overall, approximately 50 per cent of subjects believed that they had improved their memory or self-esteem, corresponding to the label on the tape, not the actual tape content.

The evidence to support the claims

Despite the lack of evidence for genuine effects, subliminal communication has become a multimillion-dollar industry. Apps and DVDs claim to improve everything from self-esteem to curing cancer. Many people seem to accept the idea of hidden messages in films or music and the idea that 'special' messages can break through into the unconscious or subconscious mind (even without knowing what consciousness is).

Subliminal messaging was dramatically introduced to the general public in the 1950s with an experiment in which the messages 'Drink Coca-Cola' and 'Eat Popcorn' were supposedly displayed for milliseconds in a cinema, resulting in a considerable increase of Coke and popcorn sales. However, this was a sham. The proponent of the 'study', ad-man James Vicary, revealed in a 1962 interview that 'the original study was a fabrication intended to increase customers for his failing marketing business' (Pratkanis, 1992).

The marketers and developers of subliminal self-help tapes, DVDs and apps claim that they 'address the subconscious mind with powerful positive hidden messages' or that they 'bypass what the human ear can hear and penetrate directly into the core of your mind'. One app on the Google Play™ site, 'Subliminal Success', claims to 'transform your mind'.

However, there is simply no evidence to support these claims. In fact, the evidence is clear that subliminal messaging *doesn't* work. In addition to the 1991 study by Anthony Greenwald and his colleagues presented in this chapter, other studies have also found no evidence to support the claims made by those who sell this pseudoscientific nonsense (Auday, Mellett & Williams, 1991; Russell, Rowe & Smouse, 1991).

In 1984 the US Army Research Institute (ARI) asked the National Academy of Sciences/National Research Council to form a committee to assess the claims of 'New Age' techniques such as neuro-linguistic programming (NLP), mind-reading and subliminal self-help tapes. The groups report concluded there was 'neither theoretical foundation nor experimental evidence' for the efficacy of subliminal self-help tapes (Swets & Bjork, 1990).

This is not to say that there is no such thing as a subliminal effect. However, there is some confusion about the difference between subliminal 'perception' and subliminal 'persuasion'. Numerous psychological studies have shown that people are capable of processing information without being aware of doing so and may be able to do so even when asleep (Wood, Bootzin, Kihlstrom & Schacter, 1992; Krishnan & Trappey, 1999).

In the 1991 study by Anthony Greenwald and his colleagues, more than a third of subjects had the illusion of improvement, and this corresponded to the label, not the actual contents of the tape. What the researchers called an 'illusory placebo effect' (Greenwald et al). People did not improve in any real way, but they *believed* that they had. This is the placebo effect at work.

The rejection of subliminal persuasion also has important implications for the study of human communication. If the body and mind can be altered by hearing the right message, then this may explain why many psychological 'fads' and pseudosciences seem so attractive.

Fads and techniques such as subliminal tapes, dream interpretation, psychic healing, faith healing, 'psychic' surgery, homeopathy, Reiki therapy, palm reading and even NLP may have their explanations in something a lot less enticing. That is the placebo effect.

So what are the big takeaways here?

- **Subliminal persuasion doesn't work.**
- **Subliminal apps and DVDs seem to work because people think they will work.** This is the placebo effect.
- **Don't waste money or time on subliminal self-help tapes, DVDs and apps.** They do not do what they say, and there is no credible research to suggest they do.

Source

Greenwald, A. G., Spangenberg, E. R., Pratkanis, A. R. & Eskenazi, J. (1991), 'Doubleblind tests of subliminal self-help audiotapes', *Psychological Science*, Vol. 2 No. 2 pp 119–22

References

Auday, B. C., Mellett, J. L. & Williams, P. M. (1991), 'Self-improvement Using Subliminal Selfhelp Audiotapes: Consumer Benefit or Consumer Fraud?' Paper presented at the meeting of the Western Psychological Association, San Francisco, California

Greenwald, A. G., Spangenberg, E. R., Pratkanis, A. R. & Eskenazi, J. (1991), 'Doubleblind tests of subliminal self-help audiotapes', *Psychological Science*, Vol. 2 No. 2 pp 119–22

Krishnan, H. S. & Trappey, C. V. (1999), 'Nonconscious memory processes in marketing: A historical perspective and future directions', *Psychology and Marketing*, Vol. 16 Issue 6 pp 451–7

Pratkanis, A. R. (1992), 'The Cargo-Cult Science of Subliminal Persuasion', *Skeptical Inquirer*, Vol. 16.3 Spring 1992

Russell, T. G., Rowe, W. & Smouse, A. D. (1991), 'Subliminal Self-Help Tapes and Academic Achievement: An Evaluation', *Journal of Counseling & Development*, Vol. 69 Issue 4 pp 359–62

Swets, J. A. & Bjork, R. A. (1990), 'Enhancing Human Performance: An Evaluation of "New Age" Techniques Considered by the U.S. Army', *Psychological Science*, Vol. 1 No. 2 pp 85–96

Wood, J. M., Bootzin, R. R., Kihlstrom, J. F. & Schacter, D. L. (1992), 'Implicit and Explicit Memory for Verbal Information Presented During Sleep', *Psychological Science*, Vol. 3 No. 4 236–9

Subliminal Success. Google Play. https://play.google.com/store/apps/details?id=com.lwi.android.subliminalsuccess

Gaining Self-Confidence. Google Play. https://play.google.com/
store/apps/details?id=com.healthyvisions.gainingselfconfidence

See also

Chapter 5 – Can your handwriting reveal your personality?

Chapter 11 – The placebo effect and communication

Chapter 24 – The Forer Effect: gullibility in action

Further reading

Druckman, D. & Swets, J. A. (Eds.) (1988), *Enhancing Human
Performance: Issues, Theories, and Techniques*. Committee
on Techniques for the Enhancement of Human Performance.
Commission on Behavioral and Social Sciences and Education.
National Research Council (National Academy Press,
Washington, D.C., 1988)

Druckman, D. & Bjork, R. A. (Eds.), *In The Mind's Eye:
Enhancing Human Performance*, Committee on Techniques
for the Enhancement of Human Performance. Commission on
Behavioral and Social Sciences and Education. National Research
Council. (National Academy Press, Washington, D.C., 1991)

McConnell, J. V., Cutler, R. L. & McNeil, E. B. (1958),
'Subliminal Stimulation: An Overview', *American Psychologist*,
Vol. 13 pp 229–42

Pratkanis, A. R. & Aronson, E. (1992), *Age of Propaganda:
The Everyday Use and Abuse of Persuasion*. New York: W. H.
Freeman

Trappey, C. (1996), 'A Meta-analysis of consumer choice and
subliminal advertising', *Psychology and Marketing*, Vol. 13
Issue 5 pp 517–30

9 WOMEN DO NOT TALK MORE THAN MEN

The talkativeness of women has been gauged in comparison not with men but with silence. Women have not been judged on the grounds of whether they talk more than men, but of whether they talk more than silent women.
Dale Spender, feminist scholar and writer (1980)

Gender and communication is a controversial and complicated area of study. However, if you ask most people who talks more, men or women, most people will answer 'women'. In fact, an Internet search of the topic will often cite the statistic that women speak approximately 20,000 words a day while men speak approximately 7,000.

This claim can be traced to Dr Louann Brizendine, an American neuropsychiatrist. In her book, *The Female Brain* (2006), she claims that women speak an average of 20,000 words per day, compared to the 7,000 spoken by men. However, given the scientific credentials of the author it is disappointing to see that her book provided no scientific evidence at all for the claim and the figures now oft quoted.

University of Pennsylvania linguistics professor Mark Liberman has been very critical of Brizendine's claims, stating that there is no basis in science for them (Liberman, 2006a). However, these claims continue to be perpetuated in self-help books and online blogs. They have become yet another online myth.

Liberman has hypothesized as to the source of the Brizendine myth and suggests:

My current best guess is that a marriage counsellor invented this particular meme about 15 years ago, as a sort of parable for couples with certain communication problems, and others have picked it up and spread it, while modulating the numbers to suit their tastes (Liberman, 2006b).

In July 2007 a team of psychologists from Washington University, the University of Arizona and the University of Texas at Austin conducted a scientific study to assess whether women really are more talkative than men (Mehl, Vazire, Ramírez-Esparza, Slatcher & Pennebaker, 2007). Published in the respected journal *Science*, the researchers conducted the first study to record systematically and analyse the quantity of words spoken by a sizable number of people.

They analysed data from 396 participants over the period from 1998 to 2004. The sample was made up of 396 university students (210 women and 186 men) in Texas, Arizona and Mexico.

The subjects' speaking was chronicled using a method for recording natural language that had been developed over eight years (Mehl, Pennebaker, Crow, Dabbs, & Price, 2001). The 'EAR' device was a digital voice recorder that unobtrusively tracked the subjects' real-world talking. It operated by periodically recording conversations in a covert way. It was impossible for participants to control or to know when the EAR was on or off (Mehl et al, 2007).

The researchers found that the average number of words spoken by men and women were almost the same, with both speaking on average 16,000 words per day. The results disproved the ratio myth of 20,000/7,000. The researchers stated:

We therefore conclude, on the basis of available empirical evidence, that the widespread and highly publicized stereotype about female talkativeness is unfounded (Mehl et al, 2007).

This result also echoed a meta-analysis conducted by the University of California, Santa Cruz in 2007 that found that across all the studies examined, men actually talked more (though the difference was small) (Leaper & Ayres, 2007). A meta-analysis is a statistical technique for combining the findings from independent studies and is considered the highest level of evidence possible in social science research (Glass, 1976).

One often-quoted brain study used to support the idea that women are more talkative than men is the work of researchers from the University of Maryland School of Medicine. This study, published in *The Journal of Neuroscience*, suggests that higher levels of FOXP2, the so-called 'language protein', are found in the brains of women (Bowers, Perez-Pouchoulen, Edwards, & McCarthy, 2013).

This study, like Brizendine's book, had journalists all excited again about the stereotype. NBC News in the USA, on its 'Today Health' website, ran an article headlined 'Chatty Cathy, listen up: New study reveals why women talk more than men' and proceeded to both repeat the 20,000/7,000 myth and the FOXP2 research to suggest women talk more than men (Kim, 2013).

However, the study was based on the vocalizations of baby rats and measured protein levels in the brains of ten dead children. Obviously, no word counts were done, and the researchers seem to have chosen not to look at the published literature on male/female word use. From this research, we could hypothesize that male rat pups have higher levels of language protein than females. However, the results should not and cannot be extrapolated to living, speaking humans.

The myth of the talkative woman

There is a popular and well-publicized stereotype that women talk more than men. However, all of the scientific research suggests this is untrue.

As mentioned above, Dr Louann Brizendine and her book *The Female Brain* is the source of the oft-quoted (20,000/7,000) myth. The book has not been well received by some of her fellow scientists. The joint reviewers in the scientific magazine *Nature* stated:

Despite the author's extensive academic credentials, The Female Brain *disappointingly fails to meet even the most basic standards of scientific accuracy and balance. The book is riddled with scientific errors and is misleading about the processes of brain development, the neuroendocrine system,*

and the nature of sex differences in general. (Young &
Balaban, 2006).

Why then is this myth so persuasive? It seems the media and the
general public simply like the idea of this myth. The Australian
feminist scholar Dale Spender suggests in the opening quote at
the beginning of this chapter that it is about male hegemony. She
is no doubt correct as stereotypes are often used by one dominant
group to exert power over another. How many young girls have
been told by their teachers to 'be ladylike and quiet'; not to be
'bold' or to 'be seen and not heard'?

This hegemonic discourse may explain why people have a problem
believing the results of scientific studies such as that by Matthias
Mehl and his colleagues (Mehl et al, 2007). It would seem that the
stereotypes about male/female communication run deep.

When we stereotype women as 'talkative' or 'chatty', we simplify
gender-based communication and ignore the scientific reality.
When we stereotype we hear and see things that we expect rather
than what is real. We jump to incorrect assumptions. We limit
our communication.

The myth – in this case, talkative women – is then perpetuated in
popular media such as books and films. This is then taken into
the workplace and women may be judged on talkativeness – not
against men, but against the stereotype. Particularly, if the 'strong
silent male' is an admired stereotype. A women who talks a lot
will then be put up as an example of the stereotype. It is easy to
see how a talkative man may not be subject to the same analysis.

The amount we speak is also about our national culture. In some
cultures, silence is seen as a highly rated communication skill,
whereas in another talking is considered more important. People
are also socialized to adopt particular gender roles based on their
cultural upbringing.

So in one culture a 'talkative' women may be going against the
cultural norm that values introversion over extroversion. In
another, being outgoing and 'chatty' may be culturally valued.
In her work on the historical perspective of Japanese women's

language formation, Mariko Bohn gives examples of old 'conduct books' that stress the importance of Japanese young women not being talkative (a talkative woman is unrefined [1698]; a woman must be careful about her language and not be talkative [1880]) (Bohn, 2011). Though the situation for women in the West may have not been a great deal different at this time.

Can we reach a firm conclusion on the question 'Do women talk more than men?'. The answer is no. In some circumstances, men may talk more than women, in others it could be reversed. The research presented here has been conducted with US college students, and that limits the generalizability of the results. However, one thing is clear, the 20,000/7,000 myth has no scientific standing. The best scientific guess at the present is that men and women probably talk about the same, though this would be significantly mediated by culture and context.

So what are the big takeaways here?

- **Word count research has found that the average number of words spoken by men and women were almost the same,** with both speaking on average 16,000 words per day.
- **If you hear someone postulating the 20,000/7,000 myth,** let them know that it has no scientific standing.
- **The prevalent and highly disseminated stereotype about female talkativeness is wrong.**
- **Women are also often labelled with the term 'gossip',** where this term is rarely used to describe a man, even one engaged in gossip.

Source

Mehl, M. R., Vazire, S., Ramírez-Esparza, N., Slatcher, R. B. & Pennebaker, J. W. (2007), 'Are Women Really More Talkative Than Men?', *Science*, Vol. 317 (5834) p 82

References

Bohn, M. T. (2011), 'Educated Japanese Young Women's Diverse Linguistic and Social Behaviours During the Meiji and Taisho Periods (1868–1926) with Implications for Japanese Language Pedagogy', Proquest, Umi Dissertation Publishing

Bowers, J. M., Perez-Pouchoulen, M., Edwards, N. S. & McCarthy, M. M. (2013), 'FOXP2 mediates sex differences in ultrasonic vocalization by rat pups and directs order of maternal retrieval', *The Journal of Neuroscience*, Vol. 33 Issue 8 pp 3276–83

Brizendine, L. (2006), *The Female Brain*. New York: Morgan Road

Glass, G. V. (1976), 'Primary, secondary and meta-analysis of research', *Educational Researcher*, Vol. 5 No. 10 pp 3–8

Hymes, D. H. (Ed.) (1964), *Language in Culture and Society*. New York: Harper & Row

Kim, E. K. (2013), 'Chatty Cathy, listen up: New study reveals why women talk more than men', *Today Heath Blog* (NBC News): http://www.today.com/health/chatty-cathy-listen-new-study-reveals-why-women-talk-more-1C8469360

Leaper, C. & Ayres, M. M. (2007), 'A Meta-Analytic Review of Gender Variations in Adults' Language Use: Talkativeness, Affiliative Speech, and Assertive Speech', *Personality and Social Psychology Review*, Vol. 11 No. 4 pp 328–63

Liberman, M. (2006), 'Sex-Linked Lexical Budgets': http://itre.cis.upenn.edu/~myl/languagelog/archives/003420.html

Mehl, M. R., Pennebaker, J. W., Crow, M. D., Dabbs, J. & Price, J. H. (2001), 'The Electronically Activated Recorder (EAR): A device for sampling naturalistic daily activities and conversations', *Behavior Research Methods, Instruments, and Computers*, Vol. 33 pp 517–23

Mehl, M. R., Vazire, S., Ramírez-Esparza, N., Slatcher, R. B. & Pennebaker, J. W. (2007), 'Are Women Really More Talkative Than Men?', *Science*, Vol. 317 (5834) p 82

Spender, D. (1980), *Man Made Language*. London: Routledge & Kegan Paul

Young, R. M. & Balaban, E. (2006), 'Review of *The Female Brain* by Louann Brizendine', *Nature*, Vol. 443 p 634 12 October

See also

Chapter 2 – Men and women are not from different planets

Chapter 27 – Cultural differences in communication

Chapter 32 – Neuro-scientific communication

Further reading

Cole, M. & Scribner, S. (1974), *Culture and Thought: A Psychological Introduction*. New York: John Wiley & Sons

Hall, E. T. (1959), *The Silent Language*. New York: Fawcett World Library

Mulac, A. & Lundell, T. L. (1986), 'Linguistic Contributors to the Gender-Linked Language Effect', *Journal of Language & Social Psychology*, Vol. 5 No. 2 pp 81–101

Mumby, D. K. & Putnam, L. L. (1992), 'The Politics of Emotion: A Feminist Reading of Bounded Rationality', *Academy of Management Review*, Vol. 17 No. 3 pp 465–86

Thomson, R. & Murachver, T. (2001), 'Predicting gender from electronic discourse', *British Journal of Social Psychology*, Vol. 40 Pt. 2 pp 193–208

10 NLP AND COMMUNICATION

Science works best when we are thoughtful and critical and scrutinize claims carefully. Our job should be to promote such thought and scrutiny.
Dr Anthony R. Pratkanis, psychologist (1995)

Neuro-linguistic programming (NLP) is a popular and well-known way of modelling communication. It has been variously claimed that NLP can improve communication, cure phobias, treat depression, eradicate learning disabilities, and that one session can eliminate certain eyesight problems such as myopia, and can even cure a common cold (Grinder & Bandler, 1975; 1976).

Developed in the 1970s by Richard Bandler and John Grinder, it had its height of popularity in the 1980s. NLP continues to be used by tens of thousands of 'NLP practitioners' and others in diverse settings today and is enthusiastically supported by those who use it, teach it and certify others to practise it. NLP is taught in universities, schools and by corporate trainers in leading organizations.

However, many psychologists and scientists describe NLP as a pseudoscience and question its efficacy (Sharpley, 1987; Heap, 2008; Witkowski, 2010). Wikipedia states that some professionals have even described NLP as a 'quasi-religion'. Druckman & Swets (1988), in a major study by the National Academy of Sciences for the US Army, concluded that there was little or no empirical evidence to support NLP (p 143).

NLP is not a unified theory; it is a collection of ideas and concepts. Some of the ideas of NLP come from classic psychology, some from psychotherapy, many were invented by Bandler and Grinder. NLP author Andy Bradbury states: 'NLP is a specific modelling process, not a person or an organization' (Bradbury, 2008). There are also a number of NLP-related techniques, some of which are faithful to Bandler and Grinder's original ideas and some that have strayed into the areas of spirituality and New Age practices.

Tomasz Witkowski is a psychologist, writer and founder of the Polish Sceptics' Club. In 2010 he published the most extensive review to date of more than 35 years of research into NLP. To avoid claims of bias, he utilized the Neuro-Linguistic Programming Research Data Base (NLP-RDB) hosted by the 'NLP Community' and held at Bielefeld University in Germany.

Witkowski found reference to 315 articles and other papers on the NLP-RDB from 1974 to 2009 (by 2015 there were 350). These papers were screened against the Master Journal List of the Institute for Scientific Information in Philadelphia (Witkowski, 2010). This list is accepted as covering the most notable and influential journals and is now known as the Science Citation Index Expanded™. Witkowski assumed that those who met the criteria for the Master Journal List would be 'less likely to have published unreliable articles'. This screening left him with 63 articles, representing 20 per cent of the NLP-RDB.

Analysis of these 63 papers (from 30 different publications) led Witkowski to claim that they were a representative sample of NLP research. Of these 63 papers, he found that 33 tested various NLP theories or claims and that 14 were discussion papers with no empirical research and thus were excluded from the analysis. He also eliminated 16 papers that apparently had nothing to do with the NLP field, leaving 33 relevant papers to be analysed.

These 33 papers made up 52.4 per cent of the initially selected sample and came from a number of publications specializing in psychology, hypnosis, counselling and business. He also noted that most of the research activity into NLP happened in the 1980s. Witkowski reported that:

- Eighteen were non-supportive of NLP principles and hypotheses (54.5 per cent)
- Nine supported NLP principles and hypotheses (27.3 per cent), and
- Six had uncertain outcomes (18.2 per cent).

Witkowski's 2010 results are consistent with reviews of the literature by Sharpley (1984; 1987), Heap (1988) and Druckman & Swets (1988). Einspruch & Forman (1985) responded to Sharpley's 1984 study claiming that the studies reviewed had serious methodological problems. They suggested that the researchers did not fully understand NLP and were often testing for things that NLP did not claim.

In a 2012 review, Witowski examined papers that had been published after 1986 in both the NLP-RDB and the PsycINFO database. He found 21 studies that explicitly described controlled, empirical studies that tested either 'NLP basic tenets' or 'NLP techniques' (Witkowski, 2012). He found that 70 per cent of studies were non-supportive, 20 per cent were partially supportive and 10 per cent were supportive of NLP.

What we know about NLP

Witkowski was conducting a literature review, not primary research and not a meta-analysis. A literature review is an accepted academic tool that can be used to analyse ideas to discover relationships and uncover hidden truths (Hart, 1999). Primary research is experimental in nature and involves the collection of data collected by the researcher. A meta-analysis is where research studies are collected and interpreted using mathematical methods similar to those used in primary data analysis (Glass, 1976).

Given that the results of a successful meta-analysis are more objective than a traditional literature review, it is a shame that Witkowski did not attempt to conduct such an analysis. Though it may be that the existing research on NLP is insufficient to conduct such a review.

NLP is marketed by a number of individuals and businesses. Anyone can use the name NLP, call themselves an 'NLP Master' and there is no agreed definition of NLP. What one person calls 'NLP' may be discredited or described as false or 'Anti-NLP' by another (Bradbury, 2015). This lack of clarity makes it particularly difficult to assess any claims made as to the usefulness or efficacy of NLP.

One of the better known NLP claims is the ability to read information from a person's eye movements or, in NLP-speak, 'eye-accessing cues' (EACs). However, this idea was thoroughly researched and discredited in the 1980s (Beck & Beck, 1984; Elich, Thompson & Miller, 1985; Druckman et al, 1988). In more recent work, Wiseman et al (2012) also dismissed the claims made by some NLP proponents that certain eye movements are reliable indicators of lying.

For example, the concept of a 'preferred representational system' (PRS) is included in the NLP literature (Stevens, 1979), and it is often claimed that communication will be more persuasive if it matches the PRS of the target person. For example, David Molden states in his book *NLP Business Masterclass* (2001) that:

Eye movement is one way of telling which of the communication channels are being used to form that representation. Is it a visual, auditory or kinaesthetic representation of the world? We actually use all three, but we may have an unconscious preference for the most developed channel and use that one most often (p 98).

In the 1980s, NLP founder Richard Bandler gave testimony that 'PRS was no longer considered an important component [of NLP]' (Druckman et al, 1988). In their 2012 book, Wake, Gray & Bourke criticized much of the established NLP research, claiming past researchers did not fully understand NLP. They stated that:

Because the researchers lacked adequate training in NLP they misunderstood the nature of the PRS and EACs as patterns and overvalued their importance to NLP (p 201).

Witkowski's extensive analysis of the existing data in 2010 and again in 2012 has shown that there is some limited empirical support for NLP, but that overwhelmingly the scientific research has not supported the claims made by NLP proponents. Witkowski concluded his 2010 review with a damning evaluation of NLP:

My analysis leads undeniably to the statement that NLP represents pseudoscientific rubbish, which should be mothballed forever (p 64).

If NLP works, as its promoters attest to, then all we can say at the present is that we do not know why it does. It may be that some of the methods taught in NLP courses increase people's observation and listening skills; it may be the placebo effect at work or NLP may have as yet unproven value. At the moment, all we know is that most of the claims made by the NLP field are not supported by peer-reviewed scientific research.

Of course, the same could also be said about the underpinning theories and efficacy of the methods adopted in many other fields of practice. A particular practice cannot be said to be efficacious in the absence of evidence-based research.

So what are the big takeaways here?

- **The overwhelming scientific evidence does not support the claims made by the proponents of NLP.**
- **In particular, the ability to use a person's eye-movement to understand their communication patterns, preferred way of communicating or to detect lying is disproven by the scientific evidence.**
- **Many of the NLP ideas popularized and tested in the 1980s, such as the PRS, have now been rejected by many in the NLP field.** What is or isn't NLP is impossible to say with any certainty due to a lack of agreement from those teaching and promoting NLP.

Source

Witkowski, T. (2010), 'Thirty-Five Years of Research on Neuro-Linguistic Programming. NLP Research Data Base. State of the Art or Pseudoscientific Decoration?', *Polish Psychological Bulletin*, Vol. 41 Issue 2 pp 58–66

References

Beck, C. E. & Beck, E. A. (1984), 'Test of the Eye-Movement Hypothesis of Neurolinguistic Programming: A rebuttal of conclusions', *Perceptual and Motor Skills*, Vol. 58 Issue 1 pp 175–6

Bradbury, A. (2008), 'Neuro-Linguistic Programming: Time for an Informed Review' (edited version) *The Skeptical Intelligencer*: http://www.bradburyac.mistral.co.uk/response.html

Bradbury, A. (2015), Honest Abe's NLP Emporium Website. FAQ 2. 'What is NLP?': http://www.bradburyac.mistral.co.uk/nlpfax02.htm

Druckman, D. & Swets, J. (Eds.), *Enhancing Human Performance: Issues, Theories and Techniques* (Committee on Techniques for the Enhancement of Human Performance, Commission on Behavioural and Social Sciences and Education: National Academy Press, Washington, D.C., 1988)

Einspruch, E. L. & Forman, B. D. (1985), 'Observations Concerning Research Literature on Neuro-Linguistic Programming', *Journal of Counseling Psychology*, Vol. 32 Issue 4 pp 589–96

Elich, M., Thompson, R. W. & Miller, L. (1985), 'Mental imagery as revealed by eye movements and spoken predicates: A test of neurolinguistic programming', *Journal of Counseling Psychology*, Vol. 32 Issue 4 pp 622–5

Glass, G. V. (1976), 'Primary, secondary and meta-analysis of research', *Educational Researcher*, Vol. 5 No. 10 pp 3–8

Grinder, J. & Bandler, R. (1975), *The Structure of Magic I*. Palo Alto, CA: Science and Behaviour Books

Grinder, J. & Bandler, R. (1976), *The Structure of Magic II*. Palo Alto, CA: Science and Behaviour Books

Hart, Chris (1999), *Doing a Literature Review: Releasing the Social Science Research Imagination*. New York: Sage

Heap, M., 'Neurolinguistic programming: An interim verdict'. In Heap, M. (Ed.) (1988), *Hypnosis: Current Clinical, Experimental and Forensic Practices*. London: Croom Helm

Heap, M. (2008), 'The validity of some early claims of neuro-linguistic programming', *Skeptical Intelligencer*, Vol. 11, 6–13

Molden, D. (2001), *NLP Business Masterclass*. London: Prentice Hall

Sharpley, C. F. (1984), 'Predicate matching in NLP: A review of research on the preferred representational system', *Journal of Counseling Psychology*, Vol. 31 No. 2 pp 238–48

Sharpley, C. F. (1987), 'Research Findings on Neurolinguistic Programming: Nonsupportive Data or an Untestable Theory?', *Journal of Counseling Psychology*, Vol. 34 No. 1 pp 103–7

Shermer, M. (2011), 'What Is Pseudoscience?', *Scientific American*: http://www.scientificamerican.com/article/what-is-pseudoscience/?page=1

Stevens, J. O. (Ed.). (1979), *Frogs into Princes: Richard Bandler and John Grinder Live*. Moab, UT: Real People Press

Wake, L., Gray, R. M. & Bourke, F. S. (Eds.) (2012), *The Clinical Effectiveness of Neurolinguistic Programming: A Critical Appraisal (Advances in Mental Health Research)*. London: Routledge

Wikipedia (2015). Neuro-linguistic programming. https://en.wikipedia.org/wiki/Neuro-linguistic_programming

Wiseman, R., Watt, C., ten Brinke, L., Porter, S., Couper, S.-L. & Rankin, C. (2012), 'The Eyes Don't Have It: Lie Detection and Neuro-Linguistic Programming', *PLoS ONE* Vol. 7 Issue 7 pp 1–5: http://www.plosone.org/article/fetchObject.action?uri=info:doi/10.1371/journal.pone.0040259&representation=PDF

Witkowski, T. (2010), 'Thirty-Five Years of Research on Neuro-Linguistic Programming. NLP Research Data Base. State of the Art or Pseudoscientific Decoration?', *Polish Psychological Bulletin*, Vol. 41 Issue 2 pp 58–66

Witkowski, T. (2012), 'A Review of Research Findings on Neuro-Linguistic Programming', *The Scientific Review of Mental Health Practice*, Vol. 9 Issue 1 pp 29–40

See also

Further reading

Bandler, R. & Grinder, J. (1979), *Frogs into princes: Neuro Linguistic Programming*. Moab, UT: Real People Press

Neuro-Linguistic Programming Research Data Base:
http://www.nlp.de/cgi-bin/research/nlp-rdb.cgi

Pratkanis, A. R. (1995), 'How to Sell a Pseudoscience', *Skeptical Inquirer*, Vol. 19 No. 4 pp 19–25

Sturt, J., Ali, S., Robertson, W., Metcalfe, D., Grove, A., Bourne, C. & Bridle, C. (2012), 'Neurolinguistic programming: A systematic review of the effects on health outcomes', *British Journal of General Practice*, Vol. 62 No. 604 pp 757–64

11 THE PLACEBO EFFECT AND COMMUNICATION

...It's very clear to see
That a...
Spoonful of sugar helps the medicine go down
The medicine go down
The medicine go down
Just a spoonful of sugar helps the medicine go down
In a most delightful way
Mary Poppins (1964, Walt Disney film)

A five-year-old boy has a terrible cough and can't sleep, his mother rather than reaching for a cough syrup, gives him a spoonful of flavoured, coloured water. His cough goes away. A spoonful of sugar doesn't just *help the medicine go down* as Mary Poppins sang but may *be* the medicine (Paul et al, 2014).

Students are told they are testing a new type of painkiller. This 'pain-killer' was a brown lotion painted on the skin. However, the students were not told that it was only water, iodine and thyme oil, none of which are painkilling medicines. Significant reductions in pain were reported, even though the painkiller was a fake (Montgomery & Kirsch, 1996).

What is going on here is the 'placebo effect'. A placebo ('I shall please' in Latin) is anything that seems to be real but is, in fact, fake. The placebo effect is the measurable and observable change in behaviour or health not attributable to the treatment that has been administered.

Scientific interest in the placebo effect has grown dramatically over the past decade (Meissner, Kohls & Colloca, 2011). The placebo effect is a real neurobiological phenomenon, and our thoughts and beliefs are critical in healing and physical wellbeing. The placebo effect has a well-documented effect on areas such as pain control, gastric ulcers, depression, asthma and even some heart conditions.

In 2013, eight Finnish researchers published an amazing study in the prestigious *New England Journal of Medicine*. The researchers conducted a randomized, double-blind trial with 146 subjects who had knee symptoms consistent with a 'degenerative medial meniscus tear', a serious knee complaint that is often treated with surgery (Sihvonen, Paavola, Malmivaara, Itälä, Joukainen, Nurmi, Kalske & Järvinen, 2013).

The researchers selected subjects who had had knee pain for more than three months and who had been unresponsive to conventional conservative treatments, such as medication and physical therapy. All the subjects had actual physical injury consistent with a tear of the medial meniscus.

The subjects, aged between 35 and 65, were randomly assigned to two groups. One group received surgery (arthroscopic partial meniscectomy) and the other received placebo (or sham) surgery. To keep the placebo or 'sham' surgery realistic, the researchers went to extraordinary lengths in both communication and methodology.

- During an initial diagnostic procedure, if a subject was confirmed to be eligible for the trial, a research nurse opened an envelope and revealed the group assignment to the surgeon (real surgery or placebo); this was not revealed to the subject.
- The numbered, opaque, sealed envelopes were prepared by a statistician with no involvement in the study.
- Only the orthopaedic surgeon and the operating room staff were made aware of the group assignment, and they did not participate in further treatment or follow-up of the subject. This way the subjects did not get any indication from their communication as to which group they were in.
- With the real surgery group, an actual surgical treatment was conducted. For the placebo surgery group, the same surgical procedure was simulated. To mimic the sensations and

sounds of real surgery, the surgeon asked for all instruments, manipulated the knee, pushed the knee with an instrument, and used suction.

- The placebo subject was kept in the operating room for the same amount of time required to perform the actual surgery.
- For both groups, post-operative care was delivered according to a standardized protocol and both groups received exactly the same follow-up from health professionals who did not know which group the subjects were in.

The subjects received a full examination after 12 months, and the findings were exceptional. There were no significant between-group differences in any primary outcome for both the genuine and the placebo surgery groups.

A year after the procedure, both groups had an equally low incidence of symptoms and were satisfied with the overall condition of their knee. Further, the subjects in the sham-surgery group were not significantly more likely than subjects in the genuine surgery group to guess that they had undergone a placebo procedure.

The placebo effect is real

The Finnish study follows on from a controversial study reported in 2002 by Bruce Moseley and his colleagues who also used placebo surgery with subjects with advanced osteoarthritis of the knee. They found that patients receiving surgical treatment did no better than those receiving placebo surgery. This study was met with unprecedented criticism and hostility, particularly from orthopaedic surgeons and their professional bodies.

What these studies and many others tell us is that the placebo effect is real, though the linkages between behaviour, brain and physical responses are not totally clear. However, the evidence of its existence is very clear. Neuroscientists such as Karin Meissner and her colleagues state that:

The placebo effect is a 'real' neurobiological phenomenon that has important implications for clinical neuroscience research and medical care (Meissner et al, 2011).

It also has important implications for the study of human communication. If the body and mind can be altered by hearing the right message then this may explain why many psychological 'fads' and pseudosciences seem so attractive. Fads and techniques such as subliminal tapes, dream interpretation, faith healing, 'psychic' surgery, homeopathy, Reiki therapy, palm reading and even neuro-linguistic programming (NLP) may have their explanations in the placebo effect.

If we believe something is making us feel better, even when it is inert, then is it still 'real'? Well, that depends on what you see as real. In the Finnish study the effects on the subjects' knees were real – they had a medical improvement based on quantifiable measures.

One of the conventional theories of how placebos work is that they are due to your expectations. If you expect a pill to do something, then the body's chemistry can cause effects similar to a real drug. Also, how strongly you believe in the (fake) treatment, also appears to have an enormous impact on the effect. The power of the message may have a significant impact on how effective a placebo is.

In the 1970s researchers at the University of California at San Francisco demonstrated that the placebo effect was related to endorphins, that is, chemicals secreted in the brain that are chemically similar to painkilling opiates (Levine, Gordon & Fields, 1978). Other researchers, though, have questioned the medical effects of placebos (Hróbjartsson & Gøtzsche, 2001).

Another important relationship to communication is the attention, care and words given when the placebo is applied. There is no doubt that when a faith healer lays their hands on someone, the homeopathic practitioner prescribes a dilution with confident words or when the Reiki therapist uses 'mystical' hand-positions, they are communicating with the person. This communication affects the expectations, feelings and even beliefs of the individual. This in turn appears to trigger the placebo effect.

In the Finnish study, the researchers went to great pains to make sure that the subjects experienced the full range of emotions, experiences and interpersonal communications, irrespective of which group they belonged to. It is not a great leap to see how administering placebo therapies or even placebo surgery with the accompanying care, confidence, touch and interpersonal communication would be an essential part of the linkage between the mind and the body.

So what are the big takeaways here?

- **The placebo effect is the measurable and observable change in behaviour or health,** not attributable to the treatment that has been administered.
- **The placebo effect is real.** The linkages between behaviour, brain and physical responses are not totally clear; however, the evidence of its existence is very clear.
- **The placebo effect explains, at least in part, why many pseudosciences seem to appear to work.**

Source

Sihvonen, R., Paavola, M., Malmivaara, A., Itälä, A., Joukainen, A., Nurmi, H., Kalske, J., Järvinen, T. L. & Finnish Degenerative Meniscal Lesion Study (FIDELITY) Group. (2013), 'Arthroscopic Partial Meniscectomy versus Sham Surgery for a Degenerative Meniscal Tear', *The New England Journal of Medicine*, Vol. 369 No. 26 pp 2515–24

References

Greenwald, A. G., Spangenberg, E. R., Pratkanis, A. R. & Eskenazi, J. (1991), 'Doubleblind tests of subliminal self-help audiotapes', *Psychological Science*, Vol. 2 No. 2 pp 119–22

Hróbjartsson, A. & Gøtzsche, P. C. (2001), 'Is the placebo powerless? An analysis of clinical trials comparing placebo with no treatment', *New England Journal of Medicine*, Vol. 344 No. 21 pp 1594–602

Levine, J. D., Gordon, N. C. & Fields, H. L. (1978), 'The Mechanism of Placebo Analgesia', *The Lancet*, Vol. 2 (8091) pp 654–7

Meissner K., Kohls, N. & Colloca, L. (2011), 'Introduction to placebo effects in medicine: mechanisms and clinical implications', *Philosophical Transactions of the Royal Society B: Biological Sciences,* Vol. 366 No. 1572 pp 1783–9

Meissner, K., Bingel, U., Colloca, L., Wager, T. D., Watson, A. & Flaten, M. A. (2011), 'The Placebo Effect: Advances from Different Methodological Approaches', *The Journal of Neuroscience,* Vol. 31 Issue 45 pp 16117–24

Montgomery, G. & Kirsch, I. (1996), 'Mechanisms of Placebo Pain Reduction: An Empirical Investigation', *Psychological Science,* Vol. 7 No. 3 pp 174–6

Moseley, J. B., O'Malley, K., Petersen, N. J., Menke T. J., Brody, B. A., Kuykendall, D. H., Hollingsworth, J. C., Ashton, C. M. & Wray, N. P. (2002), 'A controlled trial of arthroscopic surgery for osteoarthritis of the knee', *New England Journal of Medicine,* Vol. 347 Issue 2 pp 81–8

Paul, I. M., Beiler, J. S., Vallati, J. R., Duda, L. M. & King, T. S. (2014), 'Placebo Effect in the Treatment of Acute Cough in Infants and Toddlers: A Randomized Clinical Trial', *JAMA Pediatrics.* Published online October 27, 2014

Sihvonen, R., Paavola, M., Malmivaara, A., Itälä, A., Joukainen, A., Nurmi, H., Kalske, J., Järvinen, T. L. & Finnish Degenerative Meniscal Lesion Study (FIDELITY) Group. (2013), 'Arthroscopic Partial Meniscectomy versus Sham Surgery for a Degenerative Meniscal Tear', *The New England Journal of Medicine,* Vol. 369 No. 26 pp 2515–24

See also

Further reading

Aslaksen, P. M. & Flaten, M. A. (2008), 'The roles of physiological and subjective stress in the effectiveness of a placebo on experimentally induced pain', *Psychosomatic Medicine*, Vol. 70 Issue 7 pp 811–18

Beecher, H. K. (1955), 'The Powerful Placebo', *Journal of the American Medical Association*, Vol. 159 Issue 17 pp 1602–6

Meissner, K. (2009), 'Effects of placebo interventions on gastric motility and general autonomic activity', *Journal of Psychosomatic Research*, Vol. 66 Issue 5 pp 391–8

Perry, S. W. & Heidrich, G. (1981), 'Placebo response: Myth and matter', *American Journal of Nursing*, Vol. 81 pp 720–5

Zahn, T. P., Rapoport, J. L. & Thompson, C. L. (1980), 'Autonomic and behavioral effects of dextroamphetamine and placebo in normal and hyperactive prepubertal boys', *Journal of Abnormal Child Psychology*, Vol. 8 Issue 2 pp 145–60

ATTENDING SKILLS IN COMMUNICATION: THE SOLER MODEL

Learning is a result of listening, which in turn leads to even better listening and attentiveness to the other person. In other words, to learn from the child, we must have empathy, and empathy grows as we learn.
Alice Miller, psychologist and author (1923–2010)

Communicating with others is an inherently difficult process, and there are many barriers to effective communication. However, if we learn how to be attentive, to listen and to minimize those obstacles, we can improve the process enormously. Attending skills can be improved with just a little bit of knowledge, practice and application.

However, as Gerard Egan stated, these skills 'must be an extension of your humanity and not just bits of helping technology' (1986). This approach requires us to be genuine and truthful and that we should not just rely on communication 'tricks' or techniques. Attending to another person is about respect, empathy and authenticity.

Professor Gerard Egan is Professor Emeritus of Organization Development and Psychology in the Business School of Loyola University of Chicago. His classic text, *The Skilled Helper*, is the most widely used counselling text in the world. Egan's proven, step-by-step process teaches people how to become more confident and competent communicators.

In this chapter, we are going to look at part of the 'Egan Model' and focus on the micro-skills techniques that help people to tell their story. This involves the well-known SOLER approach to attending behaviour. SOLER is covered in *The Skilled Helper* in Chapter Three: Attending and Listening (1986).

Egan states that even though attending and listening seem to be simple concepts, it is amazing how often people fail to attend or listen to others. When we are talking to someone about something important, be it in an interview, or when talking to our children or someone we are trying to understand, Egan states that:

People want more than physical presence in human communication; they want the other person to be fully there, meaning psychological or social-emotional presence (1986).

When we do not attend to someone we are talking to, we miss necessary information, and we will find it hard to understand what is going on. Egan outlined five ways that you can ensure you are physically present when talking to someone. To help people understand and remember these five 'micro-skills', he created the famous acronym SOLER, which stands for:

S   Face the person **S**quarely

O   Adopt an **O**pen posture

L   At times **L**ean towards the other person

E   Maintain **E**ye contact

R   Try to **R**elax

Egan cautions that the SOLER rules should not be seen as 'absolute dictums' applied rigidly in every case. Rather that they are guidelines to help you orient yourself in a physical way to the other person (p 77). It is important to remain true to yourself and be yourself. When we come across as using a 'technique', we create a further barrier to communication.

SOLER is, however, a proven and well-respected set of guidelines. For example, the Social Care Institute for Excellence found when it reviewed the teaching of social workers that Egan's SOLER model was the most popular model taught in the UK (Diggins, 2004). The SOLER model is also used for the teaching of effective communication skills to human resource professionals, psychotherapists, police and parents. SOLER, while widely used, has not been subject to peer-reviewed critical assessment (Stickley, 2011).

Egan warns that because the technique was developed in North America, it needs to be used with caution with other cultures. Since people differ culturally in the ways in which they communicate non-verbally it is clear that the way in which people show they are paying full attention to another would also be culturally and individually different. Egan states: 'more important than a mechanical application of the SOLER guidelines is an awareness of your body as a source of communication.'

How to pay full attention to someone

The SOLER model is an excellent way of enhancing your relationship with others, particularly when dealing with difficult topics or when you need to improve and maintain rapport. Later in this book we cover listening skills in some depth, but before we can use these skills we need to learn how to pay full attention to someone and the SOLER is an ideal model to remind us how to achieve this.

Rob is talking to his 14-year-old daughter Tabatha, and things are not going that well. Let's look at what happened and how the SOLER model could be used to improve this.

Rob: *Tabatha we need to talk about this report from your teacher*

Tabatha: *No dad, not now I've gotta Skype with Mary*

Rob: *Yes Tabatha, now. Please sit down and let's talk* (glances at TV screen to check the score)

Tabatha: grumbles, *OK what?* (glances at her smartphone screen)

Rob: *OK I'm sick of hearing how you are always getting into trouble at school; you need to listen to me young woman. You will get nowhere in life unless you...* (Rob's phone beeps, he looks at the screen, ignores it) *...start applying yourself.*

Tabatha: says nothing (looks bored)

Rob: *Are you listening to me?* (arms crossed)

Tabatha: *Yes!*

Rob: *OK, will you promise to try harder in chemistry class?* (leans back)

Tabatha: (softly) *Yes, I will Dad*

Rob: *I hope so...* (pauses, glances at TV screen for game score)

Tabatha: (slowly) *OK Dad, I will, now can I go? Mary has WhatsApp'd me six times while I've been sitting here...*

Rob: *OK, but make sure you...* (Tabatha walks away and out of earshot)

Rob and Tabatha are talking, but clearly they are not communicating. Obviously Rob needs to use active listening and apply open rather than closed questions. However, even before this, he needs to look at his micro-communication skills, in particular, the physicality of communication with his teenage daughter.

Using the SOLER model, Rob needed first to adjust the seating arrangement (**S**OLER). He should be sitting directly across from Tabatha to avoid turning his body away from her. What he wants to communicate according to Egan is 'I'm with you right now'. Moving to a suitable place, away from distractions (such as the TV) is vital. Egan also states that if facing the person squarely is 'too threatening', then adopting an angled position may be appropriate.

Rob should have also adopted an open posture (S**O**LER). This means making sure his arms and legs are not crossed. Egan points out that in North American culture an open posture is typically seen as 'nondefense'. Rob needs to ensure that his posture is showing Tabatha that he is interested in what she has to say and that he is open to her thoughts and feelings.

Showing interest brings us to leaning forward (SO**L**ER). Egan suggests thinking of your upper body as if it is on a hinge and that you can move towards or away from the person you are talking to. When we lean towards someone we are saying: 'I'm interested in what you are saying.' You are paying attention to them.

The fourth part is maintaining proper eye-contact (SOL**E**R). Fifty years ago Argyle & Dean demonstrated that without eye contact, people do not feel that they are being communicated with (1965). If Rob maintains good eye contact with Tabatha, then he is demonstrating interest in what she is saying. It is important to acknowledge that eye contact has many different connotations across cultural groups (Buon, 2014).

It is important to turn off ALL screens when talking to someone. Rob and Tabatha should have turned off (not just silenced) their smartphones and the TV should be turned off. This not only prevents distraction, it sends a message of interest and attention. Consider how awful it feels when you talk to someone on the telephone and you know they are typing on their computer or scrolling their Facebook page.

The final part of the Egan model is trying to be relatively relaxed (SOLE**R**). This means not fidgeting nervously or engaging in distracting facial expressions. Rob wants to make Tabatha feel comfortable by appearing relaxed. If Rob appears anxious or nervous, he may unconsciously transfer those feelings to Tabatha. Of course, if Tabatha starts to disclose something sensitive (e.g. bullying), it is important that Rob does not appear too relaxed and demonstrates appropriate concern.

If Rob follows up the SOLER approach with active listening, open questions and appropriate empathy, he may find that his daughter is willing to open up to him. Communication with a teenager can be difficult, but by using proper micro-skills Rob can establish an appropriate helping process.

Egan stated that skilled communicators monitor the quality of their attending and listening but also recognize that no one can listen to another in an entirely unbiased and undistracted way. However, we can do things to remove distractions and turning off all screens and using the SOLER technique can go a long way to improving your communication with others.

So what are the big takeaways here?

- **Use the SOLER technique** (Sitting squarely; Open body language; Leaning forward; maintaining Eye contact; staying Relaxed).
- **Before you start to communicate with someone, remove distractions and turn off all screens** (smartphone, tablets, monitors, TVs, etc.).
- **Remember these techniques were developed in North America and, therefore, need to be approached mindfully in relation to other cultures.**

Source

Egan, G. (1986), *The Skilled Helper: A Systematic Approach to Effective Helping* (3rd ed.). Pacific Grove, CA: Brooks/Cole. Chapter Three: Attending and Listening

References

Argyle, M. & Dean, J. (1965), 'Eye-Contact, Distance and Affiliation', *Sociometry*, Vol. 28 Issue 3 pp 289–304

Buon, T. (2014), *The Leadership Coach*. London: Hodder & Stoughton

Diggins, M., *Teaching and learning communication skills in social work education* (Social Care Institute for Excellence (SCIE), London, 2004)

Egan, G. (1986), *The Skilled Helper: A Systematic Approach to Effective Helping* (3rd ed.). Pacific Grove, CA: Brooks/Cole

Stickley, T. (2011), 'From SOLER to SURETY for effective non-verbal communication', *Nurse Education in Practice*, Vol. 11 Issue 6 pp 395–8

See also

Chapter 1 – Communication is not all about body language

Chapter 13 – Discovering active listening

Chapter 15 – Space wars: why proxemics matters

Chapter 16 – Mimicry, mirroring and the chameleon effect

Chapter 19 – Paraphrasing and listening

Chapter 28 – Silence as a form of communication

Further reading

Adler, R. B. & Rodman, G. R. (1994), *Understanding human communication*. Orlando, FL: Harcourt Brace College Publishers

Egan, G. (2012), *The Skilled Helper: A problem management and opportunity development approach to helping* (10th ed.). Pacific Grove, CA: Brooks/Cole

Nakane, I. (2006), 'Silence and politeness in intercultural communication in university seminars', *Journal of Pragmatics*, Vol. 38 pp 1811–35

Power, M. R., (1998), 'Working Through Communication', Paper 13, Chapter 12: Listening: http://epublications.bond.edu.au/working_through_communication/13

Stickley, T. & Freshwater, D. (2009), 'The concept of space in the context of the therapeutic relationship', *Mental Health Practice*, Vol. 12 No. 6 pp 28–30

Sugarman, L. (1995), 'Action man: An interview with Gerard Egan', *British Journal of Guidance and Counselling*, Vol. 23 Issue 2 pp 275–87

13 DISCOVERING ACTIVE LISTENING

Arthur: *You know, it's at times like this, when I'm trapped in a Vogon airlock, with a man from Betelgeuse, and about to die of asphyxiation in deep space, that I really wish I'd listened to what my mother told me when I was young.*
Ford: *Why, what did she tell you?*
Arthur: *I don't know I didn't listen.*
Douglas Adams, Hitchhiker's Guide to the Galaxy *(radio play 1978)*

Listening is vital to communication at all levels. However, while we spend many years in school learning to read, write and speak, we spend almost no time learning to listen. Even though most experts agree that listening is a skill, it seems we don't feel it is a skill we need to develop in ourselves and others.

One way of improving listening skills is the technique of 'active listening'. The influential US psychologist Carl Rogers (1902–87) is the source of the ideas of active listening. Rogers was the founder of the 'client-centred' approach to psychotherapy. His active listening approach is also referred to by others as 'reflective listening', 'empathetic listening', 'deliberate listening' and 'relational listening'.

Although active listening is considered a fundamental communication skill, it is widely misunderstood. Few authors and trainers have read Rogers' original writings on the subject, nor analysed carefully Rogers' thinking. Arnold (2014) suggests that one reason for the widespread misunderstandings of 'Rogerian' listening may be the scarcity of close analysis of Rogers' work by scholars.

So how did Rogers actually describe active listening? What was it, how should we do it and what are the methodological limitations of the approach?

We should first note that Rogerian listening is a complex practice that was repeatedly revised over the course of Rogers' career (Arnold, 2014). In fact, Rogers actually even changed the name of the process at different times from 'active listening' (Rogers, 1957; Rogers & Farson, 1987) to 'reflective listening' (Rogers, 1958) to 'empathetic listening' (1975).

In 1987 Rogers and the psychologist and author Richard E. Farson, a former research assistant and later colleague, published a chapter in a book by the American textbook publisher, D. C. Heath and Company, *Communicating in Business Today*. This was a paper originally written by the authors in 1957 and published by the University of Chicago Industrial Relations Center as a monograph. The 1987 book was aimed at the growing corporate psychology market and in particular Rogers & Farson's chapter became a much-discussed and -used approach to listening by corporate trainers.

Rogers & Farson explain the process of active listening as:

Active listening does not necessarily mean long sessions spent listening to grievances, personal or otherwise. It is simply a way of approaching those problems which arise out of the usual day-to-day events of any job (p 590).

Rogers & Farson (1987) state that for communication to be effective it must be non-threatening. Therefore, we should avoid passing judgement on someone we are talking to and avoid being drawn into agreement or disagreement. We should avoid typical human responses such as advising, moralizing, evaluating and encouragement. The authors point out that even positive evaluations are just as blocking as negative ones.

The process of active listening is described as 'getting inside the speaker'. It is about seeing things from the speaker's point of view (POV). Communication can be significantly improved if we learn to listen effectually and that good listening is 'contagious'. The process of active listening can be explained in four simple steps.

1. **Listen for the total meaning.** Rogers & Farson explain that any message has two components: the content of the message and the underlying feelings. We need to listen for both meaning and feeling if we want to listen effectively.
2. **Respond to the feelings.** Sometimes the feelings underlying a message are more important than the content. The active listener must listen carefully to try to analyse the 'total' meaning of what the speaker is saying. This is listening with empathy.
3. **Note all cues.** Rogers & Farson remind us that not all communication is verbal and for active listening we need to look for hesitations, pauses, inflection, tone, volume, facial expression, body posture, hand and eye movements, and breathing. It is the total package of behaviour that helps the person convey their message, and we need to be alert to all of these cues.
4. **Reflect back what you think the speaker means.** As active listening is harder than it at first appears, the authors suggest we test that we have understood the speaker correctly. We do this by reflecting (repeating back) in our own words what we think the speaker means by their words and behaviour. Contrary to popular misconceptions, reflection is not a verbatim repetition of the speaker's words, but a reflecting on what you think the person is saying and feeling.

Rogers & Farson, however, caution that active listening is not an easy skill to acquire (p 594). It requires practice and personal reflection. It also requires a change in the attitude of the listener, who must have a sincere interest in the speaker and what they are trying to communicate. We must be open to a person's POV and be genuine in our concern for them as a human being.

The heart of good communication

Listening is a vital skill for the effective communicator. However, we seldom do it well. Rogers' 'active listening' is an excellent technique for improving our interpersonal communications.

Many communication problems are due to at least one of the parties not listening effectively.

Listening, and not the process of talking, is at the heart of good communication. The first step to improving your listening skills is to *stop* talking. A necessary component of listening is the proper use of silence. Most listeners speak as much if not more than the person they are listening to (Buon, 2014). Active listening is an effective technique to move the attention away from ourselves, to the other party.

Rogers & Farson (1987) state that to be effective, active listening must be 'firmly grounded in the basic attitudes of the user'. We should not attempt to use the technique unless we have a genuine concern and respect for the person speaking. False active listening will be quickly picked up by the speaker and will inhibit, not improve, communication between the parties. It is about genuine respect for the other person and their opinions, even if you disagree with them.

Active listening is a particular way of listening and responding to another person that improves mutual understanding. The listener must take care to *attend* to the speaker entirely, and then reflect back, in the listener's words, what he or she thinks the speaker has said and feels. The listener does not have to agree with the speaker – he or she must simply state what they think the speaker said. This allows the speaker to find out whether the listener understood.

Reflecting back or paraphrasing what the speaker has said is an important component of active listening, but it is also often misinterpreted or misunderstood. In 1975, Rogers stated that his earlier work on reflection was enormously misunderstood, and, as a result, he became thoroughly dissatisfied with the term 'reflection', saying that it makes him 'cringe' (Arnold, 2014).

Rogers makes it evident in his 1975 article that reflecting is definitely not a mechanical technique of repeating back the words of the speaker and is actually 'an empathic way of being with another person' (Rogers, 1975). He uses the term 'empathetic listening' to clarify this point.

If we do not practise and develop our skills in active listening properly, we can end up looking ridiculous to the speaker. If not effectively exercised, the speaker can see active listening as insincere and manipulative. The simple 'parroting' of other people's words and crass interpretations of their feelings has become the fodder for comedians mimicking ineffectual managers and psychotherapists.

You cannot use active listening all the time. Choose those situations when you need to understand precisely what someone has to say. Good examples would be in interviews, when giving feedback to someone and any conversation with a difficult emotional content (Buon, 2014). However, remember that reflecting is not merely parroting back what the person says, it is about empathy and respect.

So what are the big takeaways here?

- **The heart of good communication is not the process of talking, but that of listening.**
- **Active listening forces people to listen attentively to others.**
- **It avoids misunderstandings,** since people have to confirm that they do understand what another person has said.
- **Active listening tends to open people up, to get them to say more.**
- **By practising active listening you will find that the people you communicate with will listen to you more as well.**

Source

Rogers, C. R. & Farson, R. E., 'Active Listening' (1957). In Newman, R. G., Danziger, M. A. & Cohen, M. (Eds.) (1987), *Communicating in Business Today*. Washington, D.C.: D. C. Heath and Company

References

Adams, D. (1978), *The Hitchhiker's Guide to the Galaxy*, BBC Radio 4 play (1978 broadcast)

Arnold, K. (2014), 'Behind the Mirror: Reflective Listening and its Tain in the Work of Carl Rogers', *The Humanistic Psychologist*, Vol. 42 pp 354–69

Buon, T. (2014), *The Leadership Coach*. London: Hodder & Stoughton

Rogers, C. R. (1958), 'Listening and Understanding', *The Friend*, Vol. 116 Issue 40 pp 1248–51

Rogers, C. R. (1975), 'Empathic: An Unappreciated Way of Being', *The Counseling Psychologist*, Vol. 5 No. 2 pp 2–10

Rogers, C. R. & Farson, R. E., 'Active Listening' (1957). In Newman, R. G., Danziger, M. A. & Cohen, M. (Eds.), *Communicating in Business Today*. Washington, D.C.: D. C. Heath and Company

See also

Chapter 12 – Attending skills in communication: the SOLER model

Chapter 16 – Mimicry, mirroring and the chameleon effect

Chapter 19 – Paraphrasing and listening

Further reading

Barker, L. L. (1971), *Listening Behavior*. Englewood Cliffs, NJ: Prentice-Hall

Bolton, R. (1986), *People Skills: How to Assert Yourself, Listen to Others, and Resolve Conflicts*. Englewood Cliffs, NJ: Prentice-Hall

Grohol, J. M. (2007), 'Become a Better Listener: Active Listening', *Psych Central*: http://psychcentral.com/lib/become-a-better-listener-active-listening/0001299

Miller, W. R. & Rollnick, S. (1991), *Motivational Interviewing: Preparing People for Change*. New York: Guilford Press

Mineyama, S., Tsutsumi, A., Takao, S., Nishiuchi, K. & Kawakami, N. (2007), 'Supervisors' attitudes and skills for active listening with regard to working conditions and psychological stress reactions among subordinate workers', *Journal of Occupational Health*, Vol. 49 No. 2 pp 81–7

Myers, S. (2000), 'Empathic Listening: Reports on the Experience of Being Heard', *Journal of Humanistic Psychology*, Vol. 40 No. 2 pp 148–73

Rogers, C. R. (1951), *Client-Centered Therapy: Its Current Practice, Implications, and Theory*. Boston, MA: Houghton-Mifflin

Rogers, C. R. (1986), 'Reflection of feelings and transference', *Person-Centered Review*, Review 1 No. 4 pp 375–7

Steinbrecher, M. M. & Wilmington, S. C. (1993), *The Steinbrecher-Wilmington Listening Test*. Oshkosh, WI: M. M. Steinbrecher

Sundararajan, L. (1995), 'Echoes after Carl Rogers: "Reflective Listening" Revisited', *The Humanistic Psychologist*, Vol. 23 Issue 2 pp 259–71

Wagner, G. A. (1999), 'Further Comments on Person-Centered Approaches', *Behaviour Analyst*, Vol. 22 Issue 1 pp 53–4

Watson, K. W. & Barker, L. L. (1984), *Watson-Barker Listening Test*. New Orleans, LA: Spectra

Wolvin, A. D. & Coakley, C. G. (1996), *Listening* (5th ed.). New York: McGraw-Hill

14 RESTRICTING POWERPOINT® TO ENHANCE COMMUNICATION

Last week I got a template from a conference organizer. It seems they want every single presenter to not only use bullets for their presentations, but for all of us to use the same format! Shudder.

Seth Godin (2007), author, speaker and entrepreneur

Millions of PowerPoint® presentations are made every day, and PowerPoint has become synonymous with giving a presentation. But what if that PowerPoint presentation you have just spent three hours preparing reduces the quality of your presentation by corrupting statistical reasoning and weakening verbal and spatial thinking? Well, this is exactly what Edward R. Tufte, the legendary information design guru and professor emeritus at Yale University has suggested in his 2006 publication: *The Cognitive Style of PowerPoint: Pitching Out Corrupts Within*.

PowerPoint has been criticized before and by some influential people. In his 2006 book *Fiasco*, Pulitzer Prize-winning *Washington Post* writer Thomas E. Ricks describes how a reliance on PowerPoint slides rather than formal written orders 'seemed to some military professionals to capture the essence of Donald Rumsfeld's amateurish approach to war planning'.

Tufte explains how PowerPoint has a distinctive cognitive style that reduces the intellectual level of the content that becomes slides. Tufte provides evidence that compares PowerPoint with alternative methods for presenting information. His research uses 10 case studies, 2,000 PowerPoint slides and control samples from non-PowerPoint presentations.

In relation to cognitive style, Tufte suggests the main problems with PowerPoint are:

- A forceful and hierarchical single-path structure for organizing content
- Breaking up the narrative into fragments
- Rapid chronological sequencing of thin information
- Inappropriate design of data-graphics and tables
- PowerPoint 'Fluff'.

By Fluff, Tufte is talking about the corporate branding, irrelevant clip-art, photos, frames and over-designed symbols. Tufte also illustrates how PowerPoint slides are very low resolution compared to paper, computer screens and the visual capacities of the human eye-brain system.

As slides can only hold so much data, audiences are subjected to dozens of slides that could easily be shown on one single piece of A4 paper (consider, for example, a complex one-page spreadsheet). Tufte correctly points out that visual reasoning usually works better when evidence is shown adjacent in space within our eye span. Something that is virtually impossible in PowerPoint but very easy to do in a report or a poster.

Tufte is particularly critical of how PowerPoint templates force the use of bullet points. Tufte quotes the renowned theoretical physicist Richard Feynman on the bullet point issue in relation to his work on the first shuttle accident, the *Challenger* in 1986, who said:

Then we learned about 'bullets' – little black circles in front of phrases that were supposed to summarize things. There was one after another of these little goddamn bullets in our briefing books and slides (Feynman, 1998).

Bullet points are a major problem in PowerPoint. Bullet points encourage sloppy and lazy writing. They are too generic, particularly when dealing with complex issues. They create a staccato, summarizing flow to the presentation (Parker, 2001). Bullet points leave critical relationships unspecified (Shaw et al, 1998).

It has become a popular suggestion in the past few years to keep individual PowerPoint slides simple, with just a few words on each slide. However, Tufte would disagree. He believes that most *important* facts are too complex to be written on one slide, and warrant a written form of presentation. Tufte suggests this approach results in PowerPoint slides that are full of slogans, imprecise statements and thinly argued claims.

Tufte uses the 2005 NASA report into the 2003 *Columbia* space-shuttle disaster to argue his position. In his analysis of key PowerPoint slides used while *Columbia* was damaged but still flying, Tufte stated the slide-by-slide hierarchies inherent in PowerPoint weaken scientific argument (p 12). This should be of great concern to anyone who uses PowerPoint as a way of displaying important or technical information in their organization.

Dangers inherent in PowerPoint® communication

The Columbia Accident Investigation Board (CAIB) went even further than Tufte in its comments on PowerPoint. The CAIB said it viewed the 'endemic' use of PowerPoint by NASA officials instead of proper technical papers as an illustration of the technical communication problems at NASA (CAIB, 2003).

The Investigation Board stated in its final report that:

The Board views the endemic use of PowerPoint briefing slides instead of technical papers as an illustration of the problematic methods of technical communication at NASA (CAIB, 2003 p 191).

When Tufte criticizes PowerPoint, he is doing so not because of the technology, but due to the possibility of poor communication. He is concerned that every presentation becomes a 'pitch'. Tufte states that his research on PowerPoint applies only to serious presentations. These presentations he describes as those when the audience need to know something and they need to assess the credibility of the speaker. Tufte states that rather than providing information:

PowerPoint allows speakers to pretend that they are giving a real talk, and the audience to pretend they are listening (p 31).

Dr Jill Rider, president of the Chartered Institute for Personnel Development (CIPD) and former director general of the UK government's Cabinet Office, stated in an educational video (2009) that she required anyone who worked for her not to use PowerPoint but write a White Paper that is well articulated. Rider suggests that a written paper is a more powerful and less ambiguous way of communicating (2009).

The work by Professor John Sweller shows that it is harder to process information if it is coming at you in written and spoken form at the same time (Sweller, 1988). This is, of course, exactly what many poor presenters do, with a list of bullet points on the screen while reading out the summarized points (Buon, 2007).

Tufte states that PowerPoint does not cause much damage to 'first-rate' presenters (10 per cent) as they have strong content, self-awareness and a presentation style that neutralizes the damage caused by PowerPoint. He also suggests that the bottom 10 per cent of presenters may benefit from PowerPoint as it forces them to have some content. The remaining 80 per cent is the majority of presenters for whom the cognitive style of PowerPoint causes problems, particularly when presenting serious content.

Based on Tufte's analysis, we can see that PowerPoint has severe limitations when we need the effective communication of a message. Even if it has become ubiquitous in your organization, you can use the following steps to remove the over-reliance on PowerPoint.

1. Before you start preparing a PowerPoint presentation, ask yourself if it will be the best way to communicate your message. Would a simple print-out of a spreadsheet be more efficient?
2. Always think twice before inserting data-graphics, tables, graphs or statistical information on a PowerPoint slide.
3. Ban PowerPoint in any meeting or presentation that involves statistical, technical or complex ideas.
4. Do not have corporate-style PowerPoint templates. These often force the use of bullet points and chronological sequencing of information.

5. If you use PowerPoint, then get rid of the logos, frames, branding, clip-art, generic templates, over-designed bullet points and anything that distracts from your message.
6. Are you just preparing a set of notes for yourself? If so, then don't project your presentation, use PowerPoint on your laptop as a 'teleprompter' – without showing the slides.
7. Teach engineers and technical staff how to write professional reports and don't rely on PowerPoint as a means of written communication.

Using PowerPoint to display images, photos, video clips and other visual media is useful and can enhance learning. Merely showing your outline (or text copied from a book) risks alienating your audience and failing to communicate. Remember, people can read 3 to 4 times faster than you can speak so if you find yourself using PowerPoint, don't stand there and read out your slides. PowerPoint separates you from the audience, and ultimately them from your message.

So what are the big takeaways here?

- **Research by the information design guru Edward Tufte demonstrates that PowerPoint usually weakens verbal and spatial reasoning and almost always corrupts statistical analysis.**
- **Remember the importance of the narrative in presenting.** PowerPoint may be killing the storyteller, rhetorician or orator in you. Not everything has to be a sales pitch.
- **Before you prepare any presentation, just ask yourself if it will be the best way to communicate your message.** Would a simple printout be better than PowerPoint?

Source

Tufte, E. (2006), *The Cognitive Style of PowerPoint: Pitching Out Corrupts Within* (2nd ed.). Connecticut: Graphics Press

References

Buon, T. (2007), 'Removing PowerPoint from University lectures', *Educate*, Robert Gordon University

'*Columbia* Accident Investigation Board (CAIB) (2003) Report', vol. 1 (August 2003) pp 191

Feynman, R. P. (1988), *What do You Care What Other People Think?*. New York: Bantam Books. Cited in Tufte, E. (2006), *The Cognitive Style of PowerPoint* (2nd ed.). Connecticut: Graphics Press

Godin, S. (2007), Seth Godin's blog: http://sethgodin.typepad. com/seths_blog/2007/01/really_bad_powe.html

Parker, I. (2001), 'Absolute PowerPoint: Can a software package edit our thoughts?', *The New Yorker*, May 28: http://www. newyorker.com/magazine/2001/05/28/absolute-powerpoint

Ricks, T. E. (2006), *Fiasco: The American Military Adventure in Iraq*. New York: Penguin Press

Rider, G. (2009), 'The Limitations of PowerPoint Presentations', *50 Lessons Video Series*

Shaw, G., Brown, R. & Bromiley, P. (1998), 'Strategic Stories: How 3M is Rewriting Business Planning', *Harvard Business Review*, Vol. 76 Issue 3 pp 41–50

Sweller, J. (1988), 'Cognitive Load During Problem Solving: Effects on Learning', *Cognitive Science*, Vol. 12 Issue 2 pp 257–85

Tufte, E. (2006), *The Cognitive Style of PowerPoint, Pitching Out Corrupts Within* (2nd ed.). Connecticut: Graphics Press

See also

Further reading

Gerjets, P., Scheiter, K. & Cierniak, G. (2009), 'The Scientific Value of Cognitive Load Theory: A Research Agenda Based on the Structuralist View of Theories', *Educational Psychology Review*, Vol. 21 pp 43–54

Mayer, R. E. (2001), *Multimedia Learning*. New York: Cambridge University Press

Mayer, R. E. & Moreno, R. (2003), 'Nine Ways to reduce Cognitive Load in Multimedia Learning', *Educational Psychologist*, Vol. 38 Issue 1 pp 43–52

Miller, G. A. (1956), 'The magical number seven, plus or minus two: Some limits on our capacity for processing information', *Psychological Review*, Vol. 63 Issue 2 pp 81–97

Norman, D. A. (1993), *Things that Make Us Smart*. New York: Perseus Books p 243

Sweller, J. (1994), 'Cognitive load theory, learning difficulty and instructional design', *Learning and Instruction*, Vol. 4 Issue 4 pp 295–312

Sweller, J. (1997), 'Research points the finger at PowerPoint', *Sydney Morning Herald*, Anna Patty, Education Editor. www.smh.com.au/news/technology/powerpoint-presentations-a-disaster/2007/04/03/1175366240499.html#

Website: Edward Tufte's website: www.edwardtufte.com/tufte/powerpoint

Website: The Gettysburg PowerPoint Presentation – by Peter Norvig: www.norvig.com/Gettysburg/index.htm

Website: '*Columbia* Evidence – Analysis of Key Slide', March 18, 2003, Ask E.T. forum: http://www.edwardtufte.com/bboard/q-and-a-fetch-msg?msg_id=0000jL

15 SPACE WARS: WHY PROXEMICS MATTERS

> Jerry: *It's Elaine you don't have a problem with her do you?*
> Helen (Jerry's Mother): *We adore Elaine.*
> Jerry: *She wants to say hi, she's with her new boyfriend.*
> Helen: *What's he like?*
> Jerry: *He's nice, bit of a close talker.*
> Helen: *A what?*
> Jerry: *You'll see*
> Seinfeld *(TV episode 18:1)*

Proxemics is the study of the space requirements of people and animals, and the impact spatial distance has on behaviour, communication and society. Proxemics is a fascinating subject with many practical applications in communication, architecture, design and social planning. The term was created by the famous anthropologist Edward Hall during the 1960s and popularized in his 1966 book, *The Hidden Dimension*.

Hall argued that the way we perceive space, though derived from our senses, is formed and influenced by culture (Hall, 1966). He believed that the ways that members of different cultures interpret each other's behaviours is often misinterpreted at the level of relationship, activity and emotions. This, in turn, leads to distancing or miss-communication.

Proxemics is all about how non-verbal communication is affected by distance. These kinds of spatial relationships involve what we now call our 'comfort zones'. There are four general categories of space, as defined by Hall: intimate, personal, social-consultative and public (Hall, 1968).

In his paper of 1963, entitled *A System for the Notation of Proxemic Behavior*, Hall was not trying to suggest that all people follow a set pattern of rules when it comes to the way they unconsciously structure space. Rather, he was aiming to present 'a simple system of observation and notation with a view to standardizing the reporting of a narrow range of microcultural events'.

Hall was also interested in why someone from one country feels 'annoyed' when someone from another country gets too close; why even when we get to know a culture well we still can feel discomfort; why we take this sort of intrusion so personally; and why is there so little we apparently can do to control our feelings of discomfort?

Hall developed his theory by first examining the work of other anthropologists and psychologists who had explored ideas of space (Birdwhistell, 1952; Hediger, 1955; Goffman, 1959; Jammer, 1960; and Kilpatrick, 1961). However, in a unique approach he explored the non-verbal sensory mechanisms of kinaesthesia (muscle sense); thermal receptors (response to heat and cold); olfaction (sense of smell); vision and oral/aural (sense of hearing). Of course, many of these are processed below the level of conscious awareness.

Initially, Hall identified eight social distances; subsequently, believing these to be overly complex, he reduced it to the famous four. However, his final categorization could still be regarded as eight since each of the four was divided into two categories: 'close' and 'not-close'. The characteristics of each zone appeared in his 1966 classic book *The Hidden Dimension*, and later expanded in his 1968 paper entitled *Proxemics* published in the journal *Current Anthropology*.

The characteristics of each proxemic zone are summarized in Table 15.1. It is important though to note that Hall cautioned in his 1966 book that his descriptions of the four distance zones had been compiled from observations and interviews with middle-class, healthy, American intellectuals. He went on to say:

It should be emphasized that these generalizations are not representative of human behaviour in general – but only of the group included in the sample (p 1010).

Zone	Characteristics
Intimate Distance 0 to 8 inches	
Close	0–6 inches Touch, love-making, voice low, comforting, only those very close to us are welcome, except in some circumstances (e.g. wrestling)
Not Close	6–18 inches Hands could easily touch or grasp other, easy eye contact, smell prominent, body heat obvious, for close family and friends only
Personal Distance 1½ to 4 feet	
Close	1½–2½ feet Can hold or grasp others, physical domination possible, only partner & close others welcome, used with friends & associates
Not Close	2½–4 feet 'Arm's length', safety from others, person can be seen clearly, body heat not obvious, some smells possible, interviews
Social – Consultative Distance 4 to 12 feet	
Close	4–7 feet Focus on facial features, details of skin and hair clear, impersonal business occurs here, casual social gatherings, workplace
Not Close	7–12 feet Fine details of face lost, eye contact becomes important, formal business and social discourse, voice louder, with strangers
Public Distance over 12 feet	
Close	12–25 feet Evasive action possible (flight), sensory shifts occur, voice louder, grammar shifts, others seen peripherally, large groups
Not Close	25 feet + Truly public, distance around VIPs, person perceived 'in a setting', voice and body-language exaggerated, public zone

Table 15.1 Four Distance Zones (Hall, 1966; 1968; 1974)

Hall states that people who come from other cultures will have very different proxemic patterns. Further, environmental factors such as lighting and noise will also have an impact on how close people need to be to communicate.

Unfortunately, some corporate trainers, and others who quote Hall's work, skip this point. Suggesting that his notation system is a universal description of how humans perceive space, rather than as Hall intended – a way to allow similar events to be compared across space.

Closeness and communication

Hall's work has application to general communication, interviewing, architecture, ethnology, therapy and social planning. His wide-ranging and perceptive approach to how we use space clearly highlights how people make use of and manipulate the physical world in order to achieve different levels of closeness and communication. His four distance zones (intimate, personal, social and public) reflect the various categories of relationships and the types of space and communication applied to each zone.

While Hall's work on proxemics is generally well regarded in the research literature, there are of course criticisms. This has focused on both the theory and methodology. Durbin (1968), while commenting that Hall's work contributed significantly to the field, suggested that he had failed to explain proxemic behaviour adequately as a communication system.

Baldassare & Feller (1975) and Evans (1972) have criticized Hall's methodology, in particular his reliance on impressionistic accounts of proxemic behaviour. Baldassare & Feller (1975) criticize Hall for making sweeping generalizations concerning the proxemic behaviour of other cultures without empirical evidence, but do concede that there is scientific evidence of cross-cultural variations in proxemic behaviours.

Hall believes that people from different cultures interpret their sensory data differently and that proxemics vary from one person to another. For example, Hall points out that Americans are continually accused of 'loud talking' by non-Americans (Hall, 1966). However, Hall suggests we should understand loudness as a feature of distance, and appreciate how Americans generally do not care if they are overhead as it's part of their 'openness'. He suggests:

For the English to be overheard is to intrude on others, a failure in manners and a sign of socially inferior behaviour. However, because of the way they modulate their voices the English in an-American setting may sound and look conspiratorial to Americans (p 134).

This is an example of how people can easily misread each other's behaviour, not because of prejudice but because we interpret non-verbal behaviour differently. This quote also demonstrates how cultural norms can change over time. While this quote was probably accurate in 1966, most English people would probably agree that this idea of manners has dramatically changed over time.

In the 1970s, researchers conducted an extensive literature review of Hall's proxemics framework (Altman & Vinsel, 1977). They found some support for the idea that 'contact-cultures' (Mediterranean, Latin American and Arabic) use closer spatial distancing than other cultures. However, they found very inconsistent evidence regarding the distances used by ethnic groups within the United States.

In a later review, the American social psychologist John R. Aiello reviewed more than 700 proxemics studies (1987). This task covered a comprehensive review of the literature, a discussion of all the principal methodological issues and an analysis of proxemics findings. This insightful work is recommended to anyone who wants to understand the area of proxemics in more detail.

So what are the big takeaways here?

- Edward T. Hall's approach to the way we use space (proxemics) highlights how people make use of and manipulate the physical world in order to achieve different levels of closeness and communication.
- The four distance zones he presented were 'intimate', 'personal', 'social' and 'public'.
- Each zone has corresponding communication patterns, senses, behaviours, emotions, attitudes and social conventions.
- Different approaches to proxemics can create misinterpretations and other communication problems.
- Learning about the proxemic patterns of other cultures can result in improved cross-cultural communication.

Source

Hall, E. T. (1968), 'Proxemics', *Current Anthropology*, Vol. 9 No. 2–3 pp 83–108

References

Aiello, J. R. (1987), 'Human spatial behavior'. In Stokols, D. & Altman, I. (Eds.) (1987), *Handbook of Environmental Psychology*. New York: John Wiley & Sons

Altman, I. & Vinsel, A. M. (1977), 'Personal Space: An Analysis of E. T. Hall's Proxemics Framework'. In Altman, I. & Wohlwill, J. (Eds.) (1977), *Human Behavior and Environment*, Vol. 2. New York: Plenum

Baldassare, M. & Feller, S. (1975), 'Cultural Variations in Personal Space', *Ethos*, Vol. 3 Issue 4 pp 481–503

Birdwhistell, R. L. (1952), *Introduction to Kinesics*. Louisville, KY: University of Louisville Press

Durbin, M. A. (1968), 'Comments on Proxemics', *Current Anthropology*, Vol. 9 pp 98–9

Evans, G. W. (1972), 'Personal Space: The Experimental Approach', *Man-Environment Systems*, Vol. 2 Issue 3

Goffman, E. (1959), *The Presentation of Self in Everyday Life*. New York: Doubleday

Hall, E. T. (1963), 'A System for the Notation of Proxemic Behavior', *American Anthropologist*, Vol. 65 Issue 5 pp 1003–26

Hall, E. T. (1966), *The Hidden Dimension*. New York: Doubleday

Hall, E. T. (1968), 'Proxemics', *Current Anthropology*, Vol. 9 No. 2–3 pp 83–108

Hall, E. T. (1974), *Handbook for Proxemic Research*. Washington, D.C.: Society for the Anthropology of Visual Communication

Hediger, H. (1955), *Studies of the psychology and behaviour of captive animals in zoos and circuses*. London: Butterworths

Jammer, M. (1960), *Concepts of Space: the History of Theories of Space in Physics*. New York: New York University Press

Kilpatrick, F. P. (Ed.) (1961), *Explorations in Transactional Psychology*. New York: New York University Press

See also

Chapter 1 – Communication is not all about body language

Chapter 26 – Measuring national culture

Chapter 27 – Cultural differences in communication

Further reading

Ciolek, T. M. (1983), 'The proxemics lexicon: A first approximation', *Journal of Nonverbal Behavior*, Vol. 8 Issue 1 pp 55–79

Evans, G. W. & Wener, R. E. (2007), 'Crowding and personal space invasion on the train: Please don't make me sit in the middle', *Journal of Environmental Psychology*, Vol. 27 Issue 1 pp 90–4

Goffman, E. (1963), *Behavior in Public Places: Notes on the Social Organization of Gatherings*. New York: The Free Press

Lawson, B. (2001), *Language of Space*. London: Routledge

Uzzell, D. & Horne, N. (2006), 'The influence of biological sex, sexuality and gender role on interpersonal distance', *British Journal of Social Psychology*, Vol. 45 pp 579–97

Van Maanen, J. V. (2011), *Tales of the Field: On Writing Ethnography* (2nd ed.), Chicago Guides to Writing, Editing & Publishing. Chicago: University of Chicago Press

16 MIMICRY, MIRRORING AND THE CHAMELEON EFFECT

Karma, karma, karma, karma, karma, chameleon,
You come and go, you come and go.
Loving would be easy if your colours were like my dreams:
Red, gold and green, red, gold and green.
'Karma Chameleon' by Culture Club (1983)

People mimic others in terms of language, accent, tone, silence, posture, gesture and emotion (van Baaren, Holland, Steenaert and van Knippenberg, 2003). This behaviour has been called mirroring, mimicry and the 'chameleon effect' (suggesting the behaviour of the colour-changing lizards). Chartrand & Bargh (1999) refer to the chameleon effect as the tendency to adopt the postures, gestures and mannerisms of interaction partners.

This type of mimicry occurs outside of conscious awareness and without any intent to imitate others (Lakin, Jefferis, Cheng & Chartrand, 2003). We can distinguish between this process of automatic mimicry and a conscious intention to mimic others.

An important study into the effect of intentional mimicry was conducted by researchers at the Department of Social Psychology, at the University of Nijmegen in The Netherlands (now Radboud University Nijmegen). This was published in the *Journal of Experimental Social Psychology* (van Baaren et al, 2003). In this study, the researchers argue that:

If mimicry enhances interpersonal closeness and liking, it seems plausible that mimicking people will also make them more benevolent towards the person who imitates them (p 394).

Specifically, they wanted to test whether people being mimicked would respond more generously towards the individual who mimics them. To test this, van Baaren and his colleagues set up an experiment to assess the effect of mimicry on tipping in restaurants. Their research question was very straightforward:

Does a waitress who literally repeats what her customers order receive a larger tip than a waitress who does not mimic her customers? (p 393)

Using an American-style restaurant in southern Holland, the research team coached a waitress to repeat customers' orders back to them in 50 per cent of cases, and in the other just say something that indicated they had been heard, such as 'OK' or 'coming up'. Other than the verbal mimicry for half of the groups of customers (n = 59), the waitress was instructed to ensure that all other behaviours were the same.

Afterwards, the team calculated the size of the tip given for both groups. They found that when a waitress mimicked her customers, her tip amount significantly increased. The customers who were verbally mimicked gave marginally more often (81 per cent) than the non-mimicked group (61 per cent). The group which was mimicked gave significantly higher tips (mean = 2.97 Dutch Guilders) than the non-mimicked customers (mean = 1.76 Dutch Guilders).

At the time of the study, a Dutch Guilder was worth about 40 US cents. It is also worth noting that tipping in restaurants in the Netherlands is much less common than in places such as the United States. In the Netherlands a service charge is typically included and tips are generally a small and discretionally reward for excellent service.

As there were some methodological questions raised in this first study, the research team decided to replicate the study with some procedural changes. In this second study, a waitress was included who was not aware of the research hypothesis.

For both mimicked and non-mimicked customers, the waitress wrote down the orders in addition to any verbal responses, to ensure that the customer was clear that she understood the order. The team also analysed the average tip size for the naïve waitress before the test, to establish a baseline for tipping.

Again in this study the researchers found that the waitresses who verbally mimicked their customers received tips more often (78 per cent vs 52 per cent) and the result was significant for both the waitress who was not aware of the research hypothesis and the one who was. Statistical analysis of the tipping found that both waitresses when mimicking customers received significantly higher tips (mean = 2.73 vs 1.36 Dutch Guilders). There was no difference between the two waitresses, and they found no significant difference for the naïve waitress between the non-mimicry condition and the baseline.

Mimicry can improve communication

These studies by the Dutch team are important as they demonstrate that mimicry creates a bond between people that goes beyond the superficial and can alter behaviour. They show that people who are being mimicked become more generous to those who mimic them. The researchers state that this supports the 'adaptive function of mimicry'.

Previous work in this area has shown that when people are mimicked they have positive feelings towards the individual mimicking them. The Dutch researchers, however, have gone beyond this and show that there are behavioural consequences and advantages from mimicking. The researchers state:

Tentatively, we assume that all pro-social behaviours may be fostered by mimicry. Helping others who are in need of help, sharing resources with group members, and even the purpose of bonding and mating may be facilitated by mimicry. This way, mimicry may be a powerful tool in building and maintaining positive relationships between individuals (p 397).

While the researchers tentatively assume that all pro-social behaviours may be fostered by mimicry, there has been considerable research over the past 20 years that supports this assumption. In particular, the groundbreaking research on the attachment processes including mimicry and mirroring between the primary caregiver and infants (Stern, 1985; Beebe & Lachmann, 2002; Fonagy, Gergely, Jurist & Target, 2002; BCPSG, 2007).

Neuro-scientific research (for a detailed review, *see* Carr & Winkielman, 2014) has also highlighted the significance of automatic mimicry during our development. Of particular importance are the numerous functional magnetic resonance imaging (fMRI) studies showing that when we observe another person's behaviour traditional regions of interest (ROIs) associated with the human minor neuron system (MNS) are activated (Carr & Winkielman, 2014).

Studies have shown that we like people who mimic us (Chartrand & Bargh, 1999) and that mimicry can increase prosocial behaviour – such as being helpful to others in the vicinity and giving to charity (van Baaren et al, 2003). It appears that when we see others being kind, we are also kind to others.

One informal experiment you may like to try can show you this in action. The next time you are driving in a traffic jam, let in as many people as you can filter into your lane. There is a good chance that you will then notice other people repeating your behaviour and significantly more doing it for the next short while.

Related to mimicry is the communication technique of mirroring. Many people credit neuro-linguistic programming (NLP) with having developed the technique. This is incorrect: the founders of NLP acquired the technique from the work of psychologist Carl Rogers and the family therapist Virginia Satir, who described a 'mirroring process' that should validate and nurture clients (Satir, 1972).

It is critical to note that, just as with paraphrasing in the active listing process (*see* Chapter 13), mirroring should not be imitation or impersonation. For example, copying a person's accent (though often accidentally done) can be insulting. Mirroring is about using behaviours, language or facial expressions that resemble the other person, not exact copies of these behaviours.

So what are the big takeaways here?

- **Mimicry and mirroring works.** In the Dutch study, when a waitress mimicked her customers, her tip amount increased significantly.
- **Mimicry and mirroring connect people, creating harmonious relationships.**
- **Mimicry and mirroring have also been shown to improve the process and outcome of negotiations** (For more information on this, *see* Maddux, Mullen & Galinsky, 2008).
- **Whether intentional or automatic, mimicry and mirroring improve relationships between people.**

Source

van Baaren, R. B., Holland, R. W., Steenaert, B. & van Knippenberg, A. (2003), 'Mimicry for money: Behavioural consequences of imitation', *Journal of Experimental Social Psychology*, Vol. 39 pp 393–8

References

Beebe, B. & Lachmann, F. M. (2002), *Infant Research and Adult Treatment: Co-constructing Interactions*. Hillsdale, NJ: Analytic Press

Boston Change Process Study Group (BCPSG) (2007), 'The foundational level of psychodynamic meaning: Implicit process in relation to conflict, defence and the dynamic unconscious', *The International Journal of Psychoanalysis*, Vol. 88 Issue 4 pp 843–60

Carr, E. W. & Winkielman, P. (2014), 'When mirroring is both simple and "smart": how mimicry can be embodied, adaptive, and non-representational', *Frontiers in Human Neuroscience*, Vol. 8 Article 505: http://psy2.ucsd.edu/~pwinkiel/Carr-Winkielman_mimicry-smart_FrontiersHumanNeuro_2014.pdf

Chartrand, T. L. & Bargh, J. A. (1999), 'The Chameleon Effect: The Perception-Behavior Link and Social Interaction', *Journal of Personality and Social Psychology*, Vol. 76 No. 6 pp 893–910

Culture Club (1983); singer: Boy George; songwriters: O'Dowd, George/Moss, Jon/Craig, Michael/Hay, Roy. 'Karma Chameleon' lyrics © Sony/ATV Music Publishing LLC, Universal Music Publishing Group, BMG Rights Management US, LLC

Fonagy, P., Gergely, G., Jurist, E. & Target, M. (2002), *Affect Regulation, Mentalization and the Development of the Self*. New York: Other Press

Lakin, J. L., Jefferis, V. E., Cheng, C. M. & Chartrand, T. L. (2003), 'The Chameleon Effect as Social Glue: Evidence for the Evolutionary Significance of Nonconscious Mimicry', *Journal of Nonverbal Behaviour*, Vol. 27 Issue 3 pp 145–62

Leander, N. P., Chartrand, T. L. & Wood, W. (2011), 'Mind your mannerisms: Behavioral mimicry elicits stereotype conformity', *Journal of Experimental Social Psychology*, Vol. 47 pp 195–201

Maddux, W. W., Mullen, E. & Galinsky, A. D. (2008), 'Chameleons bake bigger pies and take bigger pieces: Strategic behavioral mimicry facilitates negotiation outcomes', *Journal of Experimental Social Psychology*, Vol. 44 No. 2 pp 461–8

Satir, V. (1972), *Peoplemaking*. Palo Alto, CA: Science and Behaviour Books

Stern, D. N. (1985), *The Interpersonal World of the Infant: A view from Psychoanalytic and Developmental Psychology*. New York: Basic Books van Baaren, R. B., Holland, R. W., Kawakami, K. & van Knippenberg, A. (1994), 'Mimicry and Prosocial Behavior', *Psychological Science*, Vol. 15 No. 1 pp 71–4

van Baaren, R. B., Holland, R. W., Steenaert, B. & van Knippenberg, A. (2003), 'Mimicry for money: Behavioural consequences of imitation', *Journal of Experimental Social Psychology*, Vol. 39 pp 393–8

See also

Chapter 1 – Communication is not all about body language

Chapter 10 – NLP and communication

Chapter 12 – Attending skills in communication: the SOLER model

Chapter 13 – Discovering active listening

Chapter 19 – Paraphrasing and listening

Further reading

Belot, M., Crawford, V. P. & Heyes, C. (2013), 'Players of Matching Pennies automatically imitate opponents' gestures against strong incentives', *Proceedings of the National Academy of Sciences of the USA*, Vol. 110 Issue 8 pp 2763–8

Chartrand, T. L. & van Baaren, R. (2009), 'Human Mimicry', *Advances in Experimental Social Psychology*, Vol. 41 pp 219–74

Cheng, C. M. & Chartrand, T. L. (2003), 'Self-Monitoring Without Awareness: Using Mimicry as a Nonconscious Affiliation Strategy', *Journal of Personality and Social Psychology*, Vol. 85 Issue 6 pp 1170–9

Lakin, J. L. & Chartrand, T. L. (2003), 'Using Nonconscious Behavioral Mimicry to Create Affiliation and Rapport', *Psychological Science*, Vol. 14 No. 4 pp 334–9

Maurer, R. E. & Tindall, J. H. (1983), 'Effect of postural congruence on client's perception of counselor empathy', *Journal of Counseling Psychology*, Vol. 30 Issue 2 pp 158–63

Neumann, R. & Strack, F. (2000), '"Mood contagion": The automatic transfer of mood between persons', *Journal of Personality and Social Psychology*, Vol. 79 Issue 2 pp 211–23

Parrill, F. & Kimbara, I. (2006), 'Seeing and Hearing Double: The Influence of Mimicry in Speech and Gesture and Observers', *Journal of Nonverbal Behavior*, Vol. 30 Issue 4 pp 157–66

Paukner, A., Suomi, S. J., Visalberghi, E. & Ferrari, P. F. (2009), 'Capuchin monkeys display affiliation toward humans who imitate them', *Science*, Vol. 325 (5942) pp 880–3

Rogers, C. R. & Farson, R. E. (1987), 'Active Listening'. In Newman, R. G., Danziger, M. A. & Cohen, M. (Eds.) (1987), *Communication in Business Today*. Washington, D.C.: Heath and Company

Savage, J. (2010), *Listening & Caring Skills: A Guide for Groups and Leaders*. Nashville, TN: Abingdon Press

Steele, H., Steele, M. & Fonagy, P. (1996), 'Associations among attachment classifications of mothers, fathers and their infants', *Child Development*, Vol. 67 Issue 2 pp 541–55

17 CHECKING YOUR EMAIL TOO OFTEN WASTES TIME

Time is the coin of your life. It is the only coin you have, and only you can determine how it will be spent. Be careful lest you let other people spend it for you.
Carl Sandburg, writer & poet (1878–1967)

Since the 1990s, email has eclipsed paper-based mail and fax to become the communication standard in the business world. While social media and instant messaging are closing in (particularly with younger people), email still holds firm.

The number of worldwide email accounts is expected to increase from 3.1 billion in 2011 to nearly 4.1 billion by year-end 2015 (Radicati, 2014). It is also suggested that the typical business email user sends and receives about 105 email messages per day and that even with spam filters roughly 19 per cent of email messages delivered to a user's email inbox constitute spam.

In one study conducted in 2012 by the McKinsey Global Institute, workers reported spending more than a quarter of the day reading and answering email (Chui et al, 2012). Email might be a great communication tool, but if you are not careful it can eat up your valuable time and interfere with interpersonal communication.

In 2002 three computer science researchers from Loughborough University in the UK presented an astounding piece of research to a software engineering conference. The researchers were interested in how employees use email and how the use of email could be more efficient. They found a significant 'interrupt effect' from email use (Jackson, Dawson & Wilson, 2002).

The study into email usage was conducted at the Danwood Group, a print and document solutions company. The company has 500 employees spread over 19 sites in the UK. The Loughborough researchers used a computer-based application to monitor employee activity. In addition, a video recorder was used to record employee activities during the day.

Sixteen employees – comprising a variety of staff roles including clerks, programmers and managers – were monitored over 28 working days. All of the subjects were using Microsoft Outlook® and were notified when new email arrived, generally every five minutes.

All the subjects' email activity was recorded and analysed to measure for 'interrupts'. The researchers defined an interrupt as 'any distraction that makes a developer stop his planned activity to respond to the interrupt's initiator'. The time it took employees to return to their work at the same work rate at which they left it was recorded and analysed.

The researchers found that it took the employees an average of 1 minute 44 seconds to react to an email notification. They also found that 70 per cent of emails were reacted to within 6 seconds, and 85 per cent were reacted to within 2 minutes. Finally, the researchers found that the time it takes the employees to recover from an email interrupt was, on average, 64 seconds.

The researchers found that the interrupt effect from emails was much higher than they had hypothesized. They found the typical reaction to the arrival of an email is to react almost immediately (within 6 seconds). Somewhat like the way Pavlov's dogs responded to the bell he rang before feeding them.

This conditioned response is most evident when people here the email 'ping' or get a 'new mail' notification – they seem almost incapable of not responding, or at least looking at the email. Of course, we also see similar behaviours with mobile-phone 'rings', text 'beeps' and instant messaging 'pops'.

The Loughborough researchers concluded that while email is less disruptive than the telephone, the way the majority of users handle their incoming email has been shown to cause significant interruptions. They note:

If an employee has set up the email application to check for email every 5 minutes then it is possible, if (s)he is a heavy user of email, that there could be 96 interruptions in a normal 8-hour working day. However, if the email application was set up to check for email every 45 minutes then the number of possible interruptions is reduced to 11 per day (p 4).

The researchers concluded their paper with a number of practical suggestions, including: email training for employees, reducing interruptions through turning off new email alerts, limiting the use of 'cc', the proper use of email subject lines, and setting the email package to check for email less frequently.

Improving email communication

Many people spend hours each day emailing. This is usually wasted time, time you can reclaim if you learn the basics of managing your email. It is pretty amazing that while email is such a common workplace tool, most people have never been taught how to use it correctly.

You should view handling your email as a communication skill that you need to develop. Email can create a sense of urgency, but most of the messages you receive are not urgent. Controlling the volume of messages you receive is not always possible, but you can learn to use email more efficiently (Buon, 2014).

In a later paper, one of the Loughborough researchers suggested that email could be costing companies more than £10,000 per employee per year (Jackson & Lichtenstein, 2011). In this paper, Dr Jackson argues that effective email training for employees and improved email management could improve staff efficiency and minimize time wasted on irrelevant and unnecessary emails (Jackson & Lichtenstein, 2011).

The research done by Jackson, Dawson & Wilson, presented here, and other subsequent studies have shown that checking your email constantly throughout the day costs you time and money. People react to email alerts in a conditioned way, and this can cause you to lose your train-of-thought and have to start over what you were doing. However, a good email strategy, such as only checking your email certain times of the day, can stop this being a problem.

Ten practical ways you can improve your email usage are:

1. Check your email at set times during the day

The research from Loughborough shows us how important this is. Do not have your email software open all the time. Check and respond to email at set times each day. For most jobs, 3–4 times a day is plenty unless you are in a customer support role.

2. Audience

Make sure you know your audience and what method of communication they prefer (email, text, letter, etc.). Don't use email for complex, emotional and sensitive communications.

3. Set the tone

Emails should be informal, but professional. Your email message reflects you and your organization, so traditional spelling, grammar and punctuation rules apply.

4. Brevity

Keep your messages brief and to the point. If you have a lot to say, send a memo, letter, or use an attachment. Make sure the subject line relates to the email content.

5. Have a strategy

Have a plan in place for how you will handle email when you do check it at set times during the day. Respond, delete or if you need to deal with it later, move it into a pending folder.

6. In-box management

Do not leave mail in the 'inbox' folder. Make sure you clear out your email inbox whenever you check your email.

7. Bcc & cc usage

Be cautious with your use of cc. Its overuse just clutters other people's inboxes. If you want less email – send less email.

8. Use of signatures

Use an email signature that includes contact information, but keep it professional and short.

9. Privacy

Remember that email isn't private. Always think of an email as a binding communication.

10. Think before you click

Never send an email when you are angry or upset. Always put in the email address you are sending to last; this way you are less likely to send the wrong email to the wrong person (Buon, 2014).

So what are the big takeaways here?

- **Research shows that checking your email constantly throughout the day costs you time and money.**
- **There is a serious interrupt effect from emails,** where you react to an email alert and this costs you time as you lose your train-of-thought and have to restart what you were doing.
- **If you set aside set times each day for checking email,** you will find yourself in 'email mode' and your emails may even be clearer, focused and accurate.

Source

Jackson, T. W., Dawson, R. & Wilson, D. (2002), 'Case Study: Evaluating the effect of email interruptions within the workplace. In: Conference on Empirical Assessment in Software Engineering (EASE), Keele University, pp 3–7

References

Buon, T. (2014), *The Leadership Coach*. London: Hodder & Stoughton

Chui, M., Manyika, J., Bughin, J., Dobbs, R., Roxburgh, C., Sarrazin, H., Sands, G. & Westergren, M. (2012), 'The social economy: Unlocking value and productivity through social technologies', *McKinsey Global Institute*

Jackson, T. W., Dawson, R. & Wilson, D. (2002), 'Case Study: Evaluating the effect of email interruptions within the workplace. In: Conference on Empirical Assessment in Software Engineering (EASE), Keele University, pp 3–7

Jackson, T. W. & Lichtenstein, S. (2011), 'Optimising e-mail communication: the impact of seminar and computer based training', *International Journal of Internet and Enterprise Management*, Vol. 7 Issue 2 pp 197–216

Radicati, S. (Ed.) (2014), 'Email Statistics Report, 2011–2015', principal analyst: Quoc Hoang. Radicati Group

See also

Further reading

Allen, D. (2001), *Getting Things Done: the Art of Stress-free Productivity*. New York: Viking

Britton, B. K. & Tesser, A. (1991), 'Effects of time-management practices on college grades', *Journal of Educational Psychology*, Vol. 83 pp 405–10

Burgess, A., Jackson, T. W. & Edwards, J. (2005), 'Email training significantly reduces email defects', *International Journal of Information Management*, Vol. 25 Issue 1 pp 71–83

Burt, C. D. B. & Kemp, S. (1994), 'Construction of activity duration and time management potential', *Applied Cognitive Psychology*, Vol. 8 Issue 2 pp 155–68

Covey, S. R. (2004), *The 7 Habits of Highly Effective People: Powerful Lessons in Personal Change*. New York: Free Press

Francis-Smythe, J. (2006), 'Time Management'. In Glicksohn, J. & Myslobodsky, M. S. (Eds.) (2006), *Timing the Future: the Case for a Time-Based Prospective Memory*. New Jersey: World Scientific

Jackson T. W., Dawson R. & Wilson, D. (2001), 'Case Study: Evaluating the use of an Electronic Messaging System in Business', Proceedings of the Conference on Empirical Assessment in Software Engineering (EASE), Keele University, pp 53–6

Macan, T. H. (1996), 'Time-management training: Effects on time behaviors, attitudes, and job performance', *Journal of Psychology*, Vol. 130 Issue 3 pp 229–36

Pavlov, I. P. (1927), *Conditioned Reflexes: An Investigation of the Physiological Activity of the Cerebral Cortex* (translated by G. V. Anrep). Oxford: Oxford University Press

Trueman, M. & Hartley, J. (1996), 'A comparison between the time-management skills and academic performance of mature and traditional-entry university students', *Higher Education*, Vol. 32 pp 199–215

Website: Prof Thomas Jackson's Email Costs Calculator: www.profjackson.com/email_cost_calculator.html

18 STOP JUDGING A BOOK BY ITS COVER

Imagine a society of saints, a perfect cloister of exemplary individuals. Crimes or deviance, properly so-called, will there be unknown, but faults, which appear venial to the layman, will there create the same scandal that the ordinary offence does in ordinary consciousnesses. If then, this society has the power to judge and punish, it will define these acts as criminal (or deviant) and will treat them as such.
Émile Durkheim, sociologist (1895)

The old saying goes 'don't judge a book by its cover'. This means that you should not jump to conclusions by outward appearance alone. However, it seems this is something we often do as human beings.

We often make up our minds about a person based solely on their outward appearance. However, once we get to know the person we may be surprised to find that the individual is very different to how we imagined. People can be stigmatized, just because of external appearance, such as scars, physical disability, skin tone or even obesity (Goffman, 1990). Stigma can interfere with effective communication in many ways. Stigma can even lead to prejudice and discrimination.

One interesting way to look at the impact of stigma and whether we judge people by their outward features is to look at the effects of applicant characteristics during a job interview. The standard job interview has been shown to be very ineffective because interviewers are overly influenced and biased by first impressions (Arvey, 1979; Cann, Siegfried & Pearce, 1981; Davison & Burke, 2000). Most research has however focused on characteristics such as obesity, gender and perceived attractiveness (McElroy, Summers & Moore, 2014).

New research conducted out of Iowa State University in the United States has taken a novel approach to this by measuring the impact that body modifications have on the perceptions of job applicants (McElroy et al, 2014). This research studied how facial piercings affect employers' impressions of a job candidate.

Facial piercings are popular body modifications and according to the researchers they are becoming increasingly common among younger adults in the United States. A survey published in the *British Medical Journal* in 2008 concluded that body piercing is common in adults in England, particularly in young women between the ages of 16 and 24 where 46.2 per cent were found to have some form of piercing on body parts other than their earlobes.

In this new study, the researchers used two samples in their research. The first group consisted of 191 undergraduate students. The second group comprised 95 full-time working adults.

Students volunteering to participate were assigned to groups and were told they would be rating a job applicant on a 'series of dimensions'. Each student was provided with a résumé (CV) of the job candidate portrayed as either a marketing or IT major, and a short description of the job to which the person was applying (a customer service job for the marketing major or a behind the scenes programming job for the IT student). The researchers then displayed a photograph (headshot) of either a male or female job candidate who did or did not have facial piercings on a screen for the subjects to view.

One male and one female confederate were recruited and had their photo taken.

To create the facial piercing condition, Photoshop was used to alter the pictures such that each photograph included an eyebrow post above the applicant's right eye and a lip ring attached to the applicant's lower lip.

The researchers then duplicated the study with full-time working adults. They used 95 part-time MBA students enrolled in an evening programme at a large university. Each participant was individually given an envelope with the experimental materials used with the undergraduates and again rated the candidates with and without piercings.

The results of the study clearly showed that facial piercings create a stigma. Facially pierced applicants are perceived as less suitable candidates for both marketing and IT positions than candidates without piercings. Further, it appears that facially pierced individuals are seen as less desirable job candidates because the piercings trigger a process where people attribute particular negative characteristics to the individual.

Judgements based on people's appearance

The students perceived the pierced individuals as more extrovert, less agreeable, less conscientious, less attractive, of more questionable character, less competent, less sociable and not as trustworthy (p 31). The second sample of working adults found pierced applicants as less conscientious, less open, having less character, being more sociable, and being less trustworthy, and not suitable for the job. Contrary to the researchers' expectations, the negative effect of piercing was greater in the student sample than in the sample of working adults.

While the study had some obvious limitations (such as using only two job applicants), it does demonstrate how we 'do judge a book by its cover'. Even though facial piercings are not uncommon and have become more socially acceptable (Wohlrab, Stahl & Kappeler, 2007), both younger and older people judge people as less suitable for a job, simply based on them.

The findings of this research suggest candidates with facial piercings are seen as less conscientious (for both samples) and less competent (for the student sample) than their non-pierced counterparts. It is clear that recruiters and interviewers were biased due to the outward appearance of facial piercings and we can assume that the same would apply to visible tattoos or other body modifications.

Further research has shown that people often make sweeping judgements about others just based on their facial features. Research suggests that it only takes 34 milliseconds for people to form a permanent impression of others (Todorov, Olivola, Dotsch & Mende-Siedlecki, 2015). People make judgements about people's leadership ability, trustworthiness, guilt, and even criminality based solely on their face (Olivola, Funk & Todorov, 2014). This has been described as 'face-ism' (Olivola et al, 2014). In a paper published in the journal *Trends in Cognitive Sciences*, the researchers state:

The fact that social decisions are influenced by facial morphology would be less troubling if it were a strong and reliable indicator of people's underlying traits. Unfortunately, careful consideration of the evidence suggests that it is not (Olivola et al, p 569).

When making decisions and judgements based on people's appearance, faces or body modifications, people are making too much out of too little information. Decisions made and conclusions drawn will often be wrong. This also leads to poor decision-making in relation to job selection or promotion, and it leads to stigmatization.

Stigma is the label that associates a person to a set of undesirable characteristics that form a stereotype. Stereotyping is, of course, useful in communication as it allows us to simplify our complex world, yet most people usually see negative rather than positive images when stereotyping (Buon, 2014).

Stigmatizing and stereotyping results in us ignoring differences between individuals and we, therefore, make quick generalizations. These generalizations are inaccurate, create barriers to effective communication and need to be avoided.

Stigmatizing individuals interferes with rational decision-making and impedes effective communication. We need to go beyond the surface and not judge people by their outward appearance.

So what are the big takeaways here?

- **If you have visible piercings, consider taking them out before you go for a job interview.** If you have other visible body modifications, consider covering them up.
- **If you are an interviewer, use proven methods such as job analysis techniques to adequately determine the needs of the job and accurately match the job to the right candidate,** don't rely on first impressions or what you feel body modifications say about the person being interviewed.
- **Stigmatizing and stereotyping makes us ignore significant differences between individuals and we make generalizations.** These generalizations, often inaccurate, create barriers to effective communication and need to be avoided.

Source

McElroy, J. C., Summers, J. K. & Moore, K. (2014), 'The effect of facial piercing on perceptions of job applicants', *Organizational Behavior and Human Decision Processes*, Vol. 125 Issue 1 pp 26–38

References

Arvey, R. D. (1979), 'Unfair discrimination in the employment interview: Legal and psychological aspects', *Psychological Bulletin*, Vol. 86 Issue 4 pp 736–65

Bone, A., Fortune, N., Nichols, T. & Norman, D. N. (2008), 'Body Piercing in England: a Survey of Piercing at Sites Other than Earlobe', *British Medical Journal*, Vol. 336 pp 1426–8

Buon, T. (2014), *The Leadership Coach*. London: Hodder & Stoughton

Cann, A., Siegfried, W. D. & Pearce, L. (1981), 'Forced attention to specific applicant qualifications: Impact on physical attractiveness and sex of applicant biases', *Personnel Psychology*, Vol. 34 pp 65–75

Davison, H. K. & Burke, M. J. (2000), 'Sex discrimination in simulated employment contexts: A meta-analytic investigation', *Journal of Vocational Behavior*, Vol. 56 Issue 2 pp 225–48

Durkheim, É. (1895), *Rules of Sociological Method* (Les règles de la méthode sociologique)

Fusilier, M. R. & Hitt, M. A. (1983), 'Effects of age, race, sex, and employment experience on students' perceptions of job applications', *Perceptual and Motor Skills*, Vol. 57 pp 1127–34

McElroy, J. C., Summers, J. K. & Moore, K. (2014), 'The effect of facial piercing on perceptions of job applicants', *Organizational Behavior and Human Decision Processes*, Vol. 125 Issue 1 pp 26–38

Olivola, C. Y., Funk, F. & Todorov, A. (2014), 'Social attributions from faces bias human choices', *Trends in Cognitive Sciences*, Vol. 18 Issue 11 pp 566–70

Todorov, A., Olivola, C. Y., Dotsch, R. & Mende-Siedlecki, P. (2015), 'Social attributions from faces: Determinants, consequences, accuracy, and functional significance', *Annual Review of Psychology*, Vol. 66 pp 519–45

Wohlrab, S., Stahl, J. & Kappeler, P. M. (2007), 'Modifying the body: Motivations for getting tattooed and pierced', *Body Image*, Vol. 4 Issue 1 pp 87–95

See also

Chapter 1 – Communication is not all about body language

Chapter 25 – Educational credentials and the racism of intelligence

Chapter 27 – Cultural differences in communication

Chapter 30 – The Obama Effect: reducing stereotyping

Further reading

Cann, A., Siegfried, W. D. & Pearce, L. (1981), 'Forced Attention to Specific Applicant Qualifications: Impact on Physical Attractiveness and Sex of Applicant Biases', *Personnel Psychology*, Vol. 34 pp 65–75

Elliott, G. C., Ziegler, H. L., Altman, B. M. & Scott, D. R. (1982), 'Understanding Stigma: Dimensions of Deviance and Coping', *Deviant Behaviour*, Vol. 3 Issue 3 pp 275–300

Goffman, E. (1990), *Stigma: Notes on the Management of Spoiled Identity*. New York: Penguin

Heatherton, T. F., Hebl, M. R., Hull, J. G., Kleck, R. E. (Eds.) (2003), *The Social Psychology of Stigma*. New York: Guilford Press

Jussim, L., Coleman, L. M. & Lerch, L. (1987), 'The nature of stereotypes: A comparison and integration of three theories', *Journal of Personality and Social Psychology*, Vol. 52 Issue 3 pp 536–46

Pingitore, R., Dugoni, B. L., Tindale, R. S. & Spring, B. (1994), 'Bias Against Overweight Job Applicants in a Simulated Employment Interview', *Journal of Applied Psychology*, Vol. 79 No. 6 pp 909–17

Shoemaker, D. J., South, D. R. & Lowe, J. (1973), 'Facial stereotypes of deviants and judgments of guilt or innocence', *Social Forces*, Vol. 51 pp 427–33

Young, A. I., Ratner, K. G. & Fazio, R. H. (2014), 'Political Attitudes Bias the Mental Representation of a Presidential Candidate's Face', *Psychological Science*, Vol. 25 pp 503–10

Zebrowitz, L. A., White, B. & Wieneke, K. (2008), 'Mere Exposure and Racial Prejudice: Exposure to Other-Race Faces Increases Liking for Strangers of that Race', *Social Cognition*, Vol. 26 Issue 3 pp 259–75

19 PARAPHRASING AND LISTENING

Most people do not listen with the intent to understand; they listen with the intent to reply.
Stephen R. Covey (1989)

As we saw in Chapter 13, active listening can be traced to the ideas of Carl Rogers (Rogers & Farson, 1957; Rogers, 1951, 1958, 1975). Essentially it is a set of verbal and non-verbal skills that improve communication by enhancing the listening process.

Active listening, also known as 'reflective listening' or 'empathetic listening', is commonly taught on training programmes for managers, interviewers, health professionals and psychotherapists. The belief is that listening is enhanced by the paraphrasing process that, while described differently by many authors, includes a set of practical skills.

These included the paraphrasing (reflecting) back to the speaker of their words and feelings, using their body language to show interest (leaning forward, eye contact) and the use of open questions and 'minimal encouragers' ('go on', 'yes', 'uh huh') to encourage the person to elaborate.

Given the pervasiveness of the paraphrasing technique, it is surprising to find that there has been very little scientific research on the efficacy of the method. Communication researchers Harry Weger, Gina Castle and Melissa Emmett have stated that most research has focused on the training of people in active listening skills, but very little research has been conducted on the effectiveness of active listening (Weger et al, 2010).

These three researchers from the University of Central Florida published an influential paper in 2010 that attempted to fill the gap in empirical research by looking at one of the most important components of active listing, that of paraphrasing.

Paraphrasing is a method where the listener repeats back to the person speaking the message that they have heard. This included both the substance of the message and the feelings perceived by the listener. Contrary to popular misconceptions, paraphrasing (or reflecting) is not a verbatim repetition of the speaker's words, but a reflecting on what the listener thinks the speaker is saying and feeling. It is not simply a 'parroting' of the speaker's words.

The researchers designed an experiment to explore how active listening responses influence perceptions of an active listener. It focused only on the paraphrasing of the speaker's message (verbal component). They used the familiar context of an interview as they believed this is where the skill of active listening is often used.

The sample consisted of 180 undergraduates from their institution enrolled in a public speaking course. The sample comprised 100 females and 80 males, and the average age was 18.5 years. Participants were recruited by telling them that the university was considering adopting a new examination policy and they were being asked for their feedback about these possible changes.

Three student interviewers were trained to paraphrase messages in response to an interviewee. One interviewer was male; the other two female. The interviewers were instructed to use either paraphrasing or, as a control, a simple acknowledgement ('OK', 'That's great', etc.). The interviewers were asked to remain 'equally involved nonverbally during both conditions by maintaining eye contact, a slight forward lean, and remaining moderately, but not overly, relaxed'.

After the interviews, the 180 participants completed a survey that contained a sham measure of their attitudes towards the university comprehensive examinations and proven clinical measures of feelings of being understood, conversational satisfaction and the social attractiveness of the interviewer.

This study was one of the first to ever scientifically test the effect of paraphrasing as part of the active listening process. Data analysis revealed that paraphrasing was associated with the social attractiveness of the listener but was not associated with participants' conversational satisfaction or perceptions of feeling understood by the listener.

Likeability and communication

It appears that when a listener paraphrases a speaker's message, the listener's likeability is increased in the mind of the speaker. The researchers suggest that this result tells us that active listeners who paraphrase a speaker's message communicate interest in the speaker's message and perhaps create a greater sense of closeness (Weger et al, 2014).

They also suggest 'paraphrasing is a verbal analogue to nonverbal mimicry' (Weger et al, 2014). This is an exciting conclusion and not one previously suggested in the literature. Here the researchers are suggesting that when paraphrasing, the listener is mimicking (or mirroring) the speaker.

Other research has described this mimicry as the 'chameleon effect' and described it as a tendency to adopt the postures, gestures and mannerisms of interaction partners (Chartrand & Bargh, 1999). This 'non-conscious mimicry' at a non-verbal level has been shown to foster relationships with others (Lakin, Jefferis, Cheng & Chartrand, 2003).

This study offers the first empirical evidence that message paraphrasing is associated with people having increased liking for the person listening to them. Likeability is an important part of the communication process, and it is obvious that we communicate more efficiently with those we like than with those we don't. This study proves that when we paraphrase we increase our likeability and hence improve the communication process.

However, paraphrasing was not associated with increases in conversational satisfaction or feeling understood by the speaker. The reasons for this are unclear. It is possible that these two elements are not associated with the paraphrasing part of active listening.

The researchers suggest two possible explanations for the unexpected result. First, they suggest that:

People may attend more to nonverbal than verbal cues in judging how they feel about an interaction or about the degree to which they feel understood. Cues such as smiling, a concerned facial expression, eye contact, and so forth could play a larger role than verbal cues to the listener's interest and concern (p 45).

The second explanation for the failure of paraphrasing to produce an increase in conversational satisfaction or perceived understanding lies in the methodology of the experiment. The researchers chose to conduct peer interviews about a change in examination policy and they acknowledge that the interviews may have been uninteresting to the subjects. It is also possible that the interviews may have generated other negative feelings, as the subjects seemed displeased with the prospect of a change of examinations policy (Weger et al, 2014).

The researchers also acknowledge the problem with using just three interviewers as the active listeners/non-active listeners. There may have been gender-related issues unexplored, or it may just be that there are some other factors at work related to the three interviewers. It is also possible that the age of the participants (both the interviewers and the subjects) and the fact that they were studying communication may have had an unintended impact on the results.

In the literature review by the Nicholson School of Communi-cation, it was reported that the research suggests that active listening is a 'trainable skill' for both professionals and non-professionals (p 36). This is also a crucial point, as it informs us that the skill of active listening can be taught, learned and developed. We should also note that paraphrasing is a vital and proven component of the technique.

To paraphrase you carefully listen to what the person is saying and then repeat, in your own words, what you think the speaker has said. You don't have to agree with the other person – simply state what you believe they have said. For example: 'So what you are telling me Ahmed is that you are really behind in your work and you think it's because of the new software?'. If Ahmed believes you have it right, he will respond with a non-verbal nod or with a 'yes that's exactly it'. If you have heard him incorrectly, he will correct you (Buon, 2014).

So what are the big takeaways here?

- **Paraphrasing is a method where the listener repeats back to the person speaking both the substance of the message and the feelings perceived by the listener.**
- **Contrary to popular misconceptions, paraphrasing (or reflecting) is not a verbatim repetition of the speaker's words,** but a reflecting on what the listener thinks the speaker is saying and feeling.
- **When we paraphrase, we increase our likeability and hence improve the communication process.**
- **You cannot use active listening all the time.** Choose those situations when you need to understand precisely what someone has to say.

Source

Weger, H., Castle, G. R., Emmett, M. C. (2010), 'Active Listening in Peer Interviews: The Influence of Message Paraphrasing on Perceptions of Listening Skills', *International Journal of Listening*, Vol. 24 Issue 1 pp 34–49

References

Buon, T. (2014), *The Leadership Coach*. London: Hodder & Stoughton

Chartrand, T. L. & Bargh, J. A. (1999), 'The Chameleon Effect: The Perception-Behavior Link and Social Interaction', *Journal of Personality and Social Psychology*, Vol. 76 No. 6 pp 893–910

Covey, S. R. (1989), *The 7 Habits of Highly Effective People: Powerful Lessons in Personal Change*. London: Simon & Schuster

Lakin, J. L., Jefferis, V. E., Cheng, C. M. & Chartrand, T. L. (2003), 'The Chameleon Effect as Social Glue: Evidence for the Evolutionary Significance of Nonconscious Mimicry', *Journal of Nonverbal Behaviour*, Vol. 27 Issue 3 pp 145–62

Rogers, C. R. (1951), *Client-Centered Therapy: Its Current Practice, Implications, and Theory.* Boston, MA: Houghton-Mifflin

Rogers, C. R. (1958), 'Listening and Understanding', *The Friend*, Vol. 116 Issue 40 pp 1248–51

Rogers, C. R. (1975), 'Empathic: An Unappreciated Way of Being', *The Counseling Psychologist*, Vol. 5 No. 2 pp 2–10

Rogers, C. R. & Farson, R. E. (1987), 'Active Listening'. In Newman, R. G., Danziger, M. A. & Cohen, M. (Eds.) (1987), *Communication in Business Today.* Washington, D.C.: Heath and Company

Weger, H., Castle, G. R., Emmett, M. C. (2010), 'Active Listening in Peer Interviews: The Influence of Message Paraphrasing on Perceptions of Listening Skills', *International Journal of Listening*, Vol. 24 Issue 1 pp 34–49

See also

Further reading

Arnold, K. (2014), 'Behind the Mirror: Reflective Listening and its Tain in the Work of Carl Rogers', *The Humanistic Psychologist*, Vol. 42 pp 354–69

Cahn, D. D. & Shulman, G. M. (1984), 'The perceived understanding instrument', *Communication Research Reports*, Vol. 1 Issue 1 pp 122–5

Hecht, M. L. (1978), 'The conceptualization and measurement of interpersonal communication satisfaction', *Human Communication Research*, Vol. 4 Issue 3 pp 253–64

Mineyama, S., Tsutsumi, A., Takao, S., Nishiuchi, K. & Kawakami, N. (2007), 'Supervisors' attitudes and skills for active listening with regard to working conditions and psychological stress reactions among subordinate workers', *Journal of Occupational Health*, Vol. 49 No. 2 pp 81–7

Sundararajan, L. (1995), 'Echoes after Carl Rogers: "Reflective Listening" Revisited', *The Humanistic Psychologist*, Vol. 23 Issue 2 pp 259–71

20 WE ARE ALL INDIVIDUALS, OR ARE WE?

Brian: *Please, please, please listen! I've got one or two things to say.*
The crowd: *Tell us! Tell us both of them!*
Brian: *Look, you've got it all wrong! You don't need to follow me, you don't need to follow anybody! You've got to think for yourselves! You're all individuals!*
The crowd: *Yes, we're all individuals!*
Brian: *You're all different!*
The crowd: *Yes, we are all different!*
Man in crowd: *I'm not*
The crowd: *Shush…Shush…Shush!*
Monty Python's Life of Brian *(1979)*

The exchange above is from the classic Monty Python film *Life of Brian*, where Brian speaks to the mob who are following him as they have mistaken him for the Messiah. We see a crowd of followers conforming to the group norms. As the crowd responds with (almost) one voice, they conform to what the group expects. The one lone voice is told to be quiet, and the group feels cohesion.

We are all both individuals and group members at the same time. However, we also know that individuals can change due to group pressure. We also know that a lone dissenting voice can have a very powerful impact on groups.

'Conformity' means to change our views or beliefs due to the influence of group pressure. A simple definition would be 'yielding to group pressures' (Crutchfield, 1955). Two of the earliest studies in the psychology of influence were conducted by Arthur Jenness from the University of Nebraska in 1932 and Muzafer Sherif from Harvard University in 1935. Both these studies found individuals conformed towards the group's view when they were uncertain of the correct answer.

Imagine you have just watched a YouTube clip of a dog playing a banjo. You think it is fake and not at all funny. But it's gone viral. The next time you see it is when with a group of friends and everyone starts laughing, saying how amazing it is. You might find yourself tempted to agree with them and laugh along, rather than appearing to be the only one who 'doesn't get it'.

In more severe circumstances, you may find yourself agreeing with group views you don't agree with or adopting fashion because everyone else is. You may even find yourself questioning what you see with your own eyes.

In one of the most cited studies in psychology, Gestalt psychologist Solomon Asch explored the issue of conformity. In the 1950s Asch Experiments, Asch was able to show that group pressure can change an individual's opinion, even when the facts are evident.

Asch's study of conformity was conducted using 50 male college students who believed that they would be part of an experiment into visual judgement – whereas in fact they were part of an exploration of conformity to group pressure.

The subjects were brought into a room where they found five to seven other students seated in a row. However, the other 'confederates' were in fact part of the study and not subjects.

The subjects were then shown two large white cards; one was the 'control' with a single line on it (*see* Figure 20.1) and one had three lines all of different lengths (*see* Figure 20.2). One of the three lines was exactly the same length as the 'control', and the other two were of varying lengths. The subjects were then asked to report, in turn, which of the lines on the second card (Figure 20.2) were the same as the single-line (Figure 20.1). The actual subject was the last to answer. The confederates answered the questions deliberately incorrectly in 12 out of 18 trials (Asch, 1951).

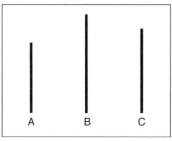

Figure 20.1   **Figure 20.2**

Asch found that overall almost a third (32 per cent) of the individuals agreed with the incorrect majority. Approximately 75 per cent of individuals went along with the incorrect group response at least once. Nearly 25 per cent of the individuals never conformed to the wrong group choices. In the control group, where there was no pressure to conform (n = 37), only 1 per cent of the subjects selected the incorrect answer.

After the study, Asch interviewed participants and asked people why they conformed. The reasons given included people reporting they the doubted their own perception; that they didn't want to cause trouble; they didn't wish to spoil the results and that the others may have been seeing an optical illusion, so they went along (Asch, 1951).

In a series of subsequent experiments, Asch found that if the individual had even one person supporting them, then conformity was reduced by at least 80 per cent. He also found that compliance increases with group size but that effect is removed when the group reaches four or five people (Asch, 1955; 1956; 1959). Later research confirmed that pressure to conform is reduced if the participant responded privately and therefore felt anonymous (Deutsch & Gerard, 1955).

The pressure to conform

Asch's research was done in the 1950s when conformity was part of the social norm in the USA. While it is often claimed his research demonstrates the power of social conformity, this is not what Asch found (Jarrett, 2008). Researchers have pointed out that Asch saw his results as a 'demonstration of independence' (Jarrett, 2008). Jarrett in an article on classic psychological myths states:

Though rarely reported, Asch's research also included the collection of qualitative data via interviews. Many participants said that although they had agreed with the group on occasions, they were certain all along that the group were wrong. This confirms the idea that participants hadn't actually been persuaded by the erroneous group majority, but rather they were attempting to play an awkward social situation in the best way possible (p 757).

Jetten & Hornsey (2014) state that when looking at how the Asch participants explained their responses, it is clear that people were trying to make sense of the conflicting views by developing theories as to why the obviously wrong answer was given. They were not just conforming blindly to the majority.

Some of the participants also indicated that they went along with the majority as the subject matter was meaningless. As one subject reported: 'If it had been a political question, I don't think I'd have agreed...' (Asch, 1952: p 469).

In the 1980s two researchers repeated Asch's study and found when using British engineering, chemistry and mathematics students, in only one out of 396 trials did individuals conform to the incorrect group (Perrin & Spencer, 1980). In a meta-analysis utilizing 133 studies from 17 countries, Bond & Smith (1996) reported that an analysis of US studies found that conformity has declined since the 1950s.

Asch used a biased sample and it is difficult to generalize his work to women and other cultures (non-Americans, non-students and older people). In their meta-analysis, Bond & Smith (1996) found that the country's individualism-collectivism was significantly related to conformity. Collectivist countries had higher levels of conformity than individualist countries.

A 2010 study conducted in Japan gives us a possible further insight into cultural differences. While women conformed at basically the same rate as Asch found, men did not. The researchers also found that the frequency of conformity was almost the same regardless of whether the majority answered unanimously or not (Mori & Arai, 2010).

Given these limitations, we should be cautious in generalizing the work of Asch to all groups of people. However, his work does show us that the group is powerful and people can feel an intense need to conform to the group's norms and opinions.

In a work setting, this tells us we should be very careful when making decisions in groups. We know that 'groupthink' (Janis, 1971) can interfere with rational group decision-making. Being aware of the power of the group can be an important first step in regulating the power of the group.

Asch's studies and subsequent research has shown that people conform relatively easily to the group. However, the studies also demonstrate that it is relatively easy to prevent it. Asch demonstrated that by introducing a second person into the group who supported the lone dissenter, conformity was significantly reduced.

In his best-selling book *The Wisdom of Crowds* (2005), James Surowiecki argues that groups of diverse people acting independently are smarter than any one person in the group. In Chapter 2 he discusses Asch's studies and states:

Ultimately, diversity contributes not just by adding different perspectives to the group but also by making it easier for individuals to say what they really think (Surowiecki, 2005).

Based on the work of Asch, this seems correct. A diverse group can prevent conformity if people do not feel they are alone in their opposing views. It is important to allow for adequate discussion and to be aware of the need to have diverse teams and the possible dangers of the group.

In their revisiting of Asch's work, Jetten & Hornsey (2014) suggest that Asch's study, rather than telling us that people readily conform to the views of the majority (as many writers suggest), actually gives us two valuable insights into positive group behaviour. These are:

- It is important for people to be validated by others
- In many situations, other people are the most useful and important source of this validation.

The dichotomy of the individual and the group is overly simplistic and not useful. Both conformity to the group and resistance against the group are 'equally rational' (Jetten & Hornsey, 2014). We are not *just* individuals nor are we *just* group members, we are all both individuals and group members at the same time.

What are the big takeaways here?

- **The pressure on people to conform to the group is persuasive.**
- **Asch's studies and subsequent research has shown that people conform relatively easily to the group.** However, the studies also demonstrate that it is relatively easy to prevent conformity.
- **In the Asch studies, people did not conform blindly to the majority.** They were trying to make sense of the conflicting views and adopting a strategy to suit.
- **The dichotomy of the individual and the group is overly simplistic and not useful.**

Source

Asch, S. E. (1951), 'Effects of group pressure upon the modification and distortion of judgments'. In Guetzkow, H. (Ed.) (1951), *Groups, Leadership and Men*. Pittsburgh, PA: Carnegie Press

References

Asch, S. E. (1951), 'Effects of group pressure upon the modification and distortion of judgments'. In Guetzkow, H.

(Ed.) (1951), *Groups, Leadership and Men*. Pittsburgh, PA: Carnegie Press

Asch, S. E. (1952), *Social Psychology*. New Jersey: Prentice-Hall

Asch, S. E. (1955), 'Opinions and Social Pressure', *Scientific American*, Vol. 193 No. 5 pp 31–5

Asch, S. E. (1956), 'Studies of independence and conformity: A minority of one against unanimous majority', *Psychological Monographs*, Vol. 70 Issue 9 pp 1–70

Asch, S. E. (1959), 'A perspective on social psychology'. In Koch, S. (Ed.) (1959), *Psychology: A study of a science.* New York: McGraw-Hill Vol. 3 pp 363–83

Bond, R. & Smith, P. B. (1996), 'Culture and Conformity: A Meta-analysis of Studies Using Asch's (1952b, 1956) Line Judgement Task', *Psychological Bulletin*, Vol. 119 No. 1 pp 111–37

Crutchfield, R. S. (1955), 'Conformity and Character', *American Psychologist*, Vol. 10 Issue 5 pp 191–8

Deutsch, M. & Gerard, H. B. (1955), 'A study of normative and informational social influences upon individual judgment', *The Journal of Abnormal and Social Psychology*, Vol. 51 Issue 3 629–36

Jarrett, C. (2008), 'Foundations of sand?', *The Psychologist*, Vol. 21 Issue 9 pp 756–9

Jetten, J. & Hornsey, M. J., 'Conformity. Revisiting Asch's line-judgement studies'. In Smith, J. R. & Haslam, S. A. (Eds.) (2012), *Social Psychology: Revisiting the Classic Studies*. London: Sage

Mori, K. & Arai, M. (2010), 'No need to fake it: Reproduction of the Asch experiment without confederates', *International Journal of Psychology*, Vol. 45 Issue 5 pp 390–7

Perrin, S. & Spencer, C. (1980), 'The Asch effect: a child of its time?', *Bulletin of the British Psychological Society*, Vol. 32 pp 405–6

Surowiecki, J. (2005), *The Wisdom of Crowds*. New York: Anchor

See also

Chapter 17 – Checking your email too often wastes time

Chapter 21 – Obedience: the communication of compliance

Chapter 22 – Communicating violence

Chapter 23 – Groupthink: revisiting the theory of error

Further reading

Abrams, D. & Hogg, M. A. (1990), 'Social identification, self-categorisation and social influence', *European Journal of Psychology*, Vol. 1 pp 195–228

Bond, R. & Smith, P. B. (1996), 'Culture and Conformity: A Meta-analysis of Studies Using Asch's (1952b, 1956) Line Judgement Task', *Psychological Bulletin*, Vol. 119 No. 1 pp 111–37

Hofstede, G. H., Hofstede, G. J. & Minkov, M. (2010), *Cultures and Organizations: Software of the Mind*. New York: McGraw-Hill Books

Janis, I. L. (1971), 'Groupthink', *Psychology Today*, Vol. 5 Issue 6 pp 43–6, 74–6

Jenness, A. (1932), 'The role of discussion in changing opinion regarding a matter of fact', *The Journal of Abnormal and Social Psychology*, Vol. 27 Issue 3 pp 279–96

Sherif, M. (1935), 'A study of some social factors in perception', *Archives of Psychology*, No. 187

Sherif, M. & Sherif, C. W. (1953), *Groups in Harmony and Tension*. New York: Harper & Row

Monty Python's Life of Brian: http://www.imdb.com/title/tt0079470/

YouTube video: 1970s reproduction of the classic study (not actual footage as often wrongly suggested): https://www.youtube.com/watch?v=NyDDyT1lDhA

21 OBEDIENCE: THE COMMUNICATION OF COMPLIANCE

> *When asked what he learned from all his people-watching,*
> *Funt replied, 'The worst thing, and I see it over and over, is*
> *how easily people can be led by any kind of authority figure,*
> *or even the most minimal signs of authority.'*
> Philip Zimbardo, 1985

How can one human commit acts of barbarism upon another? This was the question that concerned Yale professor Stanley Milgram. He was particularly interested in the human psychology that led to the Nazi Holocaust and if this willingness to obey orders could be found in 'ordinary Americans' (Milgram, 1963).

As a new professor of psychology at Yale University in the 1960s, Milgram wanted to make a name for himself. Having studied under the then-famous Solomon Asch at Princeton he was intrigued with the results of group influence found by Asch, but Milgram wanted to go further.

...it seemed to me that if, instead of having a group exerting pressure on judgments about lines, the group could somehow induce something more significant from the person, then that might be a step in giving a greater face significance to the behaviour induced by the group. Could a group, I asked myself, induce a person to act with severity against another person? (Cited in Evans, 1980: p 188)

Allen Funt was an American producer, writer and television personality and the creator and host of the famous TV show *Candid Camera* from the 1940s to 1980s

After a series of pilot studies, Milgram commenced what were to become some of the most controversial and influential experiments in social psychology (1963; 1965; 1974). He placed advertisements in various newspapers to attract participants from a wide variety of backgrounds. In addition to the pilot studies, Milgram conducted 18 different experiments, though some books seem to incorrectly imply just one.

The chosen participants were invited to Yale University to the 'elegant interaction laboratory' and were told they were to be part of an experiment into how people learn through the application of punishment. They were informed they were part of a pair of subjects where one would play the 'teacher' and the other the 'learner'. The draw was rigged, and only the participants became 'teachers'.

The task of the 'teachers' was to administer an electric shock to the learner if they gave the wrong answer to a test. In a twist, only the 'teachers' were subjects, and the 'learners' were confederates of Milgram, who would pretend to give incorrect responses and receive the electric shocks.

Milgram did not follow 'standard' scientific procedure in relation to sampling and apparatus. He carefully selected confederates to act as the 'experimenter' and 'learner' based on whom he saw as the most likely to inflict the shocks (Reicher & Haslam, 2014). He also manipulated various experimental variables to get the results he was most interested in exploring.

Milgram and his students had developed a realistic looking piece of apparatus that was to be used by the 'teacher' to give the 'learner' placed in another room a shock whenever they got an answer wrong. The apparatus, modified various times, had 30 switches labelled from 15 volts all the way up to 450 volts (*see* Figure 21.1). When he found that the 450V labelled lethal was too off-putting, he changed it to 'XXX' (Russell, 2011).

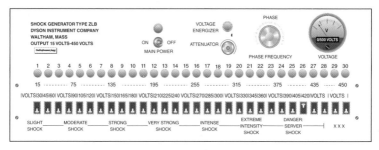

Figure 21.1 Milgram's Shock Generator (Later Version)
(Source: Milgram, 1974)

As the 'learner' deliberately gave a wrong answer, the 'teacher' delivered an increasing shock and heard the 'learner' protest as is shown in the table below. At all times, the subjects were instructed to administer the shock by the 'experimenter', who was wearing a grey lab coat. This experimenter was trained for his role and had a number of set 'prods' that he would use if the 'teacher' asked a question or to bring the subject into line (Milgram, 1963).

Over the 18 different experiments, various prods were used. The most well-known study and the one shown in the Milgram film *Obedience* is study five (Milgram, 1974). A summary of the learners' protests, the volt levels and the percentage who stopped is shown in the table below.

Volt level	Learners' comments	% who stopped
75–285V	(various comments and groans)	0%
300V	(Agonized scream) I absolutely refuse to answer any more. Get me out of here. You can't hold me here. Get me out. Get me out of here. (learner pounds on wall at 300 volts)	12.5%
315V	(Intensely agonized scream) I told you I refuse to answer. I'm no longer part of this experiment.	10%

(Continued)

Volt level	Learners' comments	% who stopped
330V	(Intense and prolonged agonized scream) Let me out of here. Let me out of here. My heart's bothering me. Let me out, I tell you. (Hysterically) Let me out of here. Let me out of here. You have no right to hold me here. Let me out! Let me out! Let me out! Let me out of here! Let me out! Let me out!	5%
345V	(No response)	2.5%
360V	(No response)	2.5%
375V	(No response)	2.5%
390-435V	(No response)	0%
450V (max)	(No response)	65%

Table 21.1 The Milgram 'Learner's' Protests (Source: Milgram, 1974)

Prior to the study, Milgram had asked 14 psychology students and some of his colleagues how far they thought the 'teachers' would go. Almost all said people would only go as high as 150 volts. The result of study five was that 26 out of 40 (65 per cent) of the subjects fully obeyed the experimenter's order to administer the maximum level of electric shock.

However, over all the Milgram studies the levels of obedience varied enormously (90 per cent to 0 per cent). This led Reicher & Haslam, in their excellent 2014 review of the experiments, to state that the studies would be better described as the 'Obedience and Disobedience' studies (p 114). While the experiments are often described in relation to how people can do terrible things, they also show how many people refuse to do these things.

People are willing to say no

It would be easy to imagine the 'teachers' as sadistic monsters who gleefully administered lethal shocks to the 'learners'. However, nothing would be further from the truth. In fact, the participants were greatly troubled by what they had to do. One observer of the experiment reported that:

I observed a mature and initially poised businessman enter the laboratory smiling and confident. Within 20 minutes he was reduced to a twitching, stuttering wreck, who was rapidly approaching a point of nervous collapse (Milgram, 1963: p 377).

It was not cruel or sadistic people who administered the highest level of shock, but ordinary, conflicted individuals. Gender was also shown not to be a factor, when a subsequent study with women also produced a 65 per cent compliance level, though Milgram reported that the women appeared to experience even more stress (Milgram, 1974).

Milgram explained his results in a number of ways, including:

- **Atmosphere:** The fact that the research took place in an impressive lab at a prestigious university. In one experiment Milgram used a 'run-down lab not associated with Yale', and the rate of obedience dropped to 48 per cent.
- **Purpose:** Milgram suggested that it was important that the experiments appeared to have an important purpose (the development of learning). People were willing to go ahead with the behaviour as they saw the overall goal of what they were doing as important.
- **Authority:** The study 'experimenter' was a middle-aged man in a lab coat, who was providing prompts and taking responsibility for the experiment. When the experimenter was an 'ordinary person' the rate of obedience dropped to 20 per cent (Milgram, 1974).
- **Commitment:** The subjects entered the experiment voluntarily and saw themselves under an obligation to aid the person conducting the experiment. They made a commitment and felt the need to follow through.
- **Presence of others:** We saw in the Asch studies that the presence of another dissenter can have a significant impact on compliance. In one experiment, Milgram used three people instead of a pair (two confederates and one subject). When the shock 'given' reached 150 volts and 210 volts the confederates refused to continue and sat on the other side of the room, the experimenter made significant efforts to get the third subject (the subject) to continue. However, almost 90 per cent refused (Milgram, 1974).

One encouraging result of Milgram's work and subsequent studies by others is that people are willing to say no. The Abu Ghraib prison scandal was exposed when Sergeant Joseph M. Darby, a US Army Reservist, handed over images of detainee abuse to the Army's Criminal Investigation Command in January 2004.

So what are the big takeaways here?

- **The results from the experiments were remarkable.** However, we have no clear understanding of why people reacted in the ways that they did.
- **The power of the Milgram studies is that they show us the factors involved in compliance and non-compliance.** Learning how others can have power over us is the first step in changing that power.
- **Obedience serves a number of purposes, both good and bad.** It can empower us to do good and help others.

Source

Milgram, S. (1963), 'Behavioral study of obedience', *The Journal of Abnormal and Social Psychology*, Vol. 67 Issue 4 pp 371–8

References

Evans, R. I. (1980), *The Making of Social Psychology*. New York: Gardner Press

Milgram, S. (1963), 'Behavioral study of obedience', *The Journal of Abnormal and Social Psychology*, Vol. 67 Issue 4 pp 371–8

Milgram, S. (1965), 'Some Conditions of Obedience and Disobedience to Authority', *Human Relations*, Vol. 18 Issue 1 pp 57–76

Milgram, S. (1974), *Obedience to Authority: An Experimental View*. New York: Harper & Row

Reicher, S. & Haslam, S. A. (2014), 'Obedience. Revisiting Milgram's shock experiments'. In Smith, J. R. & Haslam, S. A. (2014), *Social Psychology: Revisiting the Classic Studies*. London: Sage

Russell, N. J. C. (2011), 'Milgram's obedience to authority experiments: Origins and Early Evolution', *British Journal of Social Psychology*, Vol. 50 Issue 1 pp 140–62

Zimbardo, P. G. (1985), 'Laugh where we must, be candid where we can', *Psychology Today*, pp 42–7

See also

Chapter 20 – We are all individuals, or are we?

Chapter 22 – Communicating violence

Chapter 23 – Groupthink: revisiting the theory of error

Further reading

Asch, S. E. (1951), 'Effects of group pressure upon the modification and distortion of judgments'. In Guetzkow, H. (Ed.) (1951), *Groups, Leadership and Men*. Pittsburgh, PA: Carnegie Press

Blass, T. (2004), *The Man Who Shocked the World*. New York: Basic Books

Blass, T. & Schmitt, C. (2001), 'The nature of perceived authority in the Milgram paradigm: two replications', *Current Psychology*, Vol. 20 pp 115–21

De Vos, J. (2010), 'From Milgram to Zimbardo: the double birth of post-war psychology/psychologization', *History of the Human Sciences*, Vol. 23 Issue 5 pp 156–75

Freedman, J. L. & Fraser, S. C. (1966), 'Compliance without pressure: The foot-in-the-door technique', *Journal of Personality and Social Psychology*, Vol. 4 No. 2 pp 195–202

Gibson, J. T. (1991), 'Training People to Inflict Pain: State Terror and Social Learning', *Journal of Humanistic Psychology*, Vol. 31 No. 2 pp 72–87

Haritos-Fatouros, M. (1988), 'The official torturer: A learning model for obedience to the authority of violence', *Journal of Applied Social Psychology*, Vol. 18 Issue 13 pp 1107–20

Miller, A. G. (1986), *The Obedience Experiments: A Case Study of Controversy in Social Science*. New York: Praeger

Overy, R. (2011), 'Milgram and the historians', *The Psychologist*, Vol. 24 pp 662–3

Twenge, J. M. (2009), 'Change over time in obedience: The jury's still out, but it might be decreasing', *American Psychologist*, Vol. 64 Issue 1 pp 28–31

Wrightsman, L. S. (1974), 'The most important social psychological research in this generation?', *Contemporary Psychology*, Vol. 19 Issue 12 pp 803–5

22 COMMUNICATING VIOLENCE

Ralph wept for the end of innocence, the darkness of man's heart, and the fall through the air of the true, wise friend called Piggy.
William Golding, Lord of the Flies (1954)

During 2003 and 2004 US soldiers, CIA officers and civilian contractors tortured, sexually assaulted and humiliated prisoners in the Abu Ghraib Prison, 20 miles west of Baghdad, Iraq. The abuse was so accepted as normal that the soldiers were happy to take more than 2,000 photographs of themselves committing the degrading acts. The photos disgraced American credibility internationally and devastated the Bush administration's 'war on terror' rhetoric. The defence of some of the soldiers prosecuted was that they were 'only following orders' (Hersh, 2004; Graveline & Clemens, 2010).

How can one human commit acts of barbarism upon another? This was the question that concerned Yale professor Stanley Milgram in the 1960s when he conducted his studies on obedience (Milgram, 1963) (*see* Chapter 21). It also interested his former classmate, Philip Zimbardo, a full professor at Stanford University who was fascinated with how social influences can lead to extreme behaviours.

In a research study that no ethics committee would allow today, Zimbardo decided to explore the question of brutality in a prison situation. He was interested in the question of whether prison cruelty was a product of the personalities of the guards or the personalities of prisoners. Zimbardo went about creating a radical research environment to study this question.

He built himself a mock prison in the basement of the psychology department building at Stanford University (Zimbardo, 1971; Zimbardo, 1973; Haney, Banks, & Zimbardo, 1973a;

Haney & Zimbardo, 1998). This led to one of the most controversial and most quoted studies in social psychology, the 1971 Stanford Prison Experiment.

Using a team of 24 volunteers from nearly 100 applicants who had responded to an advertisement in a local city newspaper, Zimbardo decided to test issues of power, dominance, control and submission. The 24 selected subjects were given a battery of psychological tests to ensure their 'normality' and the group was then randomly split in two. One group was allocated to play the prison guards (along with titles, uniforms, police clubs, whistles, and mirror sunglasses) and the other the prisoners (assigned prison numbers, a basic uniform with no underwear and an ankle chain) (Zimbardo, 1971).

Having been 'arrested' at home (with the assistance of real police), the students who had been designated prisoners were driven in a police car to the fake prison and stripped, searched, shaved and deloused. The volunteer prison guards then placed the prisoners in a cell. The study was scheduled to last for two weeks. During the study, there were nine prisoners on 'the yard', three to a cell, and three guards on 8-hour shifts (Zimbardo, 2004).

Data was collected using video and audio recordings, interviews and tests during the study, post-experiment reports and hidden observations (Zimbardo et al, 1999). Over the next six days, the study saw the prison guards become increasingly sadistic and violent towards the prisoners. Filled with a sense of power and authority, some of the guards began humiliating and victimizing the volunteer prisoners. Both prisoners and guards began assuming their allocated roles as if they were real.

Approximately one-third of the guards started to exhibit sadistic tendencies (Haney & Zimbardo, 1998). Prisoners who tried to start a riot were punished, and those not involved were rewarded. Zimbardo introduced an informant into the prison when plans of an escape were uncovered (Haslam & Reicher, 2014).

After only 36 hours, the researchers had to remove one subject as he appeared to be suffering from acute depression and rage. On subsequent days, other prisoners were also released for similar reasons. Released prisoners were replaced with alternatives from the originally selected sample.

On the sixth day, the study was abruptly terminated as a number of the participants had become traumatized. Even Zimbardo reported he had become indoctrinated into his chosen role of prison superintendent, and it was only after his girlfriend and future wife, the psychologist Christina Maslach, intervened that he ended the experiment (Zimbardo et al, 1999).

In 2004, Zimbardo testified for the defence in the court-martial of a guard at Abu Ghraib prison. He testified that the guard's sentence should be lessened due to mitigating circumstances, arguing that his studies demonstrated that the powerful situational pressures of prison can result in terrible behaviours from an ordinary person (Haslam & Reicher, 2014).

The study inspired three major movies, *Das Experiment* (2001), *The Experiment* (2010) and *The Stanford Prison Experiment* (2015). Zimbardo is possibly the most recognised psychologist alive today (with the exception of TV's Dr Phil). In 2002 he was elected president of the American Psychological Association.

An insight into behaviour and communication

Unlike the other scientific experiments discussed in this book, Zimbardo's 1971 Stanford Prison Experiment was never published in a peer-reviewed journal and instead appears in a number of eclectic publications (*see* Zimbardo, 1953–2004). The experiment has also been criticized on methodological and ethical grounds (Banuazizi & Movahedi, 1975; Haslam & Reicher, 2014). However, this has not stopped the fascination with this study conducted more than 40 years ago.

The methodological criticisms are important as many people seem to take Zimbardo's results on face value. Alexander Haslam and Stephen Reicher revisited the Stanford Prison Experiment and raise a number of important issues related to conclusions that have been drawn from Zimbardo's work (Haslam & Reicher, 2014).

The most damning criticism is that Zimbardo's instructions to his 'guards' may have been related to their extreme behaviours (Banuazizi & Movahedi, 1975; Haslam & Reicher, 2014). The volunteer guards were issued with police clubs, bags to place over prisoner's heads, and other potentially violent props. Zimbardo did not remain neutral as most experimenters would, and instead instructed his guards to:

create in the prisoners feelings of boredom, a sense of fear to some degree, you can create a notion of arbitrariness that their life is totally controlled by us, by the system, you, me – and they'll have no privacy… they can do nothing, say nothing that we don't permit. We're going to take away their individuality (Zimbardo, 1989).

As we saw with the Asch experiments previously, what is not reported or emphasized in a study is of vital interest. Professor Zimbardo did not adequately account for the two-thirds of the volunteer guards that did not behave brutally towards the volunteer prisoners. In fact, a majority of guards asserted their authority with fair-mindedness and even kindness. An analysis of the behaviour of these guards would not be as sensational as those who were sadistic, but may produce some interesting insights into group behaviour.

A final concern with the Stanford Prison Experiment is the claim by Zimbardo that the students were 'normal' and 'healthy' individuals. A study conducted by researchers at the Western Kentucky University in the USA found that those people who respond to ads to participate in a study of 'prison life' were significantly more authoritarian than those who applied to a study without the words 'prison life' (Carnahan & McFarland, 2007).

An Australian study conducted in 1979 used three different types of prisons and the guards were instructed very differently and behaved very differently (Lovibond, Mithiran & Adams, 1979). The violence exhibited by both guards and prisoners varied across prison types but did not go anywhere near that found in the Stanford Prison Experiment. They found that when the guards were trained to respect the prisoners and to include them in decision-making, the behaviour of all the subjects was far less aggressive and extreme (Lovibond et al, 1979).

In May 2002 the British Broadcasting Corporation (BBC) broadcast a TV show called *The Experiment*. It was based on the research and guidance of Alex Haslam and Steve Reicher, psychology professors from the University of St Andrews in Scotland and the University of Exeter in England. Funded by the BBC, the eight-day study was designed to investigate the behaviour of groups that were 'unequal in terms of power, status, and resources' (Reicher & Haslam, 2006).

The study was not a direct replication of the Stanford Prison Experiment and unlike Zimbardo, Haslam & Reicher did not take an active role in the study. They also instigated a number of modern psychological research safeguards (Reicher et al, 2006). The BBC Prison Study researchers rejected the premise that group behaviour is necessarily uncontrolled, mindless and antisocial.

The researchers suggested that the way in which members of influential groups behave depends on the norms and values associated with their distinct social identity and may be either anti- or pro-social (Reicher & Haslam, 2006). The BBC Prison Study further provides a number of challenges to the work of Zimbardo.

As was mentioned above, Zimbardo testified at the trial of one of the Abu Ghraib guards, Ivan 'Chip' Frederick. However, his arguments were dismissed by the prosecution who stated that Frederick was 'an adult who could tell right from wrong'. Zimbardo's testimony that Frederick was '... a wonderful young man who did these horrible things', was also apparently ignored by the judge, who sentenced Frederick to the maximum sentence of eight years and a dishonourable discharge (Wilson, 2004).

In a letter to the editor of the *Journal of the Association for Psychological Science*, 43 faculty and doctorate-level professionals and 6 graduate students wrote:

...Our concern is that Zimbardo has misrepresented the scientific evidence in an attempt to offer a purely situational account of the antisocial acts perpetrated at Abu Ghraib. The scientific consensus, based on existing data, is that people vary in their propensity for antisocial behaviour and that environments transact with personalities. Some people are more likely to turn out to be bad apples than others, and this is particularly evident in certain situations (April 2007).

So what are the big takeaways here?

- What is not reported or emphasized in a study can be of vital interest.
- Professor Philip Zimbardo did not adequately account for the two-thirds of the volunteer guards that did not behave brutally towards the volunteer prisoners. In fact, a majority of guards asserted their authority with fair-mindedness and even kindness.
- However, the Stanford Prison Experiment remains a fascinating insight into human behaviour and communication.

Source

Philip G. Zimbardo Papers (1953–2004). [SC0750] Department of Special Collections and University Archives, Stanford University Libraries, Stanford, California: http://searchworks. stanford.edu/view/6022627

References

Banuazizi, A. & Movahedi, S. (1975), 'Interpersonal dynamics in a simulated prison: A methodological analysis', *American Psychologist*, Vol. 30 pp 152–60

Carnahan, T. & McFarland, S. (2007), 'Revisiting the Stanford Prison Experiment: Could Participant Self-Selection Have Led to the Cruelty?', *Personality and Social Psychology Bulletin*, Vol. 33 Issue 5 pp 603–14

Golding, W. (1954), *Lord of the Flies* (1st ed.). London: Faber and Faber

Graveline, C. & Clemens, M. (2010), *The Secrets of Abu Ghraib Revealed: American Soldiers on Trial*. Dulles: Potomac Books

Haney, C., Banks, C. & Zimbardo, P. (1973), 'A Study of Prisoners and Guards in a Simulated Prison', *Naval Research Review*, Vol. 9 pp 1–17. Reprinted in Elliot, A. (Ed.) (1973), *Readings About The Social Animal* (3rd ed.). San Francisco: W. H. Freeman

Haney, C. & Zimbardo, P. (1998), 'The Past and Future of U.S. Prison Policy: Twenty-Five Years After the Stanford Prison Experiment', *American Psychologist*, Vol. 53 No. 7 pp 709–27

Haslam, S. A. & Reicher, S. (2012), 'Tyranny: revisiting Zimbardo's Stanford Prison Experiments'. In Smith, J. R. & Haslam, S. A. (2012), *Social Psychology: Revisiting the Classic Studies*. London: Sage

Hersh, S. M. (2004), 'Torture at Abu Ghraib', *The New Yorker*, May 10: http://www.newyorker.com/magazine/2004/05/10/torture-at-abu-ghraib

Lovibond, S. H., Mithiran, X. & Adams, W. G. (1979), 'The effects of three experimental prison environments on the behaviour of non-convict volunteer subjects', *Australian Psychologist*, Vol. 14 pp 273–87

Milgram, S. (1974), *Obedience to Authority: An Experimental Review*. New York: Harper & Row

Reicher, S. D. & Haslam, S. A. (2006), 'Rethinking the psychology of tyranny: The BBC prison study', *British Journal of Social Psychology*, Vol. 45 pp 1–40

Wilson, J. (2004), 'Eight years for US soldier who abused prisoners', *The Guardian*, 22 October 2004, www.theguardian.com/world/2004/oct/22/usa.iraq

Philip G. Zimbardo Papers (1953–2004). [SC0750] Department of Special Collections and University Archives, Stanford University Libraries, Stanford, California: http://searchworks.stanford.edu/view/6022627

Zimbardo, P. G. (1971), 'The Stanford prison experiment'. Script of the slide show

Zimbardo, P. G. (1973), 'On the ethics of intervention in human psychological research: With special reference to the Stanford prison experiment', *Cognition*, Vol. 2 pp 243–56

Zimbardo, P. G. (1989), 'Quiet rage: The Stanford prison study video', Stanford University

Zimbardo, P. G., Haney, C., Banks, W. C. & Jaffe, D. (1982), 'The psychology of imprisonment'. In Brigham, J. C. & Wrightsman, L. (Eds.) (1982), *Contemporary issues in social psychology* (4th ed.). Monterey, CA: Brooks/Cole

Zimbardo, P. G., Maslach, C. & Haney, C. (1999), 'Reflections on the Stanford Prison Experiment: Genesis, Transformations, Consequences'. In Blass, T. (Ed.) (2000), *Obedience to authority: Current perspectives on the Milgram paradigm*. Mahwah, NJ: Erlbaum

Zimbardo, P. G. (2004), 'A situationist perspective on the psychology of evil: understanding how good people are transformed into perpetrators'. In Miller, A. G. (2004), *The Social Psychology of Good and Evil*. New York: The Guilford Press

'Not so situational', *Observer*, 2007, June/July, Vol. 20 No. 6 p 5: http://www.psychologicalscience.org/index.php/publications/observer/2007/june-july-07/not-so-situational.html

See also

Chapter 20 – We are all individuals, or are we?

Chapter 21 – Obedience: the communication of compliance

Chapter 25 – Educational credentials and the racism of intelligence

Further reading

Official experiment website: http://www.prisonexp.org/

Asch, S. E. (1956), 'Studies of independence and conformity: A minority of one against unanimous majority', *Psychological Monographs*, Vol. 70 Issue 9 pp 1–70

Haney, C., Banks, C. & Zimbardo, P. (1973), 'Interpersonal dynamics in a simulated prison', *International Journal of Criminology and Penology*, Vol. 1 pp 69–97

Haney, C. & Zimbardo, P. (1998), 'The Past and Future of U.S. Prison Policy: Twenty-Five Years After the Stanford Prison Experiment', *American Psychologist*, Vol. 53 No. 7 pp 709–27

Zimbardo, P. G. (1995), 'The psychology of evil: A situationist perspective on recruiting good people to engage in anti-social acts', *Research in Social Psychology*, Vol. 11 pp 125–33

Zimbardo, P. G., Maslach, C. & Haney, C. (2000), 'Reflections on the Stanford Prison Experiment: Genesis, Transformations, Consequences'. In Blass, T. (Ed.) (2000), *Obedience to authority: Current perspectives on the Milgram paradigm*. Mahwah, NJ: Erlbaum

Zimbardo, P. G. (2007), *The Lucifer Effect: Understanding how good people turn evil*. New York: Random House

23 GROUPTHINK: REVISITING THE THEORY OF ERROR

For it is dangerous to attach one's self to the crowd in front, and so long as each one of us is more willing to trust another than to judge for himself, we never show any judgment in the matter of living, but always a blind trust, and a mistake that has been passed on from hand to hand finally involves us and works our destruction.
Seneca the Younger (4 BCE–AD 65)

In 1971, a research psychologist at Yale University by the name of Irving Janis first presented his theory of 'groupthink'. In a nutshell, Janis proposed that highly cohesive or unified groups are likely to suppress critical analysis and will experience faulty decision-making, with flawed outcomes. He argued that groups will attempt to minimize conflict and reach consensus, but at the cost of rational decision-making (Janis, 1972).

For his research, Janis explored the failed Bay of Pigs invasion of 1961, where US-trained and -equipped soldiers attempted to overthrow Fidel Castro's Cuban government. He also looked at other group decision-making failures such as the failure of the US to be prepared for the attack on Pearl Harbor, the Korean War stalemate and the escalation of the Vietnam War (Janis, 1971).

Janis stated that 'groupthink' happens not just in government decision-making, but also in 'business, industry and any other field where small, cohesive groups make the decisions' (p 74). The theory of 'groupthink' is now taught in most business courses, widely referenced and often quoted in relation to modern fiascos such as the decision to invade Iraq based on the faith of 'weapons of mass destruction'.

Janis's work did not involve laboratory or empirical research. Rather he analysed existing cases of poor decision-making and used the behavioural scientific theory of group work and decision science to state his claims. He consulted 'hundreds' of relevant documents and historical reports about group meetings and informal conversations with group members to form his theory (p 43).

He outlined in his original 1971 paper, and the subsequent books in 1972 and 1982, the eight symptoms of 'groupthink' (Janis, 1971; 1972; Janis modified and extended his model in 1982).

- **Invulnerability:** excessive optimism that leads to extraordinary risk-taking
- **Rationale:** group constructs rationalizations in order to discount warnings and other forms of negative feedback
- **Morality:** unquestioning belief in the inherent morality of the group that then ignores any ethical or moral consequences of their decisions
- **Stereotypes:** stereotyped views of the leaders of any out-groups
- **Pressure:** direct pressure on any individual who momentarily expresses doubts about the group's shared illusions or arguments
- **Self-censorship:** individuals keep silent about any misgivings and even minimize to themselves the importance of their doubts
- **Unanimity:** The majority view is assumed to be supported by all
- **Mindguards:** Self-appointed, these group members protect the leader and fellow members from opposing or problematic information.

In his paper, Janis gives detailed accounts of the failure of the US Navy to prepare for the possibility of a Japanese attack on Pearl Harbor, despite repeated warnings; the Central Intelligence Agency's disastrous Bay of Pigs plan under the Kennedy administration; and President Lyndon B. Johnson's in-group, the 'Tuesday Cabinet', which kept escalating the Vietnam War. To Janis, 'groupthink' was a 'quick and easy' term to refer to the thinking that group members engage in when consensus seeking becomes so dominant that it overrides rational analysis of alternative courses of action (p 44).

To counteract 'groupthink', Janis proposed several remedies based on his analysis of the Marshall Plan of the Truman Administration and the handling of the Cuban Missile Crisis by President Kennedy.

1. Encourage all group members, including the group leader, to express doubts and concerns.
2. In meetings, the leader should adopt an impartial stance instead of stating at the beginning their preferences and expectations.
3. Several outside evaluation groups should be formed to work on the same question, each deliberating under a different leader.
4. Before the group reaches a final consensus, each member should discuss the group's deliberations with a trusted associate.
5. The group should invite one or more outside experts to each meeting and encourage the experts to challenge the views of the group.
6. At least one group member should be given the role of 'devil's advocate', to challenge the majority position.
7. When the issue involves relations with rivals, the group should devote significant time to assess all warning signals from the rivals.
8. When looking at alternatives, the group should divide into two or more subgroups to meet separately, under different leadership, and then come back together to argue differences.
9. After reaching a preliminary consensus, the group should hold a 'second-chance' meeting at which every member can express all residual doubts, without being attached to the previous decision (p 44).

Janis acknowledges that these nine recommendations have their disadvantages. It could lead to prolonged and costly debates when a decision requires a fast decision. It could also cause negative emotions such as depression and anger. It may cause power struggles and escalate the conflict. Finally, setting up outside evaluation groups might create security concerns. However, Janis states that he is confident that experienced leaders who understand group behaviours, power and organizational politics, will be able to apply 'one or another of the prescriptions successfully, without harmful side effects' (p 44).

Group decision-making has its limitations

Following the publication of this paper and the subsequent works on 'groupthink', others have analysed both the cases presented by Janis and other examples of poor decision-making related to 'groupthink'. In particular, the *Challenger* space shuttle disaster (Esser & Lindoerfer, 1989; Moorhead, Ference & Neck, 1991; Dimitroff, Schmidt & Bond, 2005); Iran Hostage Crisis (Smith, 1984); WorldCom's fraud (Scharff, 2005); 1990-1 Persian Gulf crisis (First Gulf War) (Yetiv, 2003); and the invasion of Iraq to find 'weapons of mass destruction' (Badie, 2010).

Given the ubiquity of 'groupthink' in business and group-work literature and instruction, it is surprising that there has been rather limited scientific evaluation and scrutiny of the theory. Possibly this is because it 'just makes common sense' and Janis has provided both the problem, the symptoms and the cure in a well-articulated and simple-to-understand idea.

In a comprehensive review of the 'groupthink' literature, James Rose from Regent University analysed numerous studies using both case studies and experiments and concluded that while groupthink occurs across a broad range of groups, experimental results are limited and give mixed results (Rose, 2011). Other researchers have also found very little empirical support for the theory of 'groupthink'.

In 2000, Won-Woo Park conducted an investigation of Janis's model, including all 24 variables (antecedent, symptoms, signs and outcomes) and found little support for the theory (Park, 2000). Looking at the *Challenger* disaster, Mark Maier noted in 2002 that new evidence regarding the accident and analysis of past evidence demonstrates convincingly that:

Challenger **was neither an example of groupthink nor an example of excessive risk taking** (Maier, p 282).

In a special issue, the journal *Organizational Behavior and Human Decision Processes* published eight papers examining Janis's work and 'groupthink' theory. There was agreement that 'groupthink' has been an influential idea. However, the scientific support for the model is rather limited (Paulus, 1998). Paulus points out the significant disagreement about the scientific status of 'groupthink'.

Roderick Kramer from Stanford University used recently reclassified documents and memoirs from those involved in the Bay of Pigs invasion and US military escalation of the Vietnam War to re-examine Janis's thesis. He suggests that this new evidence does not support Janis's original description of the processes (Kramer, 1998).

James Esser from Lamar University in the USA reviewed the literature on 'groupthink' and concluded that the research has not provided a definite validation of 'groupthink' theory and that both the quantity and quality of 'groupthink' research is rather limited. Esser proposes, however, that the greatest value of 'groupthink' theory is the thought and discussion about group decision-making that it has generated (Esser, 1998).

More than 40 years since its conception, Irving Janis's (1971) 'groupthink' theory remains a permanent fixture in the psychological and organizational literature. Notwithstanding the concerns expressed by the reviews of 'groupthink' theory, it is clear that 'groupthink' exists. The actual causes and an empirical basis for it are still unclear. However, the work of Janis remains one of the most important ideas about group decision-making of the past 50 years.

So what are the big takeaways here?

- **Group decision-making has its limitations.** Decisions made by groups can be challenged by the powerful psychological pressures that arise when group members strive for cohesion and consensus.
- **This can result in poor decision-making and 'groupthink'.**
- **'Groupthink' is the process where cohesive groups strive for consensus and avoid any critical examination of alternatives.**
- **There is little doubt that 'groupthink' happens, but current research does not adequately explain why or how.**

Source

Janis, I. L. (1971), 'Groupthink', *Psychology Today*, November, pp 43–6, 74–6

References

Badie, D. (2010), 'Groupthink, Iraq, and the War on Terror: Explaining US Policy Shift toward Iraq', *Foreign Policy Analysis*, Vol. 6 pp 277–96

Dimitroff, R. D., Schmidt, L. A. & Bond, T. D. (2005), 'Organizational behavior and disaster: A study of conflict at NASA', *Project Management Journal*, Vol. 36 Issue 1 pp 28–38

Esser, J. K. & Lindoerfer, J. L. (1989), 'Group think and the space shuttle *Challenger* accident: Towards a quantitative case analysis', *Journal of Behavioural Decision-Making*, Vol. 2 pp 167–77

Esser, J. K. (1998), 'Alive and Well after 25 years: A review of Groupthink Research', *Organizational Behavior and Human Decision Processes*, Vol. 73 Nos. 2/3 pp 116–41

Janis, I. L. (1971), 'Groupthink', *Psychology Today*, November, pp 43–6, 74–6

Janis, I. L. (1972), *Victims of Groupthink*. Boston, MA: Houghton-Mifflin

Janis, I. L. (1982), *Groupthink* (2nd ed.). Boston, MA: Houghton-Mifflin

Kramer, R. M. (1998), 'Revisiting the Bay of Pigs and Vietnam Decisions 25 Years Later: How Well Has the Groupthink Hypothesis Stood the Test of Time?', *Organizational Behavior and Human Decision Processes*, Vol. 73 Issue 2–3 pp 236–71

Maier, M. (2002), 'Ten Years After a Major Malfunction... Reflections on "The *Challenger* Syndrome"', *Journal of Management Inquiry*, Vol. 11 Issue 3 pp 282–92

Moorhead, G., Ference, R. & Neck, C. P. (1991), 'Group Decision Fiascoes Continue: Space Shuttle *Challenger* and a Revised Groupthink Framework', *Human Relations*, Vol. 44 Issue 6 pp 539–50

Park, W.-W. (2000), 'A comprehensive empirical investigation of the relationships among variables of the groupthink model', *Journal of Organizational Behavior*, Vol. 21 Issue 8 pp 873–87

Paulus, P. B. (1998), 'Developing Consensus about Groupthink after All These Years', *Organizational Behavior and Human Decision Processes*, Vol. 73 Issue 2–3 pp 362–74

Rose, J. D. (2011), 'Diverse Perspectives on the Groupthink Theory', *Emerging Leadership Journeys*, Vol. 4 Issue 1 pp 37–57

Scharff, M. M. (2005), 'Understanding WorldCom's Accounting Fraud: Did Groupthink Play a Role?', *Journal of Leadership & Organizational Studies*, Vol. 11 No. 3 pp 109–118

Smith, S. (1984), 'Groupthink and the Hostage Rescue Mission', *British Journal of Political Science*, Vol. 15 pp 117–26

Yetiv, S. A. (2003), 'Groupthink and the Gulf Crisis', *British Journal of Political Science*, Vol. 33 Issue 3 pp 419–42

See also

Further reading

Aldag, R. J. & Fuller, S. R. (1993), 'Beyond Fiasco: A Reappraisal of the Groupthink Phenomenon and a New Model of Group Decision Processes', *Psychological Bulletin*, Vol. 11 No. 3 pp 533–52

Choi, J. N. & Kim, M. U. (1999), 'The Organizational Application of Groupthink and its Limitations in Organizations', *Journal of Applied Psychology*, Vol. 84 No. 2 pp 297–306

Fuller, S. R. & Aldag, R. J. (1998), 'Organizational Tonypandy: Lessons from a quarter century of the groupthink phenomenon', *Organizational Behaviour & Human Decision Processes*, Vol. 73 Issue 2–3 pp 163–84

Janis, I. L. (1989), *Crucial Decisions: Leadership in Policymaking and Crisis Management*. New York: Free Press

McCauley, C. (1998), 'Group dynamics in Janis's theory of groupthink: Backward and forward', *Organizational Behaviour and Human Decision Processes*, Vol. 73 pp 142–62

Montanari, J. R. & Moorhead, G. (1989), 'Development of the Groupthink Assessment Inventory', *Educational and Psychological Measurement*, Vol. 49 pp 209–19

Park, W.-W. (1990), 'A review of research on Groupthink', *Journal of Behavioral Decision Making*, Vol. 3 Issue 4 pp 229–45

Turner, M. E. & Pratkanis, A. R. (1998), 'A social identity maintenance model of groupthink, *Organizational Behaviour and Human Decision Processes*, Vol. 73 pp 210–35

Whyte, G. (1998), 'Recasting Janis's Groupthink Model: The Key Role of Collective Efficacy in Decision Fiascoes', *Organizational Behavior and Human Decision Processes*, Vol. 73 Issue 2–3 pp 185–209

24

THE FORER EFFECT: GULLIBILITY IN ACTION

If all the thousands of clinical hours currently being expended in concocting clever and flowery personality sketches from test data could be devoted instead to scientific investigation (assuming we are still selecting and training clinicians to be scientists), it would probably mean a marked improvement in our net social contribution.

Professor Paul Meehl, psychologist (1956)

Bertram R. Forer was a US psychologist who was interested in personality testing. The story goes that one night he was in a nightclub, and he was accosted by a graphologist who wanted to do a 'reading' of Forer. Forer declined and offered to do a Rorschach (ink-blot) test on the graphologist. In their subsequent discussion, the graphologist claimed the 'scientific' proof of his methods was that his 'clients' affirmed the accuracy of his readings.

Forer suggested that any trained psychologist could easily replicate this result. Forer then conducted one of the most unusual experiments in the history of personality assessment, a study into 'gullibility'.

Published in 1949, Forer's paper was called *The Fallacy of Personal Validation: A Classroom Demonstration of Gullibility*. He explains the background to his research as his concern about methodological issues in personality assessment. He stated:

Personality evaluations can be, and often are, couched in such general terms that they are meaningless in terms of denotability in behaviour. Or they may have 'universal validity' and apply to everyone (Forer, 1949).

Forer created a unique study where after his students had requested being 'personality tested' he gave 39 of them an existing personality test he was working on and had discussed in class. One week later he gave each of the students a typed personality assessment. He told them he needed secrecy regarding their results and got them to read the results while sitting two seats apart.

The reason Forer needed them not to see each other's paper was that they all received the same 'personality' assessment.

He wrote the assessment using some previous work by another psychologist D. G. Paterson, but also based on some excerpts from a horoscope book. He wrote out the assessment, not as a narrative, but in a list of 13 statements. So each student was told their assessment was:

1. You have a great need for other people to like and admire you.
2. You have a tendency to be critical of yourself.
3. You have a great deal of unused capacity which you have not turned to your advantage.
4. While you have some personality weaknesses, you are generally able to compensate for them.
5. Your sexual adjustment has presented problems for you.
6. Disciplined and self-controlled outside, you tend to be worrisome and insecure inside.
7. At times you have serious doubts as to whether you have made the right decision or done the right thing.
8. You prefer a certain amount of change and variety and become dissatisfied when hemmed in by restrictions and limitations.
9. You pride yourself as an independent thinker and do not accept others' statements without satisfactory proof.
10. You have found it unwise to be too frank in revealing yourself to others.
11. At times you are extroverted, affable, sociable, while at other times you are introverted, wary, reserved.
12. Some of your aspirations tend to be pretty unrealistic.
13. Security is one of your major goals in life.

As soon as the students read 'their' 13-point assessment, they were instructed to turn over the page and rate the assessment on a scale of 0 (poor) to 5 (perfect) as to how effective it was in revealing their personality. They then were to turn the page and rate each of the 13 statements as 'true' or 'false' about themselves.

The results showed the students had been gullible. Ratings of accuracy of the test found only one student scoring the test below 4. While there were a few students who were critical of the test, most were ready to accept that the test had revealed their personality. On average, the students rated its accuracy as 4.26/5.0 (84 per cent). No different results were found for gender, age or occupational background.

Forer concluded that the claims of 'pseudo-diagnosticians' can be replicated or even surpassed by a competent psychologist just writing out vague and general personality assessments. For example, the statement:

You have a great need for other people to like and admire you

It is easy to see how this could apply to almost everyone and also how you could read your own meaning into the statement. The statement appears 'personal' to you and seems to show some 'power' of the test, the psychologist or the psychic.

If the statements are sufficiently vague, they will receive high rates of reliability and validity. Consider Forer's statement no. 7:

At times you have serious doubts as to whether you have made the right decision or done the right thing.

This is so general that no one could not apply it to themselves. Who has never, at least sometime in their life, had a serious doubt as to whether they have made the right decision or not?

The Forer Effect and communication

The Forer Effect is also sometimes referred to as the Barnum Effect, after the American showman P. T. Barnum (Meehl,

1956). The Forer Effect refers to pseudosciences that claim to analyse a person's personality using trivial tests or 'mysterious' methods. The Forer Effect is useful as it explains, at least in part, why people believe in things like astrology, tea-leaf reading and graphology.

The Forer Effect has been studied and verified by others since Forer's original study (*see* Dmitruk, Collins & Clinger, 1973; Dana & Fouke, 1979; Fichten & Sunerton, 1983; Dickson & Kelly, 1985; Tobacyk & Milford, 1988). The researchers always find the same result, people accept vague and general personality assessments as being unique to themselves.

In one later study, researchers found that subjects will give higher accuracy ratings if the subject believes that the analysis applies only to them. If the subject believes in the authority of the evaluator and the assessment lists mainly positive traits (Dickson & Kelly, 1985). This is why psychologists also call the Forer Effect the 'personal validation fallacy'.

The Forer Effect has also been found in complementary medicine. In one study 60 students gave samples of head hair and the following week were given a 'trichosis (hair) diagnosis', which consisted of 24 bland statements regarding their health (Furnham, 1994). The researcher reported 'discussions with the students afterwards showed that most had been "duped" by the procedure'. Furnham concludes that the Forer Effect could, in part, explain why patients often give positive personal testimonies for sham alternative medicine practices.

Unfortunately, there has been limited research on the cross-cultural consistency of the Forer Effect. However, one study conducted in 2009 found that Western and Chinese populations showed no notable variations (Rogers & Soule, 2009). In one German study researchers found that medical doctors were not duped by 'hair diagnoses' and they concluded that the doctors may have been too cynical to be misled (Ernst & Resch, 1995).

Derren Brown, the British magician and sceptic, on his TV programme, *Trick of the Mind*, replicated Forer's study on groups of volunteers from Hollywood, Barcelona and London. He had the volunteers sketch their hand print, write their birthdate (and time if known), and select a personal small object and put everything in a numbered envelope. After a wait, Brown gives each of the volunteers their 'personal personality assessments'. Most give them an 80 per cent to 99 per cent accuracy rating. Brown then reveals, to the volunteer's amazement, that they all have the same assessments (Brown, 2006).

The Forer Effect tells us a number of things about human communication. It tells us that we have a serious problem remaining impartial in our self-assessment when we read vague and general statements about ourselves. It also shows us how pseudoscientific frauds such as cold-readers, mediums, graphologists and psychics can deliver what appear to be accurate assessments of someone's personality.

The Forer Effect also advises caution in interpreting personality evaluations and psychometric tests given by psychologists and HR professionals. In particular, you should be careful when given overly simplistic 'personality tests' on training courses, delivered by keen, but unqualified trainers. The psychologist Professor Robert Spillane, from Macquarie University, cautions:

After rehearsing these arguments for 40 years, I conclude that personality tests are discriminatory, unreliable, invalid, and cannot predict work performance (Spillane, 2012).

Personality is very complex and not easily explained. The personality assessments we get from simplistic tests appear to be a reading of our personality, because in many respects they are. However, they are also a reading of everyone. They provide a crude estimate of 'what' we are, but they do not explain 'who' or 'why' we are.

So what are the big takeaways here?

- The Forer Effect refers to the tendency of people to rate sets of statements as highly accurate for them personally, even though the statements could apply to almost anyone.

- The Forer Effect, at least partially, explains why so many people think that pseudosciences work.
- Be very cautious when interpreting personality assessments, based on simplistic tests or evaluations. Personality is very complex and not easily explained.

Source

Forer, B. R. (1949), 'The Fallacy of Personal Validation: a Classroom Demonstration of Gullibility', *Journal of Abnormal and Social Psychology*, Vol. 44 Issue 1 pp 118–23

References

Brown, D. (2006), *Trick of the Mind*, S03E01. Channel 4, UK

Dickson, D. H. & Kelly, I. W. (1985), 'The "Barnum Effect" in Personality Assessment: A Review of the Literature', *Psychological Reports*, Vol. 57 Issue 2 pp 367–82

Ernst, E. & Resch, K. L. (1995), 'The Barnum effect in complementary medicine', *Complementary Therapies in Medicine*, Vol. 3 pp 134–7

Forer, B. R. (1949), 'The Fallacy of Personal Validation: a Classroom Demonstration of Gullibility', *Journal of Abnormal and Social Psychology*, Vol. 44 Issue 1 pp 118–23

Furnham, A. F. (1994), 'The Barnum effect in medicine', *Complementary Therapies in Medicine*, Vol. 2 Issue 1 pp 1–4

Rogers, P. & Soule, J. (2009), 'Cross-Cultural Differences in the Acceptance of Barnum Profiles Supposedly Derived From Western Versus Chinese Astrology', *Journal of Cross-Cultural Psychology*, Vol. 40 No. 3 pp 381–99

Spillane, R. (2012), 'The problem with personality tests', *Financial Review* (Australia). Published: 21 Feb 2012

See also

Further reading

Adams, B. (1997), *E Pluribus Barnum: The Great Showman and the Making of U. S. Popular Culture*. Minneapolis, MN: University of Minnesota Press

Brugger, P., Regard, M., Landis, T., Cook, N. D., Krebs, D. & Niederberger, J. (1993), '"Meaningful patterns" in visual noise: effects of lateral stimulation and the observer's belief in ESP', *Psychopathology*, Vol. 26 Issue 5–6 pp 261–5

Claridge, G., Clark, K., Powney, E. & Hassan, E. (2008), 'Schizotypy and the Barnum Effect', *Personality and Individual Differences*, Vol. 44 pp 436–44

Dana, R. H. & Fouke, H. P. (1979), 'Barnum statements in reports of psychological assessment', *Psychological Reports*, Vol. 44 pp 1215–21

Dmitruk, V. M., Collins, R. W. & Clinger, D. L. (1973), 'The "Barnum effect" and acceptance of negative personal evaluation', *Journal of Consulting and Clinical Psychology*, Vol. 41 Issue 2 pp 192–4

Fichten, C. S. & Sunerton, B. (1983), 'Popular horoscopes and the "Barnum Effect"', *The Journal of Psychology,* Vol. 114 pp 123–34

Karnes, E. & Leonard, S. D., 'Graphoanalytic and psychometric personality profiles: Validity and Barnum effects'. In Beyerstein, B. L. & Beyerstein, D. F. (1992), *The Write Stuff: Evaluation of Graphology – The Study of Handwriting Analysis*. Amherst, MA: Prometheus Books

King, R. N. & Koehler, D. J. (2000), 'Illusory Correlations in Graphological Inference', *Journal of Experimental Psychology: Applied*, Vol. 6 Issue 4 pp 336–48

Meehl, P. E. (1986), 'Causes and Effects of My Disturbing Little Book', *Journal of Personality Assessment*, Vol. 50 pp 370–5

Neter, E. & Ben-Shakhar, G. (1989), 'The Predictive Validity of Graphological Inferences: A Meta-Analytic Approach', *Personality and Individual Differences*, Vol. 10 Issue 7 pp 737–45

Randi, J., (1979), '"Cold Reading" Revisited', *The Skeptical Inquirer*, Vol. 3 Issue 4 pp 37–41

Stagner, R. (1958), 'The gullibility of personnel managers', *Personnel Psychology*, Vol. 11 Issue 3 pp 347–52

Tobacyk, J. & Milford, G. (1988), 'Paranormal beliefs and the Barnum Effect', *Journal of Personality Assessment*, Vol. 52 Issue 4 pp 737

Website: Link to YouTube video of the Derren Brown experiment (Trick of the Mind: S03E01) http://www.youtube.com/watch?v=haP7Ys9ocTk

25

EDUCATIONAL CREDENTIALS AND THE RACISM OF INTELLIGENCE

Credentialism is the process that occurs where entry qualifications for an occupation are upgraded but there is no commensurate change in the knowledge or skill requirements for the job.
'The Kirby Report', Australia (1985)

Credentials were first used in the 19th century, with the primary purpose of protecting the public by showing the competence of the professional (Husen & Postlethwaite, 1984). Over the past 60 years in the Western world, and more recently in developing countries, there has been significant growth in the number of people who have educational credentials, an increase in the number of 'credentialing' bodies and a growth in the use of educational credentials as a way of selecting people for employment (Dore, 1976; Davis, 1981; Buon & Compton, 1990; Buon, 1994).

This increased use of educational credentials has been referred to variously as: 'Diploma Disease' (Berg, 1970); 'Diplomaism' (Hapgood, 1971); 'Qualificationalism' (Dore, 1976); 'Credentialism' (Kirby, 1985); or the 'Paper – Qualifications Syndrome' (Dore & Oxenham, 1984). These various descriptive terms can be categorized under the popular heading of credentialism.

Many early social theorists have been concerned with the issue of occupational credentialism. Adam Smith, Karl Marx and Émile Durkheim were all concerned with the credentialing system. Many of the concerns expressed today about occupational credentialism echo concerns expressed by social theorists about the guilds in years gone by.

It was the French academic and philosopher, Pierre Bourdieu who was among the first to describe how the stratified system of mass education is described as a fundamental institution in the reproduction of class inequality from generation to generation. Here, educational credentials are a type of 'educational capital', passed on from one dominant group to another (Bourdieu & Passeron, 1977).

Pierre Bourdieu would be well known to sociology students and educationalists, but less well known to others. However, according to ranking provided by Thomson Reuters (previously the Institute for Scientific Information), Bourdieu is the second most quoted author in the world (Turong & Weill, 2012).

In May 1978, Bourdieu gave a talk to the MRAP (Mouvement contre le racisme) under the auspices of UNESCO. This was later published in 1978 in French in 'Cahiers: Droit et liberté' and in English as a Chapter in *Sociology in Question* (1993).

This powerful speech was called, 'The Racism of Intelligence'. Here Bourdieu points out that there is not one type of racism in the world, but multiple racisms. He suggests that there are as many racisms as there are groups who need to justify their power. For racism at its core is about power.

Bourdieu believed that this form of racism was evident in the educational credentials and titles held by the educated dominant class. It is these credentials that the dominant class uses to justify being dominant. Essentially they feel themselves to be justifiably (and essentially) superior.

In his speech, Bourdieu suggests that we should refuse to accept the biological or social foundations of 'intelligence'. He challenges the assumptions and conventions of psychological intelligence. He states that in relation to our ideas of intelligence we should not turn to science to understand intelligence, but rather we should 'try to look scientifically at the question itself'.

Bourdieu states that intelligence tests merely measure intelligence as defined by the dominant educational system. These tests of intelligence then justify the stratification and discrimination of others. He states:

Educational classification is a euphemized version of social classification, a social classification that has become natural and absolute, having been censored and alchemically transmuted in such a way that class differences turn into differences of 'intelligence', 'talent', and therefore differences of nature (p 178).

Big brains of little use

Credentialism is where the credentials for a job or a position are upgraded even though there is no skill change that makes this increase necessary. Credentialism can be seen clearly in today's workforce with the use of educational credentials as a requirement in a majority of jobs. Even jobs where credentials are not justified on any rational level.

In 1976, Ronald Dore published his book, *The Diploma Disease: Education, Qualification & Development*. In some detail, Dore explains how employers throughout the world end up using educational credentials as entry requirements for jobs, even though they are not needed – creating a qualification spiral. This has resulted in an explosion of educational bodies, both legitimate and not, issuing diplomas.

For US$600.00 and a 300-word thesis one can earn a doctorate or for US$50.00 you can have a bachelor's degree. You can complete a Ph.D. in one year for US$2,500 and get a full academic transcript and a diploma 'suitable for framing'. Class rings and other graduation regalia are extra. Unfortunately, what you are getting is defrauded by an unethical institution, a 'diploma mill'.

The plethora of online diploma mills shows us that educational credentials are a sought-after commodity – a commodity with an increasing value in the workplace. Ashenden described how a number of occupations, such as nurses, engineers, teachers, child care workers and even jockeys have gained their own exclusive educational credentials and with it the benefits of a 'closed shop'

(1988). These associations then establish entry requirements, issue credentials and increase the training time necessary for entrance into the profession.

Credentialism is also seen to support discrimination against minority or low power groups. As educational access is limited to those with power (position, money, ethnicity, gender), repressed groups are kept in their positions of relative powerlessness. In the conditioning tradition, occupational credentialism is believed to legitimatize social inequality and reinforce social hegemony.

Credentialism legitimizes inequality by making it appear natural, fair and immutable, due to the distribution of natural ability and intelligence. This process can be identified as the process of 'symbolic power' explained by Bourdieu (1977), where symbolic systems are categorized as structuring phenomenal reality through their own internal structuring. People do not see the unequal power relations on which occupational credentialism rests, since they appear to be based on rational social and economic grounds while actually maintaining class dominance.

Credentialism can be lessened if certification accurately reflects actual skill competencies and expectations of skill competencies. As Buon & Compton (1990) state, given that the entire recruitment process is aimed at predicting future success, it does not make a great deal of sense to rely on only one indicator (i.e. educational credentials). The results of at least one study support this view and suggest that employers see experience as a better indication of potential work performance than educational credentials (Buon, 1994).

This is not to suggest that education has no value, for it clearly does. Moreover, while those with higher educational credentials do appear to have higher personal incomes, it is important to note that educational credentials are not sources of revenue in their own right. We should remember that incomes are attached to occupations and not to educational credentials (Hussain, 1977).

However, the last word is left to an employer who was asked in the Buon (1994) study why they did not specify that credentials were required in a job advertisement for a training professional to work with the Aborigine Milingimbi Council in the Northern Territory:

People do not necessarily have to be a genius to be able to do the duties required. Life's teachings are often enough. It must at this stage be strongly stated that the job deals with traditional Aboriginal people who do not appreciate big brains of little use (1994).

So what are the big takeaways here?

- Pierre Bourdieu introduced us to 'IQ Racism' or the racism of intelligence.
- This form of racism was evident in the educational credentials and titles held by the educated dominant class. It is these credentials that the dominant class use to justify being dominant and to feel superior.
- The process of credentialism legitimizes inequality by making it appear natural, fair and immutable, due to the distribution of natural ability and intelligence.
- People do not see the unequal power relations on which occupational credentialism rests, since they seem to be based on rational social and economic grounds while maintaining the power of the dominant group.

Source

Talk given at a Colloquium of the MRAP, UNESCO, May 1978, published in *Cahiers: Droit et liberté* (Races, sociétés et aptitudes: apports et limites de la science) (1978), Vol. 382 pp 67–71. Reprinted in English in: Bourdieu, P. (1993), *Sociology in Question*. London: Sage

References

Ashenden, D. (1988), 'Who's Unskilled?', *Australian Society*, May pp 23–5

Berg, I. (1970), *Education and Jobs: The Great Training Robbery*. New York: Praeger

Bourdieu, P., 'Symbolic Power'. In Gleeson, D. (1977), *Identity and Structure, Issues in the Sociology of Education*. Driffield, Yorks.: Nafferton Books

Bourdieu, P. (1993), *Sociology in Question*. London: Sage

Bourdieu, P. & Passeron, J.-C. (1977), *Reproduction in Education, Society and Culture*. California: Sage

Buon, T. & Compton, R. (1990), 'Credentials, Credentialism and Employee Selection', *Asia Pacific Journal of Human Resources*, Vol. 28 Issue 4 pp 126–32

Buon, T. (1994), 'The Recruitment of Training Professionals in Australia', *Training and Development in Australia*, Vol. 21 Issue 5 pp 17–22

Davis, D. (1981), 'Back to Beginnings: Credentialism, Productivity, and Adam Smith's Division of Labour', *Higher Education*, Vol. 10 pp 649–61

Dore, R. P. (1976), *The Diploma Disease*. London: Allen and Unwin

Dore, R. & Oxenham, J., 'Educational Reform and Selection for Employment: An Overview' pp 3–40. In Oxenham, J. (Ed.) (1984), *Education Versus Qualifications?*. London: George Allen and Unwin

Hapgood, D. (1971), *Diplomaism*. New York: D. W. Brown Inc.

Husen, T. & Postlethwaite T. N. (Eds.) (1984), *The International Encyclopaedia of Education, Research and Studies*, Vol. 2.C. Oxford: Pergamon Press

Hussain, A. (1977), 'The relationship between educational qualifications and occupational structure: a re-examination', pp 103–11. In Gleeson, D. (1977), *Identity and Structure, Issues in the Sociology of Education*. Driffield, Yorks.: Nafferton Books

'Report of the Committee of Inquiry into Labour Market Programs', *The Kirby Report* (Australian Government Publishing Service, Canberra, 1985)

Truong, N. & Weill, N. (2012), 'A decade after his death, French sociologist Pierre Bourdieu stands tall', *Guardian Weekly*, 21 February: www.theguardian.com/world/2012/feb/21/pierre-bourdieu-philosophy-most-quoted

See also

Chapter 6 – Maslow was wrong; your needs are not hierarchical

Chapter 7 – The myths of emotional intelligence

Chapter 18 – Stop judging a book by its cover

Chapter 40 – Swearing, cursing and communication

Further reading

Bourdieu, P. & Passeron, J.-C. (1978), *The Inheritors: French Students and Their Relation to Culture*. Chicago: Chicago University Press

Davis, D. (1991), 'Credentialism and Related Socio-Economic Theories of Relationships between Higher Education and Work', *Encyclopaedia of Higher Education*

McClelland, D. C. (1961), *The Achieving Society*. New York: D. Van Nostrand

Porter, L. (1972), *Degrees for Sale*. New York: ARCO

Reid, R. H. (1959), *American Degree Mills*. Washington, D.C.: American Council on Education

Smith, A. (1880), *An Inquiry into the Nature and Causes of the Wealth of Nations* (Vol. 1). Oxford: Clarendon Press

Stewart, D. W. & Spille, H. A. (1988), *Diploma Mills: Degrees of Fraud*. New York: American Council on Education/Macmillan Publishing

Weber, M. (1972), 'Characteristics of a Bureaucracy'. In Gerth, H. & Mills, C. W. (Eds.) (1972), *From Max Weber*. London: Routledge and Kegan Paul

26 MEASURING NATIONAL CULTURE

Over the last several decades, culture has been one of the key research constructs in fields ranging from management and psychology to accounting and marketing. This interest was largely triggered by Hofstede's work, detailed in his 1980 book entitled, Culture's Consequences.
(Taras, Steel & Kirkman, 2012)

They are many different types of culture. These include occupational, organizational, age and even gender (Buon, 2014). However, one of the most prominent types is national culture. That is the norms, behaviours, beliefs, attitudes, customs and values that exist within the population of a country.

National culture has been defined in many ways, but possibly the most compelling explanation is that by Dutch social scientist Professor Geert Hofstede:

Culture is the collective programming of the mind distinguishing the members of one group or category of people from others (1980).

In 1965, Geert Hofstede, a Dutch social psychologist, founded the Personnel Research Department at IBM (Europe), and between 1967 and 1973 he conducted one of the largest studies ever done in relation to national values using a sample of 117,000 employees in the worldwide subsidiaries of IBM.

Hofstede first used the 40 countries with the largest groups of respondents and afterwards extended the analysis to 50 countries and 3 regions. Subsequent studies validating the earlier results have been conducted and continue to be done today.

Hofstede published his research in his academic book *Culture's Consequences* (1980). This has been translated into multiple languages, cited in thousands of peer-reviewed journals, and he is by far the most quoted social scientist in the area of cultural communication.

Hofstede concluded that the values that distinguished country cultures from each other could be statistically categorized into four groups. These groups became known as the 'Hofstede Dimensions of National Culture'. These are:

- **Power Distance**
- **Individualism versus Collectivism**
- **Masculinity versus Femininity**
- **Uncertainty Avoidance.**

Subsequently, and based on further research, additional dimensions were added to this list. A fifth dimension was added in 1991 based on research by Michael Bond, 'Long-Term Orientation' (now renamed 'Pragmatism') and also informed by data from the World Values Survey analysed by Michael Minkov.

Power Distance (PDI) refers to the degree to which the less powerful members of a society accept and expect that power is distributed unequally (Hofstede, 2010). For example, most Arabic nations score highly on power distance, reflecting the view that there are significant power distances between people, and a hierarchical order is generally accepted. Compare this to New Zealand where the low PDI score indicates support for egalitarianism and equality.

Individualism versus Collectivism (IDV) is about the degree to which individuals are integrated into groups. In individualistic societies such as the USA, emphasis is placed on personal achievements and individual rights. In contrast, in collectivist societies such as China individuals act predominantly as members of the group. As Hofstede puts it: 'this dimension is reflected in whether people's self-image is defined in terms of "I" or "we"' (Hofstede, 1980).

Masculinity versus Femininity (MAS) is not about gender in itself, rather it is about the use of power and how much a society values traditional male and female roles. Masculinity in the Hofstede scale is about a preference in society for achievement, heroism, assertiveness, material rewards and competitiveness. Femininity in the Hofstede scale is about cooperation, modesty, empathy and group consensus (Hofstede, 2010). Japan would be an example of a country with a high MAS score; in contrast, Scandinavian countries would be an example of a low MAS.

Uncertainty Avoidance (UAI) refers to the amount to which the members of a country feel uncomfortable with ambiguity and vagueness (Hofstede, 2010). In a high UAI-scoring country such as Pakistan, people aim to avoid ambiguous situations and maintain rigid codes of belief and behaviour and are intolerant of unorthodox ideas. In a low UAI country such as the UK, we are likely to find support for original ideas and very few rules. For example, in the UK new and novel ideas are embraced and encouraged whereas, in a high UAI country, these ideas may be discouraged.

Hofstede's research does not imply that all people in a particular country are programmed in the same way; he acknowledges there are considerable differences between individuals. Moreover, while we can quantify national cultures based on his research, we need to interpret the data as large-scale generalizations and Hofstede warns that without comparison to each other, a country's particular score is meaningless (Hofstede, 2010).

Understanding cultural differences

Culture shapes the way we think and behave. Avruch & Black (1993) suggest that when faced with a cultural interaction that we do not understand, we tend to interpret the others involved as 'weird' or 'wrong'. Learning about other cultures is a vital skill in improving cross-cultural communication.

Learning about Power Distance, Individualism versus Collectivism, Masculinity versus Femininity and Uncertainty Avoidance as demonstrated in the work of Hofstede is an invaluable tool as it provides a quantifiable classification of culture and how culture can be measured. His research showed that cultural differences matter.

Hofstede's work, while impressive and well regarded, does have its critics and limitations. For example, Hofstede's primary data were extracted from a pre-existing bank of employee attitude surveys and were not the product of original research. The main criticisms point to the methodology Hofstede used to analyse his data pool, and many critics have questioned the validity and reliability of his results (Dorfman & Howell, 1988; Søndergaard, 1994; Hampden-Turner & Trompenaars, 1997; Baskerville, 2003).

There are also concerns that his data may be too old to apply to today's generations, particularly given that his original data source dates from employee attitude surveys conducted around 1967 and 1973 (Jones, 2007). However, Hofstede always saw his work as exploratory, not a finished theory, and new data is still informing the original research (Hofstede, 2003).

But how can Hofstede's work have direct application to communication and work in the real world? Can the classification and quantification of national culture have a practical use? The following short anecdote may help to answer this question.

In the early 1990s, an American fast-food chain opened its first restaurant in Mainland China. They employed local staff and trained them using their corporate training programmes. HR systems from the United States were also implemented, including an 'Employee of the Month' award. This award was given to the employee whom the restaurant manager felt was the best worker over the previous month. This involved a special name badge, a cash prize and a large photo of the winner next to the service counter.

During the opening month, one employee, Li Jing, was exceptional. She was great with customers, implemented the corporate system and put in extra effort. The restaurant manager had an easy decision, and Li Jing won the first ever 'Employee of the Month' award. Within two weeks, she had resigned. The following month the award was given to Bao-Zhi, and within a month he had left as well. Something was amiss.

The American HR director thought maybe a rival restaurant was using the winner's photos to poach good workers. However, the Chinese HR assistant had a different idea and asked to visit Li Jing and Bao-Zhi at their homes and conduct an 'exit interview'. Li Jing said how she loved her job, but winning the award was so shameful she had to leave. She described how every time she had to walk past the photo she covered her eyes and felt like she would cry. Bao-Zhi also shared similar feelings; he said when the manager pinned on the badge he 'felt like his heart was being pierced'.

China scores extremely high on the Hofstede cultural norm of collectivism. This means that people do not value self-aggrandizement, and their self-image is defined in terms of the group. By suggesting, they were 'better' than the rest of their team, the restaurant manager had inadvertently made the employee feel ashamed, and the only solution was to leave. Li Jing told the HR assistant: 'It wasn't just me, the whole team deserved recognition, without them I am nothing.'

The 'Employee of the Month' award was effective in an individualistic society such as the USA, where individual achievement is applauded and would likely reinforce positive employee behaviour. However, in China the opposite was true. If the restaurant manager had looked at the cultural values for China, he never would have instituted the individual reward scheme. When a 'Team of the Month Award' was established, it did work, as it fitted the collectivist cultural norms.

So what are the big takeaways here?

- There are significant differences between individuals from and within different countries. However, we can quantify national cultures based on the research of Geert Hofstede and others.
- By understanding these differences, we can meaningfully improve our communication across cultural groups.
- Have a look at the cultural value scores for countries you know or have visited. Did the Hofstede data seem consistent with your experiences?

Source

Hofstede, G. (1980), *Culture's Consequences: International Differences in Work-Related Values.* Beverly Hills, CA: Sage Publications

References

Avruch, K. & Black, P. W. (1993), 'Conflict Resolution in Intercultural Settings: Problems and Prospects'. In Sandole, D. & Van der Merwe, H. (Eds.) (1993), *Conflict Resolution Theory and Practice: Integration and Application.* New York: St Martin's Press

Baskerville, R. F. (2003), 'Hofstede Never Studied Culture', *Accounting, Organizations and Society*, Vol. 28 Issue 1 pp 1–14

Buon, T. (2014), *The Leadership Coach.* London: Hodder & Stoughton

Dorfman, P. W. & Howell, J. P. (1988), 'Dimensions of National Culture and Effective Leadership Patterns: Hofstede revisited', *Advances in International Comparative Management*, Vol. 3 pp 127–50

Hampden-Turner, C. & Trompenaars, F. (1997), 'Response to Geert Hofstede', *International Journal of Intercultural Relations*, Vol. 21 Issue 1 pp 149–59

Hofstede, G. (1980), *Culture's Consequences: International Differences in Work-Related Values.* Beverly Hills, CA: Sage Publications

Hofstede, G. (2003), 'What is culture? A reply to Baskerville', *Accounting, Organizations and Society*, Vol. 28 pp 811–13

Hofstede, G., Hofstede, G. J., Minkov, M. (2010), *Cultures and Organizations: Software of the Mind* (Rev. and expanded 3rd ed.). New York: McGraw-Hill

Jones, M. L. (2007), 'Hofstede – Culturally questionable?', Oxford Business & Economics Conference, Oxford, UK, 24–26 June 2007

Søndergaard, M. (1994), 'Hofstede's consequences: A study of reviews, citations and replications', *Organization Studies*, Vol. 15 No. 3 pp 447–56

Taras, V., Steel, P. & Kirkman, B. L. (2012), 'Improving national cultural indices using a longitudinal meta-analysis of Hofstede's dimensions', *Journal of World Business*, Vol. 47 pp 329–41

See also

Chapter 27 – Cultural differences in communication

Chapter 28 – Silence as a form of communication

Chapter 29 – Communication and facial expressions

Further reading

Bhawuk, D. P. S. & Brislin, R. W. (2000), 'Cross-cultural training: A review', *Applied Psychology: An International Review*, Vol. 49 Issue 1 pp 162–91

Bond, M. H. (1988), 'Finding universal dimensions of individual variation in multicultural studies of values: The Rokeach and Chinese value surveys, *Journal of Personality and Social Psychology*, Vol. 55 Issue 6 pp 1009–15

Hofstede, G. & Bond, M. H. (1988), 'The Confucius Connection: From Cultural Roots to Economic Growth', *Organizational Dynamics*, Vol. 16 Issue 4 pp 5–21

Hofstede, G. (1993), 'Cultural Constraints in Management Theories', *Academy of Management Executive*, Vol. 7 No. 1 pp 81–94

Hofstede, G. (2001), *Culture's Consequences: Comparing Values, Behaviors, Institutions, and Organizations Across Nations* (2nd ed.). Thousand Oaks, CA: Sage Publications

Hofstede, G. (2002), 'The pitfalls of cross-national survey research: a reply to the article by Spector et al on the psychometric properties of the Hofstede Values Survey Module 1994', *Applied Psychology: An International Review*, Vol. 51 Issue 1 pp 170–8

Inglehart, R. (1997), *Modernization and Postmodernization: Cultural, Economic and Political Change in 43 Societies.* Princeton, NJ: Princeton University Press

Inkeles, A. (1997), *National Character: A Psycho-Social Perspective.* New Brunswick, NJ: Transaction Publishers

Kuper, A. (1999), *Culture: The Anthropologists' Account.* London: Harvard University Press

O'Leary, T. J. & Levinson, D. (1991), *Encyclopedia of World Cultures* (Vol. 1). Boston, MA: G. K. Hall & Company

Spector, P. E., Cooper, C. L. & Sparks, K. (2001), 'An International Study of the Psychometric Properties of the Hofstede Values Survey Module 1994: a Comparison of Individual and Country/Province Level Results', *Applied Psychology: An International Review*, Vol. 50 Issue 2 pp 269–81

Taras, V., Kirkman, B. L. & Steel, P. (2010), 'Examining the impact of *Culture's consequences*: A three-decade, multi-level, meta-analytic review of Hofstede's cultural value dimensions', *Journal of Applied Psychology*, Vol. 95 Issue 3 pp 405–39

Taras, V., Rowney, J. & Steel, P. (2009), 'Half a Century of Measuring Culture: Approaches, Challenges, Limitations and Suggestions Based on the Analysis of 121 Instruments for Quantifying Culture', *Journal of International Management*, Vol. 15 Issue 4 pp 357–73

Tomlinson, J. (1999), *Globalization and Culture*. Cambridge: Polity Press

Trompenaars, F. (1993), *Riding the Waves of Culture*. London: Economist Books

Voronov, M. & Singer, J. A. (2002), 'The myth of individualism-collectivism: A critical review', *Journal of Social Psychology*, Vol. 142 Issue 4 pp 461–80

Website: The Hofstede Centre: http://geert-hofstede.com

27 CULTURAL DIFFERENCES IN COMMUNICATION

*The single biggest problem in communication is
the illusion that it has taken place.*
George Bernard Shaw, Irish playwright (1856–1950)

It can be very difficult to communicate if you do not share
a common language with someone. However, cross-cultural
communication problems can also be about differences in how we
see the world, how we process information, even how we view
time (Buon, 2014). Avruch & Black (1993) suggest that when
faced with a cultural interaction that we do not understand, we
tend to interpret the others involved as 'weird' or 'wrong'.

Cultural differences in communication can also cause significant
problems. Million dollar business deals can be lost, international
conflicts can escalate and terrible injustices can happen. One
such injustice was the imprisonment of an Australian Aboriginal
woman, Robyn Kina, for murder in 1988. This case illustrates
the potential for cross-cultural communication problems and the
possible ways to minimize these issues.

Aboriginal Australians possess the world's oldest continuous
culture and were the original inhabitants of the continent of
Australia for 40,000–50,000 years before Europeans landed
in 1788. There are significant differences in social, cultural,
lifestyle and language customs between the various Aboriginal
and Torres Strait Islander people. Aboriginal people experience
disproportionate rates of disadvantage against all measures of
socio-economic status and are significantly over-represented in
the Australian prison populations (Eades, 1996).

Diana Eades, from the Department of Linguistics at the
University of New England in NSW, Australia, has argued that

language and communication issues are part of the reason for this over-representation (Eades, 1994; 1995; 1996). In a 1996 paper, in the journal *Language & Communication*, she uses the case study of Robyn Kina to present her case in a clear and compelling way.

Robyn Kina is an Aboriginal woman who was born in 1959 and grew up in the Aboriginal communities of north Queensland. In 1988, she was sentenced to life imprisonment with hard labour for the killing of her abusive de-facto spouse.

During the trial, which lasted just under four hours, Kina neither gave nor called any evidence in her defence. This decision was made by her lawyers based on their assessment of her credibility as a witness and what they described as her 'unwillingness to give evidence before a jury or to be subjected to cross-examination' (Robson, 1994).

Several years later, Australian Broadcasting Corporation (ABC) television documentary makers interviewed Kina for two documentaries about the legal and moral issues concerning victims of domestic violence who kill their violent spouse in situations of self-defence (Eades, 1996). As a result of these documentaries, the Queensland attorney-general granted a new appeal on the grounds of self-defence and provocation.

Evidence to support this appeal was apparent from the documentary interviews shown on the ABC in 1992 and 1993. Kina had been subjected to horrific sexual and emotional abuse by her spouse, Tony Black (a non-Aboriginal man). On the day she killed Black, he had threatened to rape Kina's 14-year-old niece who was living in the house with them.

Eades suggests that the most important question that her lawyers needed to answer at the appeal was 'why did Kina talk about this self-defence and provocation to TV journalists in 1991 and 1992, but not to her lawyers in 1988?' (p 217). Eades attempted to answer this question for the defence on the basis of sociolinguistics (the study of language as it relates to culture, power and society).

Eades explored the communication gap between Kina and her original lawyers, the ABC journalists and a counsellor, with whom Kina had confided. Eades's sociolinguistic analysis concluded that:

In 1988 Kina was communicating in an Aboriginal way. The lawyers who interviewed her were not able to communicate in this way, and they were not aware that their difficulties in communicating with her involved serious cultural differences (p 217).

The ways in which the lawyers interpreted Kina's use of silence and the style of direct questioning were culturally inappropriate, ineffective and would even be seen as bad mannered when applied to Aboriginal Australians. Eades also points out that at the time the lawyers had received no training in interviewing Aboriginal people (p 217, 219).

However, the ways in which both the ABC journalists and the counsellor communicated were similar to Aboriginal ways of communicating. For example, the counsellor's careful and considered use of silence, use of paraphrasing and active listening, are supportive of Aboriginal communication styles.

The journalists also took time to get to know Kina and again this would be appropriate for an Aboriginal person who would need to get to know someone before disclosing personal information. Further, they gave Kina the opportunity to give several uninterrupted narrative accounts of her story.

Based on her interview with Kina, analysis of documents in Kina's file and her knowledge of Aboriginal communication, Eades concludes that Kina's cultural differences in communication had not been taken into account in the original trial, and the appeal court agreed. The Queensland Court of Criminal Appeal accepted the sociolinguistic evidence and, as a result, Kina's murder conviction was quashed, and she was released from prison on 29 November 1993 (Pringle, 1994).

Improving cross-cultural communication

The Robyn Kina case can teach us much about cross-cultural communication problems. From the inappropriate use of interview techniques to false assumptions about silence and assumptions about personality and character based on communication barriers.

An interview is 'a speech event specific to Western societies' (Eades, 1996). However, the techniques of interview used in one culture may be entirely inappropriate in another. In the Kina case, the lawyers used both 'Western' and 'legal' styles of interviewing that focused on direct questions, establishing facts and ultimately uncovering the 'truth'. Aboriginal people prefer a free-flowing narrative, an indirect style of questioning, an acceptance of silence and are open to the possibility of multiple 'truths'.

In many other cultures, these Aboriginal ways of communicating would be seen as commendable. The acceptance of 'multiple truths' and a focus on listening rather than talking can be seen in many Arabic and Eastern cultures. Interviewing can become culturally inappropriate and ineffective if the interviewer does not take into account cultural differences in communication style.

For example, silence is an often overlooked component of communication, especially in Western culture. Eades states that her research demonstrates that silence is often wrongly interpreted by legal professionals as uncooperativeness, agreement or a lack of knowledge (Eades, 1996). When communicating, silence can mean many different things depending on the cultural background of those involved and the cultural context in which the communication takes place.

There are a number of ways in which we can improve cross-cultural communication and minimize possible barriers. These have been summarized by Buon (2014) and include:

- **Think beyond national:** When communicating across cultures, difficulties can be at national, regional, religious/ethnic, organizational, occupational and gender cultural levels.

- **Ask questions:** Most people enjoy being asked about their lives and their cultures and are happy when you show an interest in their culture.
- **Listen:** Use the skills of active listening to improve cross-cultural communication.
- **Learn:** Take the time to learn about cultural differences in communicating.
- **Avoid stereotypes:** When we stereotype we hear and see things we expect rather than what is real.
- **Honour silence:** It is important to be aware of how other cultures view silence.

In her 1996 paper, Eades explains the cultural differences in speaking and listening that divided Kina from her 1988 lawyers. These lawyers regarded Kina as a difficult and uncommunicative client. However, this was based on their beliefs about communication. If they had been properly trained and aware of how an Australian Aboriginal woman brought up in the Aboriginal environment of Queensland communicated, many terrible mistakes could have been prevented.

So what are the big takeaways here?

- **In 1988 Robyn Kina, an Australian Aboriginal woman, was convicted and received a life sentence for the murder of her de-facto husband.** The initial case lasted only four hours.
- **The Appeal Court accepted sociolinguistic evidence that Kina's cultural differences in communication had not been taken into account in the original trial,** and, as a result, Kina's murder conviction was quashed and she was released from prison in 1993.
- **If we are to understand people from cultures that are different to our own we need to understand the ways in which they communicate.** We should not ascribe personality based on the way a person communicates.

Source

Eades, D. (1996), 'Legal recognition of cultural differences in Communication: the case of Robyn Kina', *Language & Communication*, Vol. 16 Issue 3 pp 215–27

References

Avruch, K. & Black, P. W. (1993), 'Conflict Resolution in Intercultural Settings: Problems and Prospects'. In Sandole, D. & Van der Merwe, H. (Eds.) (1993), *Conflict Resolution Theory and Practice: Integration and Application*. New York: St Martin's Press

Buon, T. (2014), *The Leadership Coach*. London: Hodder & Stoughton

Eades, D., 'A case of communicative clash: Aboriginal English and the legal system'. In Gibbons, J. (Ed.) (1994), *Language and the Law*. London: Longman

Eades, D. (Ed.) (1995), *Language in Evidence: Issues Confronting Aboriginal and Multicultural Australia*. Sydney: University of New South Wales Press

Eades, D. (1996), 'Legal recognition of cultural differences in Communication: the case of Robyn Kina', *Language & Communication*, Vol. 16 Issue 3 pp 215–27

Pringle, K. L. (1994), R. *v.* Robyn Bella Kina, *Aboriginal Law Bulletin*, Vol. 3 (67) April, 14–15

Robson, F. (1994), 'The terrible trials of Robyn Kina [Good Weekend]', *The Australian*, 26 March, pp 41–5

See also

Further reading

Arthur, J. (1996), *Aboriginal English: A Cultural Study*. Melbourne: Oxford University Press

Berry, D. (2014), *Robyn Kina, Strong Aboriginal Woman: A Lifer Redeemed*. CreateSpace Independent Publishing Platform, Australia

Nakane, I. (2006), 'Silence and politeness in intercultural communication in university seminars', *Journal of Pragmatics*, Vol. 38 Issue 11 pp 1811–35

Sifianou, M., 'Silence and politeness'. In Jaworski, A. (Ed.) (1997), *Silence: Interdisciplinary Perspectives*. Berlin: Mouton de Gruyter

Website: Robyn Kina: The Book: http://robynkina.com

28 SILENCE AS A FORM OF COMMUNICATION

'Speech too is great, but not the greatest. As the Swiss Inscription says: "Sprechen ist silbern, Schweigen ist golden" (Speech is silvern, Silence is golden); or as I might rather express it: Speech is of Time, Silence is of Eternity.'
Thomas Carlyle, Sartor Resartus (1831)

Silence is an often overlooked component of communication, especially in Western culture. For example, it is often suggested that silence is greatly respected and widely used when communicating in Japan, whereas in the UK or the USA, people are likely to fill any gaps in communications with more words. However, we should be very careful in such generalizations as scientific research does not always support these conclusions (Kogure, 2007).

Silence serves a number of purposes, from demonstrating politeness (Sifianou, 1997), reducing conflict (Tannen, 1990), avoiding embarrassment (Jaworski, 1993), demonstrating anger or disinterest (Liegner, 1971), indicating interpersonal intimacy or extreme distance (Jaworski, 2000), and even increasing solidarity (Bohnet & Frey, 1999). Silence serves many purposes and is an essential component of communication.

However, silence has long been neglected in communication research. While there are many discussions in books and blogs about the 'importance' of silence, there is little scientific study into the functions and cultural components of silence.

Researcher Ikuko Nakane from the Asia Institute in Melbourne, Australia, attempted to add to the limited scientific data on silence and communication by exploring the use of silence in university seminars by different students. Specifically, she compared Japanese and Australian students' use of silence and politeness (Nakane, 2006).

The data for this study was collected at two universities in Sydney, Australia, and included interviews with 19 Japanese students; survey results from 34 lecturers; videotaped classroom interaction and interviews with three Japanese students and their Australian peers and lecturers; and other data recorded from two Japanese high schools (Nakane, 2006). The videotaped seminars were the primary focus of the paper published in the *Journal of Pragmatics* by Nakane. Nakane later published a fuller account of her overall study in a 2007 book (Nakane, 2007).

Nakane reports that 78.9 per cent of the Japanese students studying in Australian universities indicated that they were silent in classroom communication. This self-perception of silence was characterized by comments such as 'I don't talk much in class' or 'I am very quiet during discussions'.

She also reported that 73.7 per cent of the Japanese students described their Australian peers as active vocal participants in class. The lecturers running the seminars said that Japanese students generally remained silent unless nominated to speak, and this was supported by the students.

Nakane looked at various factors to account for the use of silence by Japanese students. These included language skill, educational practices and beliefs, and participants' background and history. She found 'politeness strategies' and 'orientations' seemed to have a very strong influence on the students' silence.

The Japanese students appeared to use silence as a strategy to avoid 'loss of face' due to a perception of insufficient language proficiency. It is important to note that the idea of 'losing face' in most Asian cultures is not just about preventing embarrassment to yourself, it goes much deeper and is about reputation, dignity, influence and even social class. It is also often directed towards others, helping them 'save face'.

However, Nakane found that the fear in the Japanese students went even deeper than a concern for language proficiency. It was also about the fear that the student would appear to the lecturer as not having the correct answer. This was about saving their own face. Nakane quoted one student as saying:

I must say asking questions to the lecturer is kind of scary. Because I don't have confidence in grasping the theories, I have this fear that lecturers may, in fact, spot my weakness if I ask questions. So I decide I'd better not do it (p 1816).

When to use silence

In Australia, students are encouraged from a young age to question their teachers and 'speaking up' is generally positively reinforced. Nakane reports that the Australian students' involvement was 'criticized by a number of Japanese students for its carelessness and irrelevance'. This shows a potential serious barrier to communication between Australian and Japanese students and their teachers.

In Australian universities, colleges and schools (as in the USA and the UK), classroom or tutorial participation is often assessed and forms part of a final mark. This is very rare in Asian universities, colleges or schools. Nakane found that the lecturers in his study found the Japanese students' silence as their 'major weakness'.

Nakane found that Japanese students' use of silence was not just a face-saving strategy, but that it was also about politeness (Nakane, 2006). This is an important finding, beyond the scope of the present study. Many other cultures, including Chinese and Middle Eastern, see silence as a way of demonstrating politeness; whereas in many Western cultures, keeping silent is perceived as being rude.

Many of the Australian and Japanese students in Nakane's study may have seen each other as rude for their use of silence or speaking up. The students (and the lecturers) views on silence and talking were shaped by their cultural influences and upbringings, as all cultural views are. But they need to understand where the other is coming from and be able to look at this as a positive aspect of diversity and embrace the differences to enhance communication.

In the Nakane study, she found that for Australian students and lecturers the expression of critical views or disagreement with classmates or the lecturer is regarded as a sign of engagement, enthusiasm and academic competence. This is no doubt the source of many conflicts between people of different national cultures. Understanding the role of silence, both in terms of face-saving and politeness, is vital if we are to improve cross-cultural communications.

The assumption that the Japanese prefer silence during conversational interaction, as compared to Westerners, is not proven in the scientific literature. However, studies such as that done by Ikuko Nakane, demonstrate the existence of cultural differences. They are just a lot more complicated than a particular culture's preference for silence or talk.

No matter what our culture, moments of silence in conversation can communicate important non-verbal information, as well as deeply facilitate effective communication. When someone is silent, it may be that they are conveying emotional messages or they may just be attempting to be polite. Alternatively, when we respond with silence in a conversation, our quietness can be seen by the other person as demonstrating acceptance and concern. However, silence can also be interpreted as conveying disinterest, and disengagement, leading to a breakdown in communication.

We need to be aware of when to use or not use silence. For example, while 'saying nothing' can be a very effective response in one situation, it can be the completely wrong response in another. Learning how the other party sees silence can be an important way to improve communication, particularly when dealing with someone that sees silence differently than you do.

Sometimes remaining silent is an excellent strategy, particularly when dealing with obnoxious people. In a study published in the *Journal of Social and Personal Relationships* in 2013, the researchers found that it is healthier and less mentally draining to ignore other people in some circumstances (Sommer & Yoon, 2013). The researchers concluded 'silence can be golden' – when you ignore an especially annoying person.

So what are the big takeaways here?

- We need to be consciously aware of the use of silence in our communications and not underestimate or overestimate its significance.
- Silence can be no more than a needed pause in an intense discussion or it can be a gateway to acceptance and understanding.
- Silence does not always need to be filled; sometimes saying nothing is the best thing.
- It is just as important to develop your communication skills in silence as it is to develop skills in writing, speaking or listening.

Source

Nakane, I. (2006), 'Silence and politeness in intercultural communication in university seminars', *Journal of Pragmatics*, Vol. 38 Issue 11 pp 1811–35

References

Bohnet, I. & Frey, B. S. (1999), 'The sound of silence in prisoner's dilemma and dictator games', *Journal of Economic Behavior & Organization*, Vol. 38 pp 43–57

Carlyle, T. (1831), *Sartor Resartus*

Jaworski, A. (1993), *The Power of Silence: Social and Pragmatic Perspectives*. Newbury Park, CA: Sage Publications

Jaworski, A. (2000), 'Silence and small talk'. In Coupland, J. (Ed.), *Small talk*. London: Pearson Education

Kogure, M. (2007), 'Nodding and smiling in silence during the loop sequence of backchannels in Japanese conversation', *Journal of Pragmatics*, Vol. 39 Issue 7 pp 1275–89

Liegner, E. (1971), 'The silent patient', *Psychoanalytic Review*, Vol. 61 pp 229–45

Nakane, I. (2006), Silence and politeness in intercultural communication in university seminars', *Journal of Pragmatics*, Vol. 38 Issue 11 pp 1811–35

Nakane, I. (2007), *Silence in Intercultural Communication: Perceptions and performance* (Pragmatics and Beyond New Series). Amsterdam: John Benjamins Publishing

Sifianou, M., 'Silence and politeness'. In Jaworski, A. (Ed.) (1997), *Silence: Interdisciplinary Perspectives*. Berlin: Mouton de Gruyter

Sommer, K. L. & Yoon, J. (2013), 'When silence is golden: Ostracism as resource conservation during aversive interactions', *Journal of Social and Personal Relationships*, Vol. 30 Issue 7 pp 901–19

Tannen, D. & Saville-Troike, M. (Eds.) (1985), *Perspectives on Silence*. Norwood, NJ: Ablex

Tannen, D. (1990), 'Silence as conflict management in fiction and drama: Pinter's *Betrayal* and a short story, "Great Wits"'. In Grimshaw, A. D. (Ed.) (1990), *Conflict Talk*. Cambridge: Cambridge University Press

See also

Further reading

Arlow, J. A. (1961), Silence and the theory of technique, *Journal of the American Psychoanalytic Association*, Vol. 9 pp 44–55

Braithwaite, C. A. (1990), 'Communicative Silence: a Cross-Cultural Study of Basso's Hypothesis'. In Carbaugh, D. (Ed.) (1990), *Cultural Communication and Intercultural Contact*. Hillsdale, NJ: Lawrence Erlbaum

Bruneau, T. J. (1973), 'Communicative silences: forms and functions', *Journal of Communication*, Vol. 17 pp 36–42

Buon, T. (2014), *The Leadership Coach*. London: Hodder & Stoughton

Hofstede, G. (1980), *Culture's Consequences: International Differences in Work-Related Values*. Beverly Hills, CA: Sage

Khan, M. (1963), 'Silence as communication', *Bulletin of the Menninger Clinic*, Vol. 27 pp 300–13

Kurzon, D. (1997), *Discourse of Silence*. Amsterdam: John Benjamins

29 COMMUNICATION AND FACIAL EXPRESSIONS

The movements of expression in the face and body, whatever their origin may have been, are in themselves of much importance for our welfare. They serve as the first means of communication between the mother and her infant; she smiles approval, and thus encourages her child on the right path, or frowns disapproval.

Charles Darwin (1872)

It's all in the face, or so the argument goes. Beginning with Charles Darwin's work described in his 1872 book *The Expression of the Emotions in Man and Animals*, and backed up by hundreds of published scientific papers since. We know that non-verbal communication plays a central role in communication and emotion. Even current brain research supports this idea (LeDoux, 1995).

Paul Ekman has had a distinguished career in psychological research, and has been described as one of the 100 most-eminent psychologists of the 20th century (Haggbloom et al, 2002). He focused his work on the study of emotions and, in particular, their relation to facial expressions. He is best known for his work in the late 1960s when, along with colleague Wallace Friesen, he studied the Fore people of Papua New Guinea (PNG) to test the Darwinian hypothesis that a particular set of emotions, and how they are expressed, are both innate and universal.

In 1967 and 1968, Ekman travelled to PNG to study non-verbal behaviour of the Fore people, an isolated, subsistence-oriented cultural group. The research was funded by a grant from the US Department of Defense. The aim of the study was to test Darwin's claim that facial expressions are universal and not, as many anthropologists had claimed, culturally specific and determined (Mead, 1975; Lutz & White, 1986).

Ekman & Friesen had previously conducted experiments where they had showed still photographs to people from many different cultures to test whether they saw the same emotion in the facial expressions, irrespective of their national culture (Ekman & Friesen, 1969). They found that they did.

However there was a problem with the methodology. It was possible that the people in all the countries they had tested had all been exposed to the same mass media portrayals of facial behaviours and collectively learned to name them (Ekman & Friesen, 1971).

To illuminate this confounding variable was going to be very difficult. Where can you find anyone who has not been exposed to television, movies and other forms of popular media? In PNG such a group of people existed. The people of the Fore cultural group of the South East Highlands of PNG were very isolated with only minimal contact with other peoples until the 1950s. They lived in a Neolithic culture and many had no contact at all with outsiders.

Ekman & Friesen choose 189 Fore adults and 130 Fore children to be part of their study group. They were selected on a strict criteria of minimal contact with Westerners and any form of mass media (Ekman & Friesen, 1971). Twenty-three Fore who had had extensive contact with Westerners, who had seen movies and spoke English, were chosen as a control group.

Due to language limitations and other methodological concerns, Ekman & Friesen told small stories to the subjects to describe an emotion. They then presented three photographs of Westerners (each depicting a different emotion) and asked the subject to match the appropriate one (the children were given only two).

The results were that both adults and children were able to associate the same emotion concepts with the same facial behaviours as did members of Western and Eastern literate cultures. The researchers found no differences between genders and the results for the Fore who had been Westernized were almost the same as the experimental group. Ekman & Friesen reported they had found empirical support for the universality of certain emotions. Ekman later stated:

These stone-age people, who could not have learned expressions from the media, chose the same expressions for each emotion as had the people in the 21 literate cultures. The only exception was that they failed to distinguish the fear and surprise faces from each other, although both were distinguished from anger, happiness, sadness and disgust expressions (p 308).

The expressions he found to be universal were those indicating anger, disgust, fear, happiness, sadness and surprise. Other researchers have since confirmed the universality of these six emotions. Ekman & Keltner (2014) state that almost 200 scientific studies have shown that people from entirely different cultures are able to label facial expressions with terms from a list of emotion words.

Understanding non-verbal gestures

Critics, such as Professor James Russell (1994), have questioned the methodology and internal validity of the Ekman & Friesen study. Russell has argued in some detail that the faults in the design of the Fore experiments make the conclusions of these studies impossible to interpret.

Others have also questioned the universality thesis and suggested facial expressions are socially learned and differ across cultures (Lutz & White, 1986; Mead, 1975; Leach, 1972). Russell also makes a strong argument however that the dichotomy of either universalism or difference is limiting and ultimately unhelpful to the science of communication.

The work of Ekman and his colleagues supports the idea that there are certain emotions that are common to all national cultures and that we can identify these in others. The idea of this ability to read the emotions of others was illustrated in a 1983 study by Krauss, Curran & Ferleger. In this study the researchers had US students, who did not speak Japanese, watch Japanese soap operas. The US students were able to recognize the emotions displayed by the Japanese actors, simply by observing their facial expressions (Krauss, Curran & Ferleger).

Ekman suggested there were at least six basic emotions: anger, disgust, fear, happiness, sadness and surprise. There is also support for a seventh emotion, contempt (Matsumoto, 1992; Rosenberg & Ekman, 1995; Wagner, 2000). In 1999 Ekman also introduced 15 other emotions that are distinguishable from each other. These were: amusement, anger, contempt, contentment, disgust, embarrassment, excitement, fear, pride in achievement, relief, sadness/distress, satisfaction, sensory pleasure and shame. He also conceded that guilt would be a possible addition to this list. He also suggested that interest had been proposed by other researchers though he believed it was a 'cognitive state' rather than an emotion.

Ekman also introduced the valuable concept of 'emotion families', suggesting 'each emotion is not a single affective state but a family of related states' (1999). Each family of emotions shares unique characteristics, which for Ekman are the product of evolution, while the variations within the emotion families reflect learning.

In relation to the debate over nature *versus* nurture, Ekman is clear: he states that both are at play. Emotion is seen as a physiological phenomenon influenced by our culture and learning (Ekman, 1993).

In 2014 three neuroscientists from the University of Glasgow published their work on the biology of human emotions and questioned the thesis of six basic emotions and suggested that there were only four. These were happy, sad, fear/surprise and disgust/anger (Jack, Garrod & Schyns). This research suggests that our emotional signals evolve over time with possibly only four basic emotions being biologically based and later developing socially into the six or seven facial expressions of emotion.

While Ekman and his colleagues' work has shown us the possible universality of emotion, we should not read into this a lack of cultural difference in emotion. For example, research has demonstrated cross-cultural gender differences in how emotions are experienced (Fischer et al, 2004). A meta-analysis of 162 studies showed that gender differences in smiling are both culture and age specific (LaFrance, Hecht & Paluck, 2003).

Although non-verbal communication often provides valuable information about people's emotions, we need to be careful not to take Ekman's work and apply it simplistically. There may be six or seven emotions that are universal, but this does not mean that it is easy to decode non-verbal gestures. For example, when a person's facial expression shows anger but he or she is in a frightening situation, we may incorrectly interpret the emotion as fear.

Hillary Elfenbein and Nalini Ambady from Harvard University have demonstrated that there is an in-group advantage in emotion, whereby emotional communication is generally more accurate when the people involved are from the same cultural group (2002). To put it simply, we are better at reading the emotions of those who are similar to us. The flip side to this is that we need to be careful when evaluating the emotions in those who are different from us.

Ekman states that his research has shown how people can misrepresent emotions (Ekman, 1993). He states that while good liars can mimic facial expressions to support their lies, sometimes there is what Ekman calls *leakage* in the facial and vocal expressions of the liars (Ekman & Friesen, 1969; Ekman, 1988; Ekman, 1993). However, most people are not able to detect lies, though some people are able to read lies better than others (Ekman, 1988).

Some people seem able to read the subtle 'micro-expressions' that can betray a lie. After retiring from his university in 2004, Ekman opened a private company dedicated to 'enhancing emotional awareness' and offering a number of online tools for developing skills in detecting micro-expressions.

It should be noted that even if you can naturally identify micro-expressions or have learned how to do so, this does not mean that someone is lying, simply that there is more to the story. It may be that they think, you think, they are lying. Or they think, you think, they think, they are lying. Or they think, you think, they think, you think, they are lying... (and so on). It is better to see these moments as probing points, when you dig below the surface, using all your available communication skills, to arrive at a shared understanding.

So what are the big takeaways here?

- Ekman & Friesen were able to associate the same emotion concepts with the same facial behaviours as did members of Western and Eastern literate cultures.
- The six expressions they found to be universal were those indicating anger, disgust, fear, happiness, sadness and surprise.
- While it appears likely that emotions are biologically programmed, the way we control our emotions, what triggers and how we perceive emotions is culturally determined.

Source

Ekman, P. & Friesen, W. V. (1971), 'Constants Across Cultures in the Face and Emotion', *Journal of Personality and Social Psychology*, Vol. 17 Issue 2 pp 124–9

References

Darwin, C. (1872), *The Expression of the Emotions in Man and Animals*. London: John Murray

Ekman, P. (1988), 'Lying and Nonverbal Behavior Theoretical Issues and New Findings', *Journal of Nonverbal Behavior*, Vol. 12 Issue 3 pp 163–75

Ekman, P. (1993), 'Facial expression of emotion', *American Psychologist*, Vol. 48 pp 384–92

Ekman, P. (1999), 'Basic Emotions'. In Dalgleish, T. & Power, M. J. (Eds.) (1999), *Handbook of Cognition and Emotion*. New York: John Wiley & Sons

Ekman. P. & Friesen, W. V. (1969), 'The Repertoire of Nonverbal Behavior: Categories, Origins, Usage, and Coding', *Semiotica*, Vol. 1 pp 49–98

Ekman, P. & Friesen, W. V. (1971), 'Constants Across Cultures in the Face and Emotion', *Journal of Personality and Social Psychology*, Vol. 17 Issue 2 pp 124–9

Ekman P. & Keltner, D. (2014), 'Darwin's Claim of Universals in Facial Expression Not Challenged': https://www.paulekman.com/uncategorized/darwins-claim-universals-facial-expression-challenged/

Elfenbein, H. A. & Ambady, N. (2002), 'On the Universality and Cultural Specificity of Emotion Recognition: A Meta-Analysis', *Psychological Bulletin*, Vol. 128 pp 203–35

Fischer, A. H., Rodriguez Mosquera, P. M., van Vianen, A. & Manstead, A. S. R. (2004), 'Gender and culture differences in emotion', *Emotion*, Vol. 4 Issue 1 pp 87–94

Haggbloom, S. J., Warnick, R., Warnick, J. E., Jones, V. K., Yarbrough, G. L., Russell, T. M., Borecky, C. M., McGahhey, R., Powell, J. L., III, Beavers, J. & Emmanuelle, M. (2002), 'The 100 most eminent psychologists of the 20th century', *Review of General Psychology*, Vol. 6 Issue 2 pp 139–52

Jack, R. E, Garrod, O. G. B. & Schyns, P. G. (2014), 'Dynamic Facial Expressions of Emotion Transmit an Evolving Hierarchy of Signals over Time', *Current Biology*, Vol. 24 Issue 2 pp 187–92

Krauss, R. M., Curran, N. M. & Ferleger, N. (1983), 'Expressive conventions and the cross-cultural perception of emotion', *Basic and Applied Social Psychology*, Vol. 4 pp 295–305

LaFrance, M., Hecht, M. A. & Paluck, E. L. (2003), 'The Contingent Smile: A Meta-Analysis of Sex Differences in Smiling', *Psychological Bulletin*, Vol. 129 Issue 2 pp 305–34

Lutz, C. & White, G. M. (1986), 'The Anthropology of Emotions', *Annual Review of Anthropology*, Vol. 15, 405–36

Matsumoto, D. (1992), 'More evidence for the universality of a contempt expression', *Motivation & Emotion*, Vol. 16 Issue 4 pp 363–8

Mead, M. (1975), 'Review of 'Darwin and Facial Expression', *Journal of Communication*, Vol. 25 pp 209–13

Rosenberg, E. L. & Ekman, P. (1995), 'Conceptual and methodological issues in the judgment of facial expressions of emotion', *Motivation & Emotion*, Vol. 19 Issue 2 pp 111–38

Russell, J. A. (1994), 'Is There Universal Recognition of Emotion From Facial Expression? A Review of the Cross-Cultural Studies', *Psychological Bulletin*, Vol. 115 No. 1 pp 102–41

Wagner, H. L. (2000), 'The accessibility of the term "contempt" and the meaning of the unilateral lip curl', *Cognition & Emotion*, Vol. 14 Issue 5 pp 689–710

See also

Chapter 1 – Communication is not all about body language

Chapter 4 – Does everybody lie?

Chapter 26 – Measuring national culture

Chapter 27 – Cultural differences in communication

Further reading

Bell, C. (1806), *Essays on the anatomy of expression in painting* London: Longman, Hurst, Rees & Orme

Carroll, J. M. & Russell, J. A. (1997), 'Facial expressions in Hollywood's portrayal of emotion', *Journal of Personality and Social Psychology*, Vol. 72 Issue 1 pp 164–76

Ekman, P., Sorenson, E. R. & Friesen, W. V. (1969), 'Pan-cultural elements in facial displays of emotions', *Science*, Vol. 164 (3875) pp 86–8

Guilford, J. P. (1929), 'An experiment in learning to read facial expression', *Journal of Comparative Psychology*, Vol. 24 pp 191–202

Izard, C. E. (1990), 'Facial expressions and the regulation of emotions', *Journal of Personality and Social Psychology*, Vol. 58 Issue 3 pp 487–98

Knapp, M. L. & Hall, J. A. (2005), *Nonverbal Communication in Human Interaction* (6th ed.). Belmont, CA: Wadsworth

LaBarre, W. (1947), 'The Cultural Basis of Emotions and Gestures', *Journal of Personality*, Vol. 76 Issue 1 pp 49–68

LeDoux, J. E. (1995), 'Emotion: Clues from the Brain', *Annual Review of Psychology*, Vol. 46 pp 209–35

Russell, J. A. & Fernández-Dols, J. M. (Eds.) (1997), *The Psychology of Facial Expression*. Cambridge: Cambridge University Press

Video abstract of the 2014 Glasgow study: http://www.cell.com/current-biology/abstract/S0960-9822(13)01519-4

Website: Paul Ekman's corporate website. https://www.paulekman.com

THE OBAMA EFFECT: REDUCING STEREOTYPING

A stereotype is '...a fixed, over generalized belief about a particular group or class of people'
Cardwell (1996)

The main advantages of stereotypes are that they simply save time. For example: 'I have dealt with Welsh people for years, and I know that they prefer …' Alternatively: 'The new clients are all mechanical engineers, so we know they will like …'.

Stereotyping allows us to simplify our complex world as it reduces how much thinking we have to do when we meet a new person. It is something we all do and sometimes the assumptions are also correct, at least to some degree.

The problem with stereotypes is that they usually, ignore significant differences between people, and we think things that are inaccurate (e.g. 'all Arabs are… '). When we stereotype, we hear and see things we expect rather than what is real. We jump to incorrect assumptions. We limit our communication.

Stereotypes are often used by one dominant group to dehumanize certain groups based on race, religion or physical characteristics. Stereotypes can even offer a rationalization for discrimination against marginalized groups.

When Barack Obama ran and was subsequently elected as president of the United States, he challenged commonly held stereotypes of African Americans. Research has shown that white Americans often see African Americans in a negative, stereotypical way (Jewell, 1993; Plous & Williams, 1995; Moody, 2012). Could the positive counter-stereotypical example of Barack Obama reduce the negative stereotypes held by white Americans? This is what an extraordinary study attempted to uncover in 2009.

In 2008–9, seven researchers from Florida State University and the University of Wisconsin decided to explore the Obama presidential campaign. Would the resulting high levels of exposure to a positive, counter-stereotypic black exemplar have an impact on prejudice and stereotyping among non-black participants? (Plant et al, 2009).

In 2002, Irene Blair from the University of Colorado at Boulder demonstrated that stereotypes and prejudice were not rigid, and these views can be modified in people if they are exposed to positive counter-stereotypes (Blair, 2002). Researchers Dasgupta & Greenwald (2001) conducted two experiments that revealed that exposure to admired black exemplars (e.g. the actor Denzel Washington) and disliked white exemplars (e.g. the serial killer Jeffrey Dahmer) significantly weakened instinctive pro-white attitudes.

In the Obama study, the researchers conducted two studies involving students at a midwestern university who participated in exchange for course credit. In the first study, 229 students completed a test called the Implicit Association Task (IAT). This instrument, widely available online, measures the strength of automatic associations people have in their minds.

Many people have shown that they are faster to associate positive words with names of white people rather than black people. Further research has demonstrated that non-black respondents show substantial anti-black bias when using this test (Amodio & Devine, 2006).

The results of Study 1 were dramatic. The researchers found no anti-black bias on either the evaluative IAT or the stereotyping IAT D-score, with neither being significantly different from zero. The researchers stated that:

These findings stand in stark contrast to prior work that has consistently found evaluative and stereotype IAT scores significantly greater than zero (Plant et al, 2009).

The second study examined whether decreases in prejudice resulted from increased associations between black people and traits associated with Obama as a political figure. Seventy-nine students performed a decision task assessing the strength of association between 'black primes' (an unconscious stimulus) and government-related words.

In contrast to Study 1, there was some evidence of anti-black bias on the evaluative IAT. However, this was substantially lower than scores obtained by the researchers previously. Overall, the researchers concluded that their findings indicate that the extensive exposure to Obama resulted in a drop in stereotyping of African Americans (Plant et al, 2009).

Stereotyping limits communication

There is substantial research to suggest that many people hold implicit biases (stereotypes) against such groups as non-whites, women, gay people, Arabs, etc. For example, word association tasks asking subjects to pair positive and negative words with black or white faces: most are much speedier to match black faces with negative words than with positive ones.

These stereotypes are pervasive. Almost everyone possesses them, even people whose declared beliefs are anti-stereotypical. Most people seem to hold positive stereotypes about their own groups. Though many even hold implicit biases against their own group.

Stereotypes often ignore significant differences between individuals and can reinforce negative thoughts about others. When we stereotype, we jump to incorrect assumptions and limit our critical thinking. Also, we, usually, see negative rather than positive images when stereotyping (Buon, 2014).

Stereotyping can limit our communication with others. We set up barriers to communication that are both implicit and explicit. We limit our chances to learn and develop interpersonally with those from other groups.

For example, if I have unconscious stereotypical views about Africans being corrupt, women being poor at science, or Arabs being lazy, these beliefs may stop me communicating effectively with people from these groups. My stereotypical views may limit my ability to process new information and communicate effectively.

Stereotyping can interfere with rational decision-making. A stereotypical view of one group can cause us to reject a job applicant because we hold incorrect views about that group. It could even enable us to believe it is OK to discriminate against particular groups or, worse, cause us to hate certain groups.

However, the research on Obama has encouraging implications. That is, that implicit biases are non-rigid. It appears they can easily change and to change they just need alternative positive information. We need to be flexible and be open to changing our views of others.

The hidden associations that we have formed as individuals can be unlearned. The exposure to positive information about other groups can change our beliefs. We can stop the unconscious activation of stereotypes in the first place rather than try to control their impact once they are activated. This conclusion has strong implications for the way we communicate about minority groups and the way we reduce discrimination.

With the Obama study, there are some methodological concerns. For example, the authors acknowledge that their results are based on correlational data and may not, therefore, conclusively demonstrate causal relations between the variables (Plant et al, 2009). Of course, this is a limitation of all correlational research.

Because the study involved a naturally occurring set of events (the campaign and election of Obama), the researchers could not control the level and impact of the exposure to Obama. Further, the longevity of the positive effect on participants has not been examined. We simply cannot be sure that the subjects' reduction in stereotyping lasts.

Also, as the study took place when President Obama was in his 'honeymoon' period, would the positive effect diminish if Obama's popularity is significantly reduced when he leaves office. In fact, in September/October 2014 President Obama's 'approval ranking' was at 43 per cent, a significant reduction from 67 per cent in January 2009 (Gallup, 2014).

What impact this might have on the stereotyping of African Americans is unclear. A president's legacy can take many years to be fully established. The midterm election results made it clear that a majority of voters were unhappy with Obama's performance as a president; the long-term impact his presidency will have on black stereotyping remains unknown.

So what are the big takeaways here?

- **Extensive exposure to Barack Obama in his presidential campaign and subsequent election resulted in a drop in stereotyping of African Americans by white students who previously held negative views.**
- **The hidden associations that we have formed as individuals can be unlearned.**
- **Exposing ourselves to positive examples of minorities, and other groups of whom we hold stereotypical views, can reduce our implicit biases and improve our communication skills.**

Source

Plant, E. A., Devine, P. G., Cox, W. T., Columb, C., Miller, S. L., Goplen, J. & Peruche, B. M. (2009), 'The Obama effect: Decreasing implicit prejudice and stereotyping', *Journal of Experimental Social Psychology*, Vol. 45 pp 961–4

References

Amodio, D. M. & Devine, P. G. (2006), 'Stereotyping and evaluation in implicit race bias: Evidence for independent constructs and unique effects on behavior', *Journal of Personality and Social Psychology*, Vol. 91 No. 4 pp 652–61

Blair, I. V. (2002), 'The Malleability of Automatic Stereotypes and Prejudice, *Personality and Social Psychology Review*, Vol. 6 pp 242–61

Buon, T. (2014), *The Leadership Coach*. London: Hodder & Stoughton

Cardwell, M. (1996), *Dictionary of Psychology*. Chicago IL: Fitzroy Dearborn

Dasgupta, N. & Greenwald, A. G. (2001), 'On the Malleability of Automatic Attitudes: Combating Automatic Prejudice with Images of Admired and Disliked Individuals', *Journal of Personality and Social Psychology*, Vol. 81 Issue 5 pp 800–14. Cited in Blair, I. V. (2002), 'The Malleability of Automatic Stereotypes and Prejudice', *Personality and Social Psychology Review*, Vol. 6 pp 242–61

Gallup Poll: http://www.gallup.com/poll/116479/barack-obama-presidential-job-approval.aspx

Jewell, K. S. (1993), *From Mammy to Miss America and Beyond: Cultural Images and the Shaping of US Social Policy*. New York: Routledge

Moody, M. (2012), 'New Media-Same Stereotypes: An Analysis of Social Media Depictions of President Barack Obama and Michelle Obama', *The Journal of New Media & Culture*, Vol. 8 Issue 1

Plant, E. A., Devine, P. G., Cox, W. T., Columb, C., Miller, S. L., Goplen, J. & Peruche, B. M. (2009), 'The Obama effect: Decreasing implicit prejudice and stereotyping', *Journal of Experimental Social Psychology*, Vol. 45 pp 961–4

Plous, S. & Williams, T. (1995), 'Racial Stereotypes From the Days of American Slavery: a Continuing Legacy', *Journal of Applied Social Psychology*, Vol. 25 Issue 9 pp 795–817

See also

Chapter 2 – Men and women are not from different planets

Chapter 18 – Stop judging a book by its cover

Chapter 25 – Educational credentials and the racism of intelligence

Chapter 27 – Cultural differences in communications

Further reading

Allport, G. W. (1954), *The Nature of Prejudice*. Reading, MA: Addison-Wesley

Banaji, M. R. & Hardin, C. D. (1996), 'Automatic Stereotyping', *Psychological Science*, Vol. 7 No. 3 pp 136–41

Devine, P. G. (1989), 'Stereotypes and prejudice: Their automatic and controlled components', *Journal of Personality and Social Psychology*, Vol. 56 pp 5–18

Eagly, A. H. & Steffen, V. J. (1984), 'Gender Stereotypes Stem From the Distribution of Women and Men into Social Roles', *Journal of Personality and Social Psychology*, Vol. 46 pp 735–54

Eden, A., Maloney, E. & Bowman, N. D. (2010), 'Gender Attribution in Online Video Games', *Journal of Media Psychology*, Vol. 22 pp 114–24

Greenwald, A. G., Poehlman, T. A., Uhlmann, E. L. & Banaji, M. R. (2009), 'Understanding and Using the Implicit Association Test: III. Meta-analysis of predictive validity', *Journal of Personality and Social Psychology*, Vol. 97 Issue 1 pp 17–41

Greenwald, A. G., McGhee, D. E. & Schwartz, J. L. K. (1998), 'Measuring Individual Differences in Implicit Cognition: The Implicit Association Test', *Journal of Personality and Social Psychology*, Vol. 74 No. 6 pp 1464–80

Greer, T. M., Vendemia, J. M. C. & Stancil, M. (2012), 'Neural correlates of race-related social evaluations for African Americans and white Americans', *Neuropsychology*, Vol. 26 Issue 6 pp 704–12

Hart, A. J., Whalen, P. J., Shin, L. M., McInerney, S. C., Fischer, H. & Rauch, S. L. (2000), 'Differential response in the human amygdala to racial outgroup vs ingroup face stimuli, *Neuroreport: An International Journal for the Rapid Communication of Research in Neuroscience*, Vol. 11 Issue 11 pp 2351–5

McConahay, J. B., Hardee, B. B. & Batts, V. (1981), 'Has Racism Declined in America? It Depends on Who is Asking and What is Asked', *Journal of Conflict Resolution*, Vol. 25 No. 4 pp 563–79

Stewart, T. L., Weeks, M. & Lupfer, M. B. (2003), 'Spontaneous stereotyping: A matter of prejudice?', *Social Cognition*, Vol. 21 pp 263–98

31 COMMUNICATION STARTS WITH THE EYES

Perhaps in all too many cases they are full of ancient traditional hokum from the culture about the eyes being the windows of the soul, and things being seen in them that might not otherwise be revealed – which seems to be one of the most misguided ideas I've ever known.

H. S. Sullivan (1954), psychoanalyst

It is widely believed that insufficient or excessive eye contact can create communication barriers. It is also suggested that 'appropriate' eye contact during a conversation shows attentiveness and interest. It is often also often quoted that the eyes are the 'windows to the soul'. But what is the basis for these claims? What is the actual function of eyes during interpersonal communication and do the eyes serve a critical communication function in humans?

Patterns of eye contact differ enormously across cultures. Eye contact that is too intense in one culture may be acceptable in another. For example, in many Asian cultures a lack of eye contact towards someone in authority signifies respect, while in Western cultures a lack of eye contact may be seen to indicate insincerity.

When compared to telephone or email, it is suggested that having face-to-face communication allows people to communicate more quickly and better understand unclear messages (McGrath & Hollingshead, 1993). It is also suggested that eye contact and touch are the only two ways that people can make direct contact with each other (Heron, 1970). It appears that we rely on eye contact to communicate on a conscious and unconscious level (Sato, Okada & Toichi, 2007).

The white of the human eye (the sclera) has a unique and important function. It is unique in humans as in most animals only the iris of the eye is visible. The size and the shape of the sclera can indicate fear, interest, and the direction of a person's gaze. When we are under stress our eyes open wide and the sclera appears larger.

We use our eyes to transmit social cues (verbal or non-verbal hints) that inform our communication with others. However, it is unclear whether the ability to distinguish between different social cues indicated by the eyes exists early in development and can, for this reason, be considered a critical feature of the human social makeup.

In an article published in the online journal, *Proceedings of the National Academy of Sciences*, researchers from the Max Planck Institute for Human Cognitive and Brain Sciences in Germany and the University of Virginia in the United States attempt to answer this question (Jessen et al, 2014). The researchers conducted two experiments to discover the mechanisms that underpin sensitive responding to human eyes in babies.

In the first experiment, they explored whether babies' detection of signals sent through body language signs (social cues) from someone's eyes, occurs in the absence of conscious awareness or thought. In the second experiment, they examined whether the detection of these social cues can be seen in response to information gained solely from the white of the eye (the sclera) (Jessen et al, 2014: p 16209).

The researchers used electro-encephalography (EEG) to measure the brain activity of 7-month-old babies while showing them images of eyes wide open, narrowly opened, and with direct or averted gazes. They hypothesized that the unconscious detection of social cues from scleral information should be evident early in the development of humans.

In the first experiment, the babies viewed images of eyes for only 50 milliseconds while electrodes attached to their heads measured their brain activity. Jessen & Grossmann found that the babies were able to discriminate unconsciously between fearful and non-fearful eyes. Fearful-looking eyes triggered strong results in the infants' brains (Jessen & Grossmann, 2014).

In the second experiment, the researchers examined whether, in addition to emotional cues, babies could also detect more subtle cues from human sclera in relation to gaze direction. They found that babies did show brain responses that differed when viewing direct gaze eyes compared to averted gaze. An averted fearful gaze elicited weaker electric signals in frontal regions of the brain that are responsible for higher cognitive abilities and attention.

The researchers concluded that fear and gaze detection in babies occurs unconsciously and is based on social cues from the white of the eyes. There is a fast and efficient social signal detection mechanism in the human child's brain that is likely to provide a foundation for the development of communication skills. This demonstrates that human eyes serve an essential function in communication and that these functions emerge early in human development (Jessen & Grossmann, 2014).

Eyes and human communication

To fully understand the role of the eyes in human communication, researchers are using brain research to explore the specific brain processes that connect to eye contact. Humans are the only primates with a large and highly visible white part of the eye (the sclera). Human eyes provide cues about a person's emotional state and their attentional focus (Jessen & Grossmann, 2014).

The Jessen & Grossmann study shows us that the human eye with its prominent white area facilitates social and cooperative interactions among humans. Our ability to detect social cues from the eyes of others starts early in our development and confirms the importance of eye contact. People can perceive the emotional state of others and the whites of our eyes are central to this process.

One reason why human eyes have such importance is that the eyes tell us about emotion in the other person. Understanding the feelings of others is an essential part of effective communication (Rogers, 1975; Rogers & Farson, 1987). Whether this is the detection of fear or the speaker's attentional focus, it is a vital part of the communication process.

Decoding non-verbal cues such as eye contact and gaze is an important communication skill. Possessing this skill is associated with good social relationships and supportive social support systems (Riggio & Zimmerman, 1991). We should see eye contact as an ability that we need to understand and develop.

When we communicate, we should be aware of the role of our eyes. Human eyes provide cues about a person's emotional state and where they are focusing their attention. Both functions rely on the whites of our eyes and Jessen & Grossmann have shown that these operate even in the absence of conscious awareness in both adults and babies. Our prominent sclera serves critical communicative functions during human communication (Jessen & Grossmann, 2014).

Eye contact is an essential part of the communication process and is linked to empathy and rapport building. People at an unconscious level appear to search each other's eyes and faces for positive or negative emotion. The meeting of eyes arouses strong emotions and can be an important component of intimacy. Eye contact creates moments of empathy and can increase the intimate bond between people.

Eyes play a crucial role in human communication, as they allow us to perceive others as having rational minds (Looser & Wheatley, 2010). The human eye is unique when compared to other primates. For example, the whites of our eyes allow others to see what we are looking at and notice when our focus changes direction.

The Jessen & Grossmann study provides neurological evidence for the unconscious detection of emotion through the whites of our eyes by infants. Their findings demonstrate the existence of fast, efficient and reliable social cue detection mechanisms in a baby's brain. This supports the contention that human eyes developed to facilitate communication with the eyes of other people.

A lack of eye contact can in some circumstances be a sign of shyness or disinterest. However, it is also easy to misinterpret a lack of eye contact. In some cultures averting the eyes is a sign of good manners and respect, in others it is a sign of insincerity or dishonesty. Whether or not the eyes are 'the windows to the soul', they do reveal a great deal about what we are interested in and how we are feeling.

So what are the big takeaways here?

- This study shows us that the human eye with its prominent white area facilitates communication among humans.
- Our ability to detect social cues from the eyes of others starts early in our development and confirms the importance of eye contact.
- Be aware of the importance of eye contact in communication. However, remember to take into account cultural differences.

Source

Jessen, S. & Grossmann, T. (2014), 'Unconscious discrimination of social cues from eye whites in infants', *Proceedings of the National Academy of Sciences of the United States of America*, Vol. 111 No. 45 pp 16208–13

References

Heron, J. (1970), 'The Phenomenology of Social Encounter: The Gaze', *Philosophy and Phenomenological Research*, Vol. 31 No. 2 pp 243–64

Jessen, S. & Grossmann, T. (2014), 'Unconscious discrimination of social cues from eye whites in infants', *Proceedings of the National Academy of Sciences of the United States of America*, Vol. 111 No. 45 pp 16208–13

Looser, C. E. & Wheatley, T. (2010), 'The Tipping Point of Animacy. How, When, and Where We Perceive Life in a Face', *Psychological Science*, Vol. 21 No. 12 pp 1854–62

Max Planck Institute (2014), 'Babies subconsciously process emotions', Research News website. October 31, 2014: http://www.mpg.de/8727811/Jessen_EmotionsBabies

McGrath, J. E. & Hollingshead, A. B., 'Putting the "group" back into group support systems: Some theoretical issues about dynamic processes in groups with technological enhancements'. In Jessup, L. M. & Valacich, J. S. (Eds.) (1993), *Group support systems: New perspectives*. New York: Macmillan

Riggio, R. E. & Zimmerman, J. A. (1991), 'Social skills and interpersonal relationships: influences on social support and support seeking'. In Jones, W. H. & Perlman, D. (Eds.) (1991), *Advances in Personal Relationships, Relationships. Vol. 2*. London: Jessica Kingsley

Rogers, C. R. (1975), 'Empathic – An Unappreciated Way of Being', *The Counseling Psychologist*, Vol. 5 No. 2–10

Rogers, C. R. & Farson, R. E. (1987), 'Active Listening'. In Newman, R. G., Danziger, M. A. & Cohen, M. (Eds.) (1987), *Communication in Business Today*. Washington, D.C.: Heath and Company

Sato, W., Okada, T. & Toichi, M. (2007), 'Attentional shift by gaze is triggered without awareness', *Experimental Brain Research*, Vol. 183 Issue 1 pp 87–94

Sullivan, H. S. (1954), *The Psychiatric Interview*. New York: W. W. Norton

Tickle-Degnen, L. & Rosenthal, R. (1992), 'Nonverbal aspects of therapeutic rapport'. In Feldman, R. S. (Ed.) (1992), *Applications of nonverbal behaviour theories and research*. Hillsdale, NJ: Lawrence Erlbaum

See also

Chapter 1 – Communication is not all about body language

Chapter 10 – NLP and communication

Chapter 32 – Neuro-scientific communication

Further reading

Ekman, P. (2001), *Telling Lies: Clues to Deceit in the Marketplace, Politics, and Marriage.* New York: W. W. Norton & Company

Jessen, S. & Grossmann, T. (2015), 'Neural signatures of conscious and unconscious emotional face processing in human infants', *Cortex*, Vol. 64 pp 260–70

Senju, A. & Johnson, M. H. (2009), 'The eye contact effect: Mechanisms and development', *Trends in Cognitive Sciences*, Vol. 13 Issue 3 pp 127–34

Whalen, P. J. et al (2004), 'Human Amygdala Responsivity to Masked Fearful Eye Whites', *Science*, Vol. 306 No. 5704 p 2061

Wiseman, R., Watt, C., ten Brinke, L., Porter, S., Couper, S.-L. & Rankin, C. (2012), 'The Eyes Don't Have It: Lie Detection and Neuro-Linguistic Programming', *PLOS ONE*, Vol. 7 No. 7 e40259

32 NEURO-SCIENTIFIC COMMUNICATION

*'[Before phrenology] all we knew about the brain was
how to slice it...'*
Richard Chenevix, phrenologist (1828)

Phrenology is a famous 19th-century pseudoscience that claimed you could judge a person's mental abilities and personality by examining the bumps or indentations on their head as these corresponded to brain lobes found in postmortem studies (Gall, 1808). This idea has been popularized with the 'phrenology head', a porcelain model on which a person's characteristics are illustrated.

While phrenology is now thoroughly discredited, psychologists Chamorro-Premuzic & Furnham (2010) have argued that the current enthusiasm for brain imaging, such as functional magnetic resonance imaging (fMRI), is 'really no more than a form of electrical phrenology'. The distinguished professor of psychology Warren Tryon has recently stated that:

...modern brain imaging studies do not offer any greater explanation than phrenology did. They associate brain structures with psychological and behavioural functions but associations are not explanations (Tyron, 2014).

Two American researchers, David McCabe and Alan Castel, were interested in the idea that brain images have a persuasive influence on the public perception of neuro-scientific studies (McCabe & Castel, 2008). So they conducted three experiments to test if the image of the brain has an effect on the perceived scientific quality of an article.

Experiment 1 involved 156 US undergraduates between the ages of 18 and 25. The student volunteers were given three fictional articles to read about neuroscience research. These were based on traditional news service articles and included no image, a bar graph or a brain image depicting the critical results.

After reading each article, participants were asked to rate their agreement with three statements about the quality of the article, if the title was descriptive of the work and, most importantly, if the 'scientific reasoning in the article made sense'. No difference was found for the 'title question' nor between the 'no image' and 'bar graph' articles. However, the researchers did find a moderate but significant difference in the articles that were accompanied by a brain image. These articles received the highest ratings of scientific reasoning and quality.

Experiment 2 with 128 US students was conducted to test if it was just the fact that the brain image looked 'scientific' that made it score higher. So they devised an experiment where they could test whether it was the more visually complex brain images (when compared to bar graphs) that influenced judgements of scientific reasoning. This involved comparing two of the original articles with either brain images as before and articles with complex topographical maps of the brain.

McCabe & Castel found that the texts with a brain image received higher ratings for scientific reasoning than those accompanied by a topographical map. They therefore concluded that it was not simply the visual complexity of the brain images that influenced ratings of scientific reasoning.

Experiment 3 was designed to take a broader view of the findings beyond the first two experiments. In this, the researchers used a real news service article, 'Can Brain Scans Detect Criminals?' (BBC website), that summarized a study published in the journal *Nature*. This allowed for an analysis of materials as they would be found in the 'real-world' and to assess what happens if the article reviewed contained no errors in scientific reasoning.

In this third experiment, 108 US students read the BBC website article and answered two questions related to: (1) whether the article was a good summary of the results and (2) if they agreed with the conclusion given. For half of the participants, the last paragraph of the article included text of a researcher criticizing the conclusion.

They found that for the question regarding whether subjects agreed with the conclusion reached in the article that the ratings of agreement were higher when the brain image was present. However, the effect of criticism being present or not was not significant.

McCabe & Castel concluded that the use of brain images influenced ratings of the scientific merit of the reported research, compared to identical articles including no image, a bar graph or a topographical map. This supports the belief that there is something particularly persuasive about brain images with respect to the way they communicate credibility.

The complexities of human behaviour and communication

Brain research is often popularized in the media. However, the media often oversells the results of such research. For example, it has been claimed that brain research shows that:

- People are in love with their iPhone
- Men and women are fundamentally different in how they communicate
- You can identify a criminal's brain.

All of this is untrue, but provides a clickable and sensational headline (click-bait). McCabe and Castel state:

Many scientists, particularly cognitive neuroscientists and ethicists, are concerned about how the data from fMRI studies are being interpreted, particularly by the lay media and the general public, both of whom have shown a tendency to oversimplify and misrepresent conclusions from brain imaging studies (p 344).

Understanding scientific data is a complicated process. Moreover, deciphering the complexities of the journal article is hard even for experienced scientists. Many media departments of universities and research institutes also release captivating media releases of studies designed to gain attention. Sometimes the headlines of these studies are designed primarily to attract attention in a crowded media space:

Brain study finds link between chocolate and sex

Rather than a truthful headline that conveys scientific fact:

Brain study finds tryptophan link to mating behaviour in mice

Scientific communication is complex and has a number of distinct problems. These include scientific misconduct such as fraud, partiality and plagiarism. It also involves the culture of scientific writing, with problems such as publication bias and the 'publish or perish' mentality. Publish or perish refers to the pressure on academics to publish so as to gain promotion.

From the McCabe & Castel (2008) paper, we have seen that images of brains have an especially persuasive influence on the public perception of scientific research. This is likely to extend to research related to thought, emotion, behaviour, personality and communication. The public has a fascination with brain imaging research and the media as always meets this need. However, we need to be careful not to be misled or deceived.

The researchers in this study argue that brain images are influential because they provide a physical basis for the abstract brain and that this appeals to people's 'affinity for reductionistic explanations of cognitive phenomena' (McCabe & Castel, 2008). Reductionism is about trying to explain something by reference to only one factor, in this case neural activity in the brain. Although a degree of reductionism is often necessary for theorizing, the problem is that this can ignore the complexities of human behaviour and communication.

Modern brain scans such as fMRI, computed tomography (CT), positron emission tomography (PET) and electro-encephalography (EEG) are amazing tools that have broad application in medicine, neuropsychology and communication research. For example, fMRI is a non-invasive technique for measuring brain activity. It can be used to produce colourful activation maps showing which parts of the brain are involved in a particular mental process. However, it only measures the secondary physiological correlates of neural activity – it is not a direct measure.

In this study, we have seen how colourful brain images seem to appeal to us in a way that limits our critical evaluation. There are negative consequences of using brain images in scientific communication as they can artificially inflate the credibility of research. We as readers and consumers of scientific communication need to be aware of this.

So what are the big takeaways here?

- **Neuroscience has had amazing breakthroughs over the past 20 years;** however, brain scans cannot be used to read people's emotions or thoughts.
- **When you see an image of a brain in a news story, blog, scientific paper or product research,** be careful you are not overly influenced by the picture rather than the science.
- **fMRI is an excellent tool for brain research** but fMRI is not a genuine quantitative measure of mental activity. It answers the 'what' but not the 'why'.
- **The reductionist nature of brain research can over-simplify complex questions and ignore the complexities of human behaviour and communication.**

Source

McCabe, D. P. & Castel, A. D. (2008), 'Seeing is believing: The effect of brain images on judgments of scientific reasoning', *Cognition*, Vol. 107 Issue 1 pp 343–52

References

Chamorro-Premuzic, T. & Furnham, A. (2010), *The Psychology of Personnel Selection*. New York: Cambridge University Press

Chenevix, R. (1830), 'Phrenology': Article of the *Foreign Quarterly Review*, 1 January Treuttel, Würtz, and Richter. Free e-book accessed at: https://play.google.com/store/books/details?id=lPN2fzGGWwkC&rdid=book-lPN2fzGGWwkC&rdot=1

Gall, F.-J. (1808), 'Discours d'ouverture, lu par M. le Docteur Gall... à la première séance de son cours public sur la physiologie du cerveau', le 15 janvier. Firmin Didot, Paris

McCabe, D. P. & Castel, A. D. (2008), 'Seeing is believing: The effect of brain images on judgments of scientific reasoning', *Cognition*, Vol. 107 Issue 1 pp 343–52

Tryon, W. W. (2014), 'Brain Imaging as Modern Phrenology', *SciTech Connect*: http://scitechconnect.elsevier.com/brain-imagining-modern-phrenology/#.VN9Dme8fx9A

See also

Further reading

BBC website: 'Can brain scans detect criminals?' 21 September 2005: http://news.bbc.co.uk/1/hi/health/4268260.stm

Bourdieu, P. (1988), *Homo Academicus*. Cambridge: Polity Press

Dobbs, D. (2005), 'Fact or Phrenology?', *Scientific American Mind*, Vol. 16 pp 24–31

Poldrack, R. A. (2006), 'Can cognitive processes be inferred from neuroimaging data?', *Trends in Cognitive Sciences*, Vol. 10 Issue 2 pp 59–63

Ted Talk by neuroscientist Dr Molly Crockett (2012), 'Beware Neuro-Bunk': http://www.ted.com/talks/molly_crockett_beware_neuro_bunk

Tryon, W. W. (2014), *Cognitive Neuroscience and Psychotherapy: Network Principles for a Unified Theory*. New York: Academic Press

Vul, E., Harris, C., Winkielman, P. & Pashler, H. (2009), 'Puzzlingly High Correlations in fMRI Studies of Emotion, Personality, and Social Cognition', *Perspectives on Psychological Science*, Vol. 4 No. 3 pp 274–90

Weisberg, D. S., Keil, F. C., Goodstein, J., Rawson, E. & Gray, J. R. (2008), 'The Seductive Allure of Neuroscience Explanations', *Journal of Cognitive Neuroscience*, Vol. 20 Issue 3 pp 470–7

33 OUR BRAIN CANNOT COPE WITH TOO MUCH INFORMATION

distringit librorum multitudo
[the abundance of books is distraction]
Seneca the Younger (4 BCE–AD 65)

Your brain is amazing and can do amazing things. However, it cannot cope with having too much information thrown at it at once. It goes into overload, a bit like trying to do too many things at once on your computer.

The commonly cited capacity is the so-called magic number of 7 ± 2 (Miller, 1956). That is, the brain can only hold seven (plus or minus two) pieces of information at one time. More recently, some researchers have even suggested that this could be less than seven.

Your working memory (what used to be called short-term memory) can process only limited amounts of information at a time. This limitation of working memory means that we invariably fail to understand new material if it is sufficiently complex (Sweller, 1999). Long-term memory, on the other hand, stores knowledge and skills on a more-or-less permanent basis. Long-term memory has no known limits to its capacity.

The pioneer of this work is Professor John Sweller of the University of New South Wales in Australia. His work is about cognitive load theory. This work deals with the interaction of information and mental structures and the implications of that interaction for instruction and instructional design (Sweller, 1999). For example, when using PowerPoint® to present information we should understand that it is harder to process information if it is coming at you in written and spoken form at the same time.

Learners often use a problem-solving strategy called means-ends analysis. Means-end analysis is a problem-solving method in which the problem is broken down into sub-goals, and each step to solve the problem tries to move closer to the solution. Sweller proposes problem-solving by means-ends analysis requires a relatively large amount of cognitive processing capacity, which may not be devoted to learning.

Sweller advocates that instructional designers should prevent cognitive load by designing instructional materials that do not involve problem-solving. Examples of alternative instructional materials would include worked-examples and goal-free problems.

An example of a worked-example would be a step-by-step illustration of how to perform a task such as creating a folder in Gmail or solving a mathematical problem. A goal-free problem is a problem with a non-specific goal. For example, instead of solving a particular problem specifically, such as 'calculate the correct solution', the learner is given more general wording such as 'calculate as many solutions as you can'.

In his classic 1988 study, Professor Sweller used 24 Australian high-school students (aged 15–16 years) from a Sydney high school. All had been introduced previously to the sine, cosine and tangent ratios in mathematics classes.

In the study, the high-school students were given a sheet explaining and giving examples of the use of the sine, cosine and tangent ratios and had to solve six problems. When each problem was solved, they were required precisely to reproduce the original diagram and the correct solution of the problem preceding the one that had just been solved. Subjects were informed that their primary task was to solve the problem.

The 24 students were put into two groups of 12 with one group having a conventional goal and the other a nonspecific goal. Both groups were required to memorize and reproduce the givens and solutions of the problems as a secondary task. Time and errors for each of the solution and reproduction phases were recorded.

Sweller found that there was no difference in total time to solve the six problems between groups. However, he also found that the cognitive load imposed by one task interfered with performance on the other. More excess capacity appears to be available after solving a non-specific goal problem when compared with solving a conventional problem.

Sweller concluded that traditional problem-solving through means-ends analysis imposes a heavy mental load and that the intellectual effort required by conventional problem-solving may not assist in schema acquisition, that is, knowledge stored in the long-term memory. Sweller suggests that schema acquisition is 'possibly the most important component of problem-solving expertise' (p 284). Therefore, an emphasis on problem-solving may, in fact, limit rather than enhance learning.

Keeping things simple

Cognitive load theory has become one of the most important theories in educational psychology. While Sweller's ideas have been applied to the areas of instructional design, it also has implications for learning and development, training and even corporate communication.

This is not to suggest that there are no criticisms of this work. For example, the theory has been criticized for its conceptual clarity (Schnotz & Kürschner 2007) and for the methodology used to create the theory (Gerjets, Scheiter & Cierniak, 2009; de Jong, 2010). However, even these critics have commented on the importance and general common sense of the theory.

Cognitive load theory tells us that designing instructional materials should take into consideration the way the brain processes information. If our working memory becomes overloaded, nothing ends up in long-term memory, and if nothing ends up in long-term memory, nothing has been learned or properly understood. Teachers, educators and corporate trainers should design instructional materials based on the learners' cognitive processing abilities.

At the root of cognitive learning theory is schema formation. A schema is a mental framework that helps us organize and understand information. Knowledge is stored in long-term memory in schemata (Kirschner, 2002). Skill development is about building amassed numbers of increasingly complex schemas.

Chipperfield (2004) states that cognitive load theory is based on five principles of cognitive learning.

- That short-term memory (working memory) is limited in capacity to about seven informational units.
- Long-term memory is unlimited in capacity and is where all information and knowledge is stored.
- Knowledge is stored in long-term memory as schemas or schemata.
- Schemas, no matter how large or how complex, are treated as a single entity in working memory.
- Schemas can become automated.

When we are instructing, teaching or coaching others we should also be aware of the limits suggested by cognitive load theory. For example, the traditional method of setting people problems to solve may not work as well as giving learners problems with the solutions. Limit the load on working memory by using goal-free problems or worked examples. Sweller suggests:

Looking at an already solved problem reduces the working memory load and allows you to learn. It means the next time you come across a problem like that, you have a better chance at solving it (Sweller, 1997).

When designing instructional materials or other presentation materials, we should provide illustrations or diagrams without text or labels if possible, keeping cognitive load to a minimum. If text is necessary, then it should be placed on the diagram, rather than separately. This should reduce cognitive load and, therefore, improve learning (Sweller, 1999).

This would also apply to corporate communications. If you are developing multimedia or other materials for the purposes of communicating a particular message, then you should keep cognitive load to a minimum. Multimedia adds an additional layer to the message that may result in excessive cognitive load.

Do not overuse music, animation, colour or fonts in corporate communications or you may overload the learner before the idea or skill is learned. Keeping things simple is the best way to ensure retention and efficient communication.

One interesting implication for cognitive load theory applies to the use of PowerPoint® in training and education. Sweller states:

The use of the PowerPoint presentation has been a disaster, it should be ditched. It is effective to speak to a diagram, because it presents information in a different form. But it is not effective to speak the same words that are written, because it is putting too much load on the mind and decreases your ability to understand what is being presented (Sweller, 1997).

So what are the big takeaways here?

- **According to Cognitive Load theory,** we can only process a small amount of new information at any one time before storing it in our long-term memory.
- **We should also remember that it is harder to process information if it is delivered in both written and verbal ways at the same time.**
- **If you are developing multimedia or other materials for the purposes of communicating a particular message,** then you should not overload the working memory of recipients of your message by using unnecessary multimedia.
- **Keeping things simple is the best way to ensure retention and effective communication.**

Source

Sweller, J. (1988), 'Cognitive Load During Problem Solving: Effects on Learning', *Cognitive Science*, Vol. 12 Issue 2 pp 257–85

References

Chipperfield, B. (2004), 'Cognitive Load Theory and Instructional Design' (Unpublished paper), Educational Communications and Technology, University of Saskatchewan, April: http://etad.usask.ca/802papers/chipperfield/index.htm

de Jong, T. (2010), 'Cognitive load theory, educational research, and instructional design: some food for thought', *Instructional Science*, Vol. 38 pp 105–34

Gerjets, P., Scheiter, K. & Cierniak, G. (2009), 'The scientific value of cognitive load theory: A research agenda based on the structuralist view of theories', *Educational Psychology Review*, Vol. 21 pp 43–54

Kirschner, P. A. (2002), 'Cognitive load theory: implications of cognitive load theory on the design of learning', *Learning and Instruction*, Vol. 12 pp 1–10

Miller, G. A. (1956), 'The magical number seven, plus or minus two: Some limits on our capacity for processing information', *Psychological Review*, Vol. 63 Issue 2 pp 81–97

Schnotz, W. & Kürschner, C. (2007), 'A Reconsideration of Cognitive Load Theory', *Educational Psychology Review*, Vol. 19 pp 469–508

Sweller, J. (1988), 'Cognitive Load During Problem Solving: Effects on Learning', *Cognitive Science*, Vol. 12 Issue 2 pp 257–85

Sweller, J. (1994), 'Cognitive load theory, learning difficulty, and instructional design', *Learning and Instruction*, Vol. 4 Issue 4 pp 295–312

Sweller, J. (1997), 'Research points the finger at PowerPoint', Anna Patty, Education Editor, *Sydney Morning Herald*. April 4, 2007: http://www.smh.com.au/news/technology/powerpoint-presentations-a-disaster/2007/04/03/1175366240499.html#

Sweller, J, (1999), *Instructional Design in Technical Areas*. Melbourne: ACER Press

See also

Chapter 14 – Restricting PowerPoint® to enhance communication

Chapter 17 – Checking your email too often wastes time

Chapter 33 – Our brain cannot cope with too much information

Chapter 36 – Turning off your smartphone can make you work smarter

Further reading

Anderson, J. R. (1982), 'Acquisition of cognitive skill', *Psychological Review*, Vol. 89 Issue 4 pp 369–406

Bannert, M. (2002), 'Managing cognitive load – recent trends in cognitive load theory', *Learning and Instruction*, Vol. 12 pp 139–46

Cooper, G. (1990), 'Cognitive load theory as an aid for instructional design', *Australasian Journal of Educational Technology*, Vol. 6 Issue 2 pp 108–113

Cowan, N. (2001), 'The magical number 4 in short-term memory: A reconsideration of mental storage capacity', *Behavioral and Brain Sciences*, Vol. 24 Issue 1 pp 87–114

De Groot, A., 'Perception and memory versus thought: Some old ideas and recent findings'. In Kleinmuntz, B. (Ed.) (1966), *Problem Solving*. New York: Wiley

Mayer, R. E. (2001), *Multimedia Learning*. New York: Cambridge University Press

Mayer, R. E. & Moreno, R. (2003), 'Nine Ways to Reduce Cognitive Load in Multimedia Learning', *Educational Psychologist*, Vol. 38 Issue 1 pp 43–52

Sweller, J. & Cooper, G. A. (1985), 'The use of worked examples as a substitute for problem solving in learning algebra', *Cognition and Instruction*, Vol. 2 pp 59–89

Tufte, E. R. (2006), *The Cognitive Style of PowerPoint* (2nd ed.). Graphics Press

34 READING A GOOD BOOK MAY IMPROVE YOUR EMPATHY

*... being empathic is a complex, demanding, strong
yet subtle and gentle way of being*
Carl Rogers, psychotherapist (1975)

Empathy is about feeling what another person feels. The word is derived from the Ancient Greek word *empatheia* ('affection' or 'passion'), the ability to understand things outside ourselves. The use of empathy was an important part of the psychological counselling techniques taught by Carl Rogers. Empathy in communication studies is often described as 'standing in another person's shoes'.

Closely related to empathy is Theory of Mind processes (ToM). ToM refers to our ability to characterize and understand other people's thoughts and feelings. While still under much debate, ToM has been defined as:

the everyday ability to attribute independent mental states to self and others in order to predict and explain behaviour (Premack & Woodruff, 1978).

In a fascinating study conducted in New York City, researchers found evidence that literary fiction improves a reader's capacity to understand what others are thinking and feeling (Kidd & Castano, 2013). Psychologist Emanuele Castano and doctoral candidate David Comer Kidd conducted five experiments, involving 697 online volunteers through Amazon's Mechanical Turk service.

The researchers looked at:

> literary fiction
> popular fiction (romance and adventure stories)
> non-fiction
> 'not reading at all'

... and any impact on ToM. To overcome any issues with defining 'literariness' the researchers used books acknowledged by literary prize jurors (Kidd & Castano, 2013).

In Experiment 1, 86 participants read three short literary fiction and three short non-fiction texts. They then completed a number of ToM tests. Experiment 2 involved 114 participants and used different texts and different ToM tests. Experiment 3 involved 69 subjects and replicated the literary fiction versus popular fiction comparison. Experiment 4 introduced new texts and involved 72 subjects. Experiment 5 was a replication of Experiment 4 and used 356 subjects to test for the influence of subject variables such as education, age and gender (p 378).

The works of fiction had to depict 'at least two characters' and the non-fiction works had to be about 'a nonhuman subject'. The literary texts used were:

- *The Runner* by Don DeLillo
- *Blind Date* by Lydia Davis
- *The Chameleon* by Anton Chekhov
- *The Round House* by Louise Erdrich
- *The Tiger's Wife* by Téa Obreht
- *Salvage the Bones* by Jesmyn Ward
- *Corrie* by Alice Munro
- *Leak* by Sam Ruddick
- *Nothing Living Lives Alone* by Wendell Berry
- *Uncle Rock* by Dagoberto Gilb
- *The Vandercook* by Alice Mattison

The popular fiction choices were:

- *Space Jockey* by Robert A. Heinlein
- *The Sins of the Mother* by Danielle Steel
- *Gone Girl* by Gillian Flynn
- *Cross Roads* by Wm. Paul Young
- *Too Many Have Lived* by Dashiell Hammett
- *Lalla* by Rosamunde Pilcher
- *Jane* by Mary Roberts Rinehart

The non-fiction texts were articles from the *Smithsonian* magazine:

- *How the Potato Changed the World*
- *Bamboo Steps Up*
- *The Story of the Most Common Bird in the World*

After they finished reading the passages (literary, popular or non-fiction), or not reading at all, the participants took a test that measured their ability to understand other people's thoughts and emotions. The five experiments used a combination of four different ToM tests: reading the mind in the eyes (RMET), the positive affect/negative affect scale (PANAS), the diagnostic analysis of non-verbal accuracy test (DANV) and the Yoni test (YONI) (p 379).

The researchers found a small but statistically significant difference between the literary and popular fiction readers. The results of the five experiments showed that reading short passages of literary fiction raised participants' ability to discern people's emotions from pictures of their eyes or faces.

In some cases, the benefit extended to superior performance on a ToM picture test that involved using visual or verbal cues to identify what a person was thinking or desiring. No such effects were found after reading non-fiction or popular fiction.

Empathy and communication

The results are quite surprising, after reading just short passages of literary fiction, people demonstrated better empathy. Many literary types got very excited about this research result, possibly on a moral basis. However, we need to be cautious in interpreting the results.

The researchers were also rather confounded by their results. A comparison of the linguistic characteristics of literary and popular fiction showed limited differences, with the exception of the frequency of negative emotion words.

The researchers suggest it is the way literary books 'engage their readers creatively as writers ... The absence of a single authorial perspective prompts readers to enter a vibrant discourse with the author and her characters' (p 379). However, the researchers do state that their research is only preliminary and requires much more study.

There are also a number of methodological issues with the study, including the use of the Mechanical Turk paid sample, other sampling issues, results with small significance scores, problems with interpretation of the ToM tests and no discussion on the length of the impact on subjects.

Nonetheless, if replicated in further research, there could be significant educational and social implications of these findings, including what type of literary fiction should be included in educational curricula for students of all ages.

If reading literary fiction does increase empathy, there could be other social implications. Such as:

- We need to encourage young people to read more quality literature
- Funding should be made available to distribute literary fiction at a reduced cost
- We should encourage the reading of literary fiction in prisons, juvenile correctional institutions and other similar institutions
- We should encourage the reading of literary fiction by those in certain occupations, including nurses, doctors, counsellors, therapists, corporate leaders and even military personnel.

This research also shows us the importance of empathy in day-to-day communication. When communicating with others, try to be an empathetic listener. Empathy is all about attempting to understand the feelings of the other person – putting yourself in that person's shoes. Genuine empathy is the ability to understand another's person's perspective. When you listen with empathy, you set aside your views and beliefs so that you can enter the other person's world (Buon, 2014).

When we are trying to communicate with another person, we need to communicate acceptance. You do not want to communicate to the sender that it is not acceptable for them to feel the way they do (Buon, 2014). Empathy is not the same as sympathy, which tends to introduce rather than eliminate communication barriers.

When communicating with others, try to avoid using phrases such as:

'I'm so sorry that…' **sympathizing**

'You have to…' **ordering**

'You'll be fine…' **minimizing**

'You ought to…' **moralizing**

'Why don't you…' **advising**

'What you need is…' **analysing**

The research also shows us that unlike popular fiction, in which characters are frequently predictable, literary fiction tends to question stereotypes, challenging the reader to identify with new viewpoints. The reduction of stereotyping is one of the keys to good communication.

So what are the big takeaways here?

- **Empathy is all about trying to understand the feelings of the person you are talking to. Putting yourself in that person's shoes.**
- **Reading a good book makes you better able to communicate with others by increasing your empathy.**

- **Genuine empathy is the ability to understand another person's perspective.** When you listen with empathy, you set aside your views and beliefs so that you can enter the other person's world.

Source

Kidd, D. C. & Castano, E. (2013), 'Reading Literary Fiction Improves Theory of Mind', *Science*, Vol. 342 No. 6156 pp 377–80

References

Buon, T. (2014), *The Leadership Coach*. London: Hodder & Stoughton

Kidd, D. C. & Castano, E. (2013), 'Reading Literary Fiction Improves Theory of Mind', *Science*, Vol. 342 No. 6156 pp 377–80

Premack, D. & Woodruff, G. (1978), 'Does the chimpanzee have a theory of mind?', *Behavioral and Brain Sciences*, Vol. 1 Issue 4 pp 515–26

Rogers, C. R. (1975), 'Empathic: An Unappreciated Way of Being', *The Counseling Psychologist*, Vol. 5 No. 2 pp 2–10

See also

Chapter 7 – The myths of emotional intelligence

Chapter 35 – Using big words doesn't make you look smarter

Chapter 36 – Turning off your smartphone can make you work smarter

Further reading

Carruthers, P. & Smith, P. K. (Eds.) (1996), *Theories of Theories of Mind*. Cambridge: Cambridge University Press

Djikic, M., Oatley, K. & Moldoveanu, M. C. (2013), 'Reading other minds: Effects of literature on empathy', *Scientific Study of Literature*, Vol. 3 pp 28–47

Goel, V., Grafman, J., Sadato, N., Hallet, M. (1995), 'Modeling Other Minds', *NeuroReport*, Vol. 6 Issue 13 pp 1741–6

Mar, R. A., Oatley, K. & Peterson, J. (2009), 'Exploring the link between reading fiction and empathy: Ruling out individual differences and examining outcomes', *Communications*, Vol. 34 pp 407–28

Shamay-Tsoory, S. G. (2011), 'The Neural Bases for Empathy', *The Neuroscientist*, Vol. 17 No. 1 pp 18–24

Siegal, M. & Varley, R. (2002), 'Neural systems involved in "theory of mind"', *Nature Reviews Neuroscience*, Vol. 3 Issue 6 pp 463–71

Website: Amazon Mechanical Turk: http://www.mturk.com

The literary texts used in the Kidd & Castano 2013 study:

- *Corrie* by Alice Munro (*The New Yorker*, 2008)
- *Leak* by Sam Ruddick (*The Threepenny Review*, 2012)
- *Nothing Living Lives Alone* by Wendell Berry (*The Threepenny Review*, 2012)
- *Uncle Rock* by Dagoberto Gilb (Free online eBook from *The New Yorker*, 2010)
- *The Vandercook* by Alice Mattinson (*Ecotone*, Spring 2011)
- *The Runner* by Don DeLillo (in *The Angel Esmeralda*, Scribner, 2011)
- *Blind Date* by Lydia Davis (in *The Collected Stories of Lydia Davis*, Farrar, Straus & Giroux, New York, 2009)
- *The Chameleon* by Anton Chekhov (in *Anton Chekhov's Short Stories*, Matlow, R. E. (Ed.) (Norton, New York, 1979; original work published 1884)
- *The Round House* by Louise Erdrich (HarperCollins, New York, 2012)
- *The Tiger's Wife* by Téa Obreht (Random House, New York, 2011)
- *Salvage the Bones* by Jesmyn Ward (Bloomsbury, New York, 2011)

35 USING BIG WORDS DOESN'T MAKE YOU LOOK SMARTER

> *One of the really bad things you can do to your writing is to dress up the vocabulary, looking for long words because you're maybe a little bit ashamed of your short ones. This is like dressing up a household pet in evening clothes. The pet is embarrassed and the person who committed this act of premeditated cuteness should be even more embarrassed.*
>
> Stephen King, writer (2002)

A modern curse, in relation to writing, is the 'synonym' shortcut in Microsoft Word®. This allows the writer to right-click and chose an alternative, typically more complex or bigger word. For example 'start' can be replaced with 'commencement', 'end' replaced with 'termination', and 'model' replaced with 'paradigm'.

The reason for this practice is that the writer assumes that the use of the longer or more complex word makes them look smarter to the reader. If you see the word, 'diminutive' rather than 'short', do you assume the writer is more intelligent?

Professor Daniel Oppenheimer from Princeton University has examined the impact of using long words over shorter ones and assessed how the writers are perceived. He reported that in a survey of 110 Stanford undergraduates asked about their writing habits, most of them admitted that they had made their writing more complex in order to appear smarter (Oppenheimer, 2006).

As a result of his research, Oppenheimer was awarded the 2006 Ig® Nobel Prize in Literature for his paper 'Consequences of Erudite Vernacular Utilized Irrespective of Necessity: Problems with Using Long Words Needlessly'. The Ig Nobel Prize is a satire on the Nobel Prizes, organized by the magazine *Annals of Improbable Research*. The stated aim of the prizes is to 'honour achievements that first make people laugh, and then make them think'.

Given that most texts on writing encourage people to avoid overly complex words, Oppenheimer was interested in why the majority of people admitted to deliberately increasing the complexity of their language to give the impression of intelligence. His research explored the extent to which this strategy is effective.

In a series of five experiments, Oppenheimer examined students' responses to writing samples for which the complexity of the font or vocabulary was systematically manipulated. The research was an investigation into the strategy of complexity and asked how the loss of fluency due to needless complexity in a text impacts the reader's assessments of the writer's perceived intelligence.

In the first three experiments, the researcher used personal statements, sociology dissertation abstracts and philosophical essays with groups of volunteer students. The results suggested that, contrary to prevailing wisdom, increasing the complexity of the text does not cause the writer to seem more intelligent. In fact the opposite appears to be true (Oppenheimer, 2006).

One experiment showed that reducing fluency by manipulating the standard font leads to the judgement of lower intelligence. Oppenheimer produced two versions of a document, one used an italicized 'Juice ITC' font, and the original version was in regular 'Times New Roman'. Both versions used 12-point typeset. He found that people tended to rate the intelligence of writers using an easy-to-read font (Times) as higher (Oppenheimer, 2006).

A further experiment demonstrated that if the source of the reduced fluency is obvious, participants will discount their lack of fluency, which reverses the direction of the effect. In this experiment, Oppenheimer provided samples of text printed with 'standard' and 'low' printer toner levels. The low toner levels made the text harder to read, but readers were able to identify the toner as being responsible, and therefore didn't blame the authors (Oppenheimer, 2006).

In an interview about this research on the *ScienceDaily* website, Oppenheimer points out that his study is not about long words in general, but about using long words *unnecessarily*. He states that anything that makes a document hard to read will reduce the readers' evaluations of the document and its author.

One thing seems certain: write as simply and plainly as possible and it's more likely you'll be thought of as intelligent
D. M. Oppenheimer, *ScienceDaily* (2005).

The author points out that you cannot conclude from his results that using long words is always a problem. The study used a small sample of Stanford students as the raters, and this makes it difficult to generalize the results over a wider population. He also notes that experts in a given field who are more familiar with their jargon may react differently to simple writing than novices would (Oppenheimer, 2006).

Consider the reader

Look at the following words and phrases. Which seem clearer and easier to understand?

verisimilitude	or	**truth**
a majority of	or	**most**
egalitarian	or	**equal**
unassuming	or	**modest**
it would appear that	or	**apparently**
notwithstanding the fact	or	**although**
splendiferous	or	**amazing**
fastidious	or	**fussy**
acquiesce	or	**agree**
a number of	or	**some**
discontinue	or	**stop**
formulate	or	**plan**
in a timely manner	or	**on time**
in lieu of	or	**instead**

past history	or	**history**
thoroughly understand	or	**understand**
sesquipedalian	or	**long-winded**

Most people would agree that the second word is clearer, less complicated and easier to understand. Simple writing makes you look smarter, not less intelligent.

Writing in clear and simple language focuses on the reader. This doesn't mean you have to 'dumb down' your writing, but try to write in a clear and unambiguous style that suits your reader. For example, if you are writing for a highly technical audience then the use of technical jargon or acronyms may speed up understanding.

Consider your reader: say what you mean using the simplest words that work. This does not necessarily mean using simple words, but using words that the reader will understand. Before you use a thesaurus or right-click for a synonym in MS Word®, ask yourself if you are using the word to make something clear or to look smart. If it is the latter, don't change the word.

The purpose of writing is to reveal meaning with a minimum of difficulty. So writers should use active, rather than passive verbs. For example: 'The Committee has approved this project' rather than 'Approval has been given by the Committee for this project'. You communicate more effectively when you adopt the active voice and when you write using shorter sentences. Short sentences produce a clear, easily read style, particularly for factual material.

You should avoid the abstract word and the cliché. Don't write: 'as a consequence' when you could just write 'so'. Do not write: 'by virtue of' when you could have written 'by'. Trim the fat off wordy phrases and your reader will thank you.

It is also worth noting that writing in clear and plain language can remove an accessibility barrier for people with visual impairment or dyslexia. It aids text-to-speech software. It can also assist with translation between languages. Writing in plain language makes the text more accessible to everyone.

Be careful in your writing and take the advice of George Orwell, who suggested six rules for writing that are just as valid today as they were when he wrote them in 1946:

- Never use a metaphor, simile or other figure of speech which you are used to seeing in print.
- Never use a long word where a short one will do.
- If it is possible to cut a word out, always cut it out.
- Never use the passive where you can use the active.
- Never use a foreign phrase, a scientific word, or a jargon word if you can think of an everyday English equivalent.
- Break any of these rules sooner than say anything outright barbarous (Orwell, 1946).

Rule two is particularly relevant to this chapter and the research by Oppenheimer. If you 'never use a long word where a short one will do', the research suggests that not only will you be a better writer, but you will be more likely to be seen as intelligent. If you have a preference for the complex word over the simple, you may become pleonastic (using unnecessary words) or a sesquipedalian (a user of long words; long-winded).

So what are the big takeaways here?

- **Contrary to prevailing wisdom, increasing the complexity of a text does not make the writer seem more intelligent.** In fact, the opposite appears to be true.
- **Write clearly and simply, and the research suggests that not only will you be a better writer, but you will be more likely to be thought of as intelligent.**
- **Before you use a thesaurus or right-click for a synonym in MS Word®,** ask yourself if you are using the word to make something clear or to look smart. If it's the latter, don't change the word.

Source

Oppenheimer, D. M. (2006), 'Consequences of Erudite Vernacular Utilized Irrespective of Necessity: Problems with Using Long Words Needlessly', *Applied Cognitive Psychology*, Vol. 20 Issue 2 pp 139–56

References

John Wiley & Sons, Inc. (2005, November 1), 'The Secret of Impressive Writing? Keep It Plain And Simple'. In *ScienceDaily*: www.sciencedaily.com/releases/2005/10/051031075447.htm

King, S. (2002), *On Writing: A Memoir of the Craft.* New York: Pocket Books

Oppenheimer, D. M. (2006), 'Consequences of Erudite Vernacular Utilized Irrespective of Necessity: Problems with Using Long Words Needlessly', *Applied Cognitive Psychology*, Vol. 20 Issue 2 pp 139–56

Orwell, G., 'Politics and the English Language', *Horizon*, London, April 1946

See also

Chapter 7 – The myths of emotional intelligence

Chapter 34 – Reading a good book may improve your empathy

Chapter 40 – Swearing, cursing and communication

Further reading

Batstone, R. (1994), *Grammar*. Oxford: OUP

Casanave, C. P. (2004), *Controversies in Second Language Writing: Dilemmas and Decisions in Research and Instruction.* Ann Arbor, MI: University of Michigan Press

Cheek, A. (2010), 'Defining plain language', *Clarity*, Vol. 64 pp 5–15

Gunning, R. (1968), *The Technique of Clear Writing*. New York: McGraw-Hill

Kimble, J. (1990), 'Strike three for legalese', *Michigan Bar Journal*, Vol. 418

Paltridge, B. (2004), 'Academic writing', *Language Teaching*, Vol. 37 Issue 2 pp 87–105

Pennebaker, J. W. & King, L. A. (1999), 'Linguistic Styles: Language Use as an Individual Difference', *Journal of Personality and Social Psychology*, Vol. 77 No. 6 pp 1296–1312

Reber, R. & Schwarz, N. (1999), 'Effects of perceptual fluency on judgments of truth', *Consciousness and Cognition*, Vol. 8 Issue 3 pp 338–42

Website: Plain English Campaign: https://www.plainenglish.co.uk

36 TURNING OFF YOUR SMARTPHONE CAN MAKE YOU WORK SMARTER

Technology can be our best friend, and technology can also be the biggest party pooper of our lives. It interrupts our own story, interrupts our ability to have a thought or a daydream, to imagine something wonderful because we're too busy bridging the walk from the cafeteria back to the office on the cell phone.
Steven Spielberg, filmmaker (2002), Wired Interview

Smartphones have become a ubiquitous and pervasive way to communicate. Thirty years ago such a device was the dream of science fiction writers and many people fantasized about owning their own *Star Trek* Communicator. Today you can carry around a small device that allows you to make video calls around the globe, use interactive maps of the whole planet, collect your email, play games, watch movies, use millions of apps, visit websites 24/7 and even make the occasional phone call.

There is no doubt that the smartphone has changed the way we communicate. For many people, it has allowed for cheaper and more efficient communication between family and friends. It has allowed workers to be in touch with their organizations and customers anytime and has even allowed some people to adopt more flexible working hours. This is why many organizations supply smartphones to their employees.

However, new research suggests that turning off your smartphone may make you work smarter. Especially if you turn it off at night before you sleep. Moreover, the 'always-on' culture promoted by the smartphone may, in fact, be hurting us in ways we have not yet considered.

In two studies, researchers using a sample of US workers found that people who used their smartphones for business purposes at night were more tired and less engaged the following day on the job (Lanaj, Johnson & Barnes, 2014).

The first study involved 82 managers enrolled in a weekend MBA class. Participants completed surveys on their smartphone usage, sleep and work engagement. They had an impressive 68 per cent response rate from the managers.

The second study involved a varied group of 161 employees (with a 61 per cent response rate) utilizing the Mechanical Turk. Mechanical Turk is a service from Amazon where people can complete simple tasks in exchange for a small payment and is often used by researchers.

This second study was done to explore if other late-night activities, such as using a computer or watching TV, would affect the results for smartphone use. It was designed to confirm the results found in the first study, with a wider cross-section of workers.

Across both studies, the surveys showed that night-time smartphone use had an adverse effect on sleep, made people feel depleted the next morning and subsequently made them less engaged at work the next day. This means that people who use their smartphones at night for work-based communication have significant adverse impacts on their job performance the next day.

The second study confirmed the results of the first study and further found that smartphones had a greater negative effect than watching television and using laptop and tablet computers (Lanaj et al, 2014).

The researchers also found that the adverse effects of morning depletion on daily work engagement may be lessened if the worker has a high level of control over their job. They stated:

We also found some support that the negative effects of morning depletion on daily work engagement may be buffered by job control, such that depletion impairs work engagement only for employees who experience low job control (p 11).

Turn off your phone

Sleep is an important factor in our physical and mental health. Sleep affects our ability to communicate, pay attention and even listen (Pilcher et al, 2007). During sleep, we undergo a number of brain processes that help us to function during the day. There is no set amount of sleep that is appropriate for everyone; some people need more sleep than others (MHF, 2011). However, sleep remains a complex process, and much of it continues to be a mystery to sleep scientists and psychologists.

While using your smartphone for work at night may have many benefits, it also has a serious impact on your ability to sleep and consequently on your performance the next day.

Consider the case of John Smart. John is a successful HR manager, who works for a multinational company.

John's company gave all the team an iPhone last year. At first John was delighted, it was the latest model and it looked great. It was a nice symbol of his status as an important person in the hierarchy, and all expenses were paid. He could even use it for 'personal use'. The 'personal use' bit was a bit vague, as John didn't understand the need for some people to use 'social networks' and he wouldn't be caught dead playing one of those silly computer games.

However, the new smartphone would make it easy to check his email and work messages. He may even be able to use it to access files on the company intranet.

At first it was great. John felt he was more productive; he could reply instantly to emails and at home he didn't have to boot up the laptop to check a message or get a file.

However, John also noticed that he was increasingly using the smartphone to communicate with the office, particularly the overseas branches, after hours.

He would find himself checking emails last thing at night and again first thing in the morning. If he heard the smartphone beep, he would stop everything he was doing (even talking to his wife or children) and run for the smartphone. Anyway, while he was indeed using it a lot, this smartphone seemed to be making him work more efficiently.

Then John attended a 'Time Management' seminar run for managers. While he already knew most of what he heard, one idea intrigued him. The instructor suggested the participants keep a 'Time Log' for the next week and write down all they did in half-hour blocks, and then analyse the results.

After a week, he was shocked to see that he was working on average 12 hours a day. However, what was more shocking was the amount of time he was spending on the smartphone after hours. In one week, it totalled more than ten hours. On one night alone he spent three hours on the phone dealing with work issues – all before he went to bed.

John realized that he was increasingly using his smartphone late at night, and this was having an impact on his sleep. He was waking up tired and feeling depleted and during the day he was often exhausted and distracted.

Things had to change. He started to turn off the smartphone when he got home and told his team to contact him by landline only in an emergency. He did not keep the phone on unless there was a pre-arranged reason to do so and didn't keep the phone next to his bed. He decided only to check his email at set times during the day as he was taught on the Time Management course. He even encouraged his team to do the same.

After four weeks, John found that his efficiency had improved. He was available for emergencies, but people soon learned not to expect instant replies to non-urgent messages at night or on the weekend. John slept better, worked better and felt better.

In 2013, Germany's Ministry of Labour and Social Affairs stopped its managers from calling or emailing staff out of hours except in emergencies (Vasagar, 2013). Other German firms including Volkswagen, BMW and Deutsche Telekom have taken similar measures. Volkswagen, for example, stops forwarding emails to staff from its company servers half an hour after the end of the working day.

In 2014, in France, an agreement was made by employer groups and trade unions in the technology sector to have contracted managers (only) turn off professional phones and emails when not at work, while employers are required to ensure there is no pressure for workers to communicate after hours (Lauchlan, 2014).

Smartphones are an excellent way for communicating outside of the office, particularly because they provide people with instant access to electronic communication. However, the findings of the study discussed here suggest that the late-night use of smartphones for work communication may interfere with sleep, and leave the employees exhausted in the morning and less efficient during the day.

So what are the big takeaways here?

- The late-night use of smartphones for work communication may interfere with sleep, and leave you less smart during the day.
- Turn off your smartphone at a specific time each night – say 8 or 9pm. Of course, there are some jobs where you need to be on-call and can't turn off your smartphone.
- If you are in a position to do so, consider implementing a team or an organizational rule about outside of work hours' use of smartphones.

Source

Lanaj, K., Johnson, R. E. & Barnes, C. M. (2014), 'Beginning the workday yet already depleted? Consequences of late-night smartphone use and sleep', *Organizational Behavior and Human Decision Processes*, Vol. 124 Issue 1 pp 11–23

References

Kennedy, L. (2002), 'Spielberg in the Twilight Zone', *Wired*: http://archive.wired.com/wired/archive/10.06/spielberg_pr.html

Lanaj, K., Johnson, R. E. & Barnes, C. M. (2014), 'Beginning the workday yet already depleted? Consequences of late-night smartphone use and sleep', *Organizational Behavior and Human Decision Processes*, Vol. 124 Issue 1 pp 11–23

Lauchlan, S. (2014), 'Mon Dieu! Les Français n'ont pas interdit email après 18 heures' *diginomica* (April 11): http://diginomica.com/2014/04/11/mon-dieu-les-francais-nont-pas-interdit-email-apres-18-heures/#.U_EAKfldV8E

Mental Health Foundation (MHF) (2011), 'Sleep Matters: The Impact of Sleep on Health and Wellbeing'

Pilcher, J. J., McClelland, L. E., Moore D. D., Haarmann, H., Baron, J., Wallsten, T. S. & McCubbin, J. A. (2007), 'Language performance under sustained work and sleep deprivation conditions', *Aviation, Space, and Environmental Medicine*, Vol. 78 (Suppl. 5) B25–B38

Vasagar, J. (2013), 'Out of hours working banned by German labour ministry', *The Telegraph*: http://www.telegraph.co.uk/news/worldnews/europe/germany/10276815/Out-of-hours-working-banned-by-German-labour-ministry.html

See also

Chapter 6 – Maslow was wrong; your needs are not hierarchical

Chapter 12 – Attending skills in communication: the SOLER model

Chapter 33 – Our brain cannot cope with too much information

Chapter 34 – Reading a good book may improve your empathy

Further reading

Akerstedt, T., Fredlund, P., Gillberg, M. & Jansson, B. (2002), 'Work load and work hours in relation to disturbed sleep and fatigue in a large representative sample', *Journal of Psychosomatic Research*, Vol. 53 pp 585–8

Barnes, C. M. (2011), '"I'll sleep when I'm dead": Managing those too busy to sleep.', *Organizational Dynamics*, Vol. 40 Issue 1 pp 18–26

Huhman, H. R. (2011), 'Owning a Smartphone May Pressure Workers into Putting in More Hours', *Business Insider*: http://articles.businessinsider.com/2011-08-30/strategy/30025454_1_smartphone-texts-and-emails-cell-phone

Sonnentag, S., Binnewies, C. & Mojza, E. J. (2008), '"Did You Have a Nice Evening?" A Day-Level Study on Recovery Experiences, Sleep, and Affect', *Journal of Applied Psychology*, Vol. 93 Issue 3 pp 674–84

The Economist, (10 March 2012). 'Slaves to the smartphone: The horrors of hyperconnectivity—And how to restore a degree of freedom': http://www.economist.com/node/21549904?fsrc=scn/fb/wl/ar/slavestothesmartphone

Website: Amazon Mechanical Turk: http://www.mturk.com

Everyone is living for everyone else now. They're doing stuff so they can tell other people about it. I don't get all that social media stuff, I've always got other things I want to do – odd jobs around the house. No one wants to hear about that.
Karl Pilkington, TV personality (2013)

Social networks have undoubtedly changed the way we communicate in the 21st century. These sites offer people a way to communicate in a (semi) autonomous way and to communicate with friends, family, colleagues and 'pseudo-friends' through posted content, comments, 'likes', photos and videos. Prior to the donation of the World Wide Web by CERN to the world in 1994, the earlier forms of social media consisted of Bulletin Board Systems (BBS), Usenet, AOL and CompuServe.

Launched in February 2004, Mark Zuckerberg founded Facebook along with his fellow Harvard University students. Facebook is currently the most popular social media site in the world with 1.44 billion monthly active users as of 31 March 2015 (Facebook, 2015). However, there is some discussion about younger people turning away from Facebook to newer sites such as Instagram, Snapchat and Vine.

Given the ubiquitous nature of social media it is surprising that there has been a limited amount of scientific study into the impact of social media on communication and most of the published literature is based on small samples from student populations. A large number of the previous studies also relied exclusively on self-reported usage data, which may introduce further methodological issues.

In recent times, researchers have started exploring the connection between personality and Internet usage and social media usage, in particular. However, there are significant problems with collecting reliable data on the Internet, and social media usage and privacy concerns have further limited research into social media users.

In 2015, three researchers from the Palo Alto Research Center in California attempted to rectify this lack of scientific data by conducting a detailed scientific study into Facebook usage. The researchers developed a Facebook application to directly receive data from Facebook users across a broad spectrum (Shen, Brdiczka & Liu, 2015: p 32).

The researchers recruited 1,327 subjects from all over the US. The mean age of the participants was 29 years, with ages ranging from 18 to 71 years; 57 per cent were female and 43 per cent male (p 34).

They did not rely on self-reports of user behaviour, but instead developed a Facebook app called iPersonality that was able to retrieve information directly from Facebook accounts. The advantage of this was summarized by the researchers as follows:

…While the existing research limited features to demographics and high-level usage (spent time, count of friends, groups, albums and photos), direct retrieval enables us to calculate much finer-grained signals that are salient to the audience yet never explored by researchers before, such as written content and interactions with friends (p 33).

From each participant's Facebook account, the researchers calculated 154 features, covering demographics, profile descriptions, produced content and interactions with friends (p 35). In particular, they were interested in traits related to 'neuroticism' and 'extraversion'.

Neuroticism relates to emotional stability and those who are more 'neurotic' tend to have feelings of guilt, anger, depression and anxiety. *Extraversion* refers to sociability and the directing of one's interest outwards towards others. Those who are more 'extrovert' tend to show feelings of gregariousness and seek social stimulation.

The researchers reported that Facebook users who score highly on 'neuroticism' tend to write longer posts, use more negative sentiment words and strongly subjective words in their posts (p 35). These Facebook users were more successful in gaining social support from others on Facebook. Their posts get significantly more comments from friends, usually of a positive and supportive nature (p 35).

The researchers also found that those who scored highly for 'extroversion' had significantly more Facebook friends than 'introverts', and they engage more energetically in Facebook activities (posts, status updates, etc.). Further, 'extroverts' get more comments and 'likes' from friends. However, the percentage of friends commenting or liking it is much lower than 'introverts' (p 35).

Finally, the researchers concluded that their results suggest that there are some strong indicators of personality traits on Facebook, and they propose to further explore other personality traits beyond those of neuroticism and extroversion.

Judging others by their postings

This research study claims that you can infer a person's personality, at least in relation to 'extroversion' and 'neuroticism', from their social media usage. They demonstrated the existence of correlations between people's Facebook behaviours and their personality. These results may have significant implications for communication research, personality study, the development of new social media platforms and even for the precise targeting of advertising.

Social media offers the user the ability to depict themselves without restriction or facing many of the barriers that occur in regular face-to-face communication. People judge others by what they post, comment, link to and like.

In the business world, HR departments are reported to access potential candidates and existing employees' Facebook, Twitter and other social media postings to assess their suitability for a position. However, there is little scientific evidence of how common this practice is. The actual percentage of employers using social media for background checks (or those who will admit to doing so) is probably small particularly due to the potential legal and privacy issues involved.

However, there are a number of well-publicized cases where social media usage has lost someone a job. In 2013, 17-year-old Paris Brown was appointed one of the UK's first Youth Police and Crime Commissioners. Brown soon faced calls to resign from the £15,000-a-year position when news reports said she had used her Twitter account to post racist and anti-gay comments; following continued criticism in the media and on social media sites, she stepped down from the role, saying she was 'quitting in the interests of the young people of Kent' (BBC, 2013).

The proposition that a person's personality could be inferred from their social media postings also raises a number of ethical and legal issues for employers and HR professionals. Employers using social media to monitor their employees could be breaching data protection legislation or privacy laws in the UK. In the USA, it could involve breaches of discrimination, equal employment and other Federal employment laws.

The research by Shen, Brdiczka and Liu also tells us that your personality may be evident to others in your social media postings. The researchers stated that Facebook users who scored high on the 'neurotic' scale shared personally identifying information more often. They also suggested that those who scored high on 'extroversion' had significantly more Facebook friends than 'introverts' (p 37).

Other people take notice of your comments both consciously and unconsciously. Like all communication, there are multiple channels at work. It is likely that people will judge you by the way you communicate online. They will judge your communication skills and style, but they may also judge your personality, with or without foundation.

People are very complex and their personalities are equally complex and elusive. Simplistic explanations of personality should not be drawn from a person's 'online' world, as this may differ from their authentic self. For example, it has been shown that many people do not always tell the whole truth about themselves in online dating profiles. Research has also shown that some people edit their 'selfies' posted online if they *self-objectify* (Meier & Gray, 2013; Fox & Rooney, 2015). Self-objectification is viewing yourself from the outside, as through the eyes of others.

Social networking websites such as Facebook have become a primary method of communication and self-expression for many people. But people will make judgements about you by what you post online, including potential employers or even potential life partners. These judgements may extend to suppositions about your personality.

Postings on social media are also increasingly coming under law enforcement scrutiny. Posting violent threats, harassment, or promoting hatred can lead to prosecution in many countries. It is very wise to think before you click post and, advisably, never post on social media when you are angry, tired or emotional.

So what are the big takeaways here?

- The research by Shen, Brdiczka & Liu indicates that some aspects of your personality may be evident to others in your social media postings.
- People judge others by their posts and comments.
- It is very wise to think before you click post, and never post on social media when you are angry, tired or emotional.

Source

Shen, J., Brdiczka, O. & Liu, J. (2015), 'A study of Facebook behavior: What does it tell about your Neuroticism and Extraversion?', *Computers in Human Behavior*, Vol. 45 pp 32–8

References

BBC News, 'Paris Brown: Kent youth PCC resigns after Twitter row' (9 April 2013): http://www.bbc.co.uk/news/uk-england-22083032

Facebook (2015). Facebook Inc. newsroom: http://newsroom. fb.com/company-info/

Fox, J. & Rooney, M. C. (2015), 'The Dark Triad and trait self-objectification as predictors of men's use and self-presentation behaviours on social networking sites', *Personality and Individual Differences*, Vol. 76 pp 161–5

Meier, E. P. & Gray, J. (2013), 'Facebook photo activity associated with body image disturbance in adolescent girls', *Cyberpsychology, Behavior, & Social Networking*, Vol. 17 pp 199–206

Parker, S., 'Karl Pilkington: What I've Learned', *Esquire* Magazine, 19 September 2013: http://www.esquire.co.uk/culture/film-tv/4862/karl-pilkington-what-ive-learned/

Shen, J., Brdiczka, O. & Liu, J. (2015), 'A study of Facebook behavior: What does it tell about your Neuroticism and Extraversion?', *Computers in Human Behavior*, Vol. 45 pp 32–8

See also

Further reading

Amichai-Hamburger, Y. & Vinitzky, G. (2010), 'Social network use and personality', *Computers in Human Behavior*, Vol. 26 Issue 6 pp 1289–95

Ehrenberg, A. L., Juckes, S. C., White, K. M. & Walsh, S. P. (2008), 'Personality and self-esteem as predictors of young people's technology use', *Cyberpsychology & Behaviour*, Vol. 11 Issue 6 pp 739–41

Landers, R. N. & Lounsbury, J. W. (2006), 'An investigation of Big Five and narrow personality traits in relation to Internet usage', *Computers in Human Behavior*, Vol. 22 Issue 2 pp 283–93

McKenna, K. Y. A. & Bargh, J. A. (1998), 'Coming out in the age of the Internet: identity "demarginalization" through virtual group participation', *Journal of Personality and Social Psychology*, Vol. 75 pp 681–94

Nie, N. H. (2001), 'Sociability, Interpersonal Relations, and the Internet: Reconciling Conflicting Findings', *American Behavioural Scientist*, Vol. 45 No. 3 pp 420–35

Wellman, B., Haase, A. Q., Witte, J. & Hampton, K. (2001), 'Does the Internet Increase, Decrease, or Supplement Social Capital? Social Networks, Participation, and Community Commitment', *American Behavioral Scientist*, Vol. 45 No. 3 pp 436–55

38 ONLINE COMMUNICATION: WHY DO PEOPLE TROLL?

Trolling: to make a deliberately offensive or provocative online post with the aim of upsetting someone or eliciting an angry response from them.

Oxford Dictionaries *(2015)*

In the UK people have been jailed for it, in Australia it has been met with greater Internet regulation and in the US it has resulted in online scams and litigation. Trolling behaviour on social media boards, blogs or forums has become a much-discussed method of anti-social online communication.

The origin of the word *troll* is contested, with some believing it comes from the Old Norse word 'troll' referring to the antisocial and slow-witted creatures that make life difficult for travellers. Others claim it comes from the fishing technique of dragging a baited hook from a moving boat. However, given the early Internet and bulletin boards' fondness for dungeons and dragons, the Norse origin seems most likely.

Trolling is also often confused with 'flaming' (posting rude comments), online harassment, cyberbullying and spam. One useful definition found in the online *Urban Dictionary* defines it as: 'The art of deliberately, cleverly, and secretly getting people mad' (2015).

In 2014, three psychological researchers from Canada published the results of two online studies exploring Internet trolling (Buckels, Trapnell & Paulhus, 2014). The researchers asked 1,215 people from the United States to complete an online questionnaire. The researchers defined trolling in their study as 'the practice of behaving in a deceptive, destructive, or disruptive manner in a social setting on the Internet with no apparent instrumental purpose' (Buckels et al, 2014).

Even though there is much discussion in the media and online about trolling behaviour, there has been very little scientific research into the phenomenon. The researchers suggest that with behaviours such as cyberbullying the perpetrators' identities and intent are usually clear; however, with trolling we know very little about who the trolls are and why they engage in such communication methods.

Buckels, Trapnell & Paulhus used the personality variables described as the *Dark Tetrad* of personality – narcissism, Machiavellianism, psychopathy and sadistic personality in their study. This builds on the *Dark Triad* (Jonason, Jones & Lyons, 2013) by adding the category of *sadism* (Buckels, Jones & Paulhus, 2013). To test for these dark personality traits the researchers used the *D3* (Paulus & Jones, 2015) and the *44-item Big Five Inventory* (John & Srivastava, 1999).

Sadism is about gaining pleasure from inflicting physical or psychological pain on others. In the study, the researchers used two measures to test for sadism: the *SSIS* (O'Meara, Davies, & Hammond, 2011) and the *VAST* (Paulhus & Jones, in press). They also produced a questionnaire on commenting behaviour that measured overall commenting frequency and the participants' preferred activity when commenting online (Buckels et al, 2014 p 98).

In the first study, the researchers focused on predicting enjoyment of trolling, as opposed to other online social activities, such as chatting. This study involved 418 paid participants selected from Amazon's Mechanical Turk website (42.4 per cent female, and with a mean age of 29.2). In the second study, they utilized 188 Canadian psychology student (55 per cent female; a mean age of 21.15) and 609 US residents (43 per cent female; and a mean age of 35.04) recruited from Mechanical Turk.

This larger and more diverse sample in the second study allowed the researchers to test their theories about the unique contributions of the Dark Tetrad to trolling behaviour, in particular, that of sadism. The research also developed a new test of trolling for this study called the Global Assessment of Internet Trolling scale (GAIT), which assessed trolling behaviour, identification and enjoyment (p 99).

In the first study, the researchers found that across all participants, the mean number of commenting hours per day was 1.07. Men reported greater numbers of hours posting comments than women. A total of 23.8 per cent of participants expressed a preference for debating issues, 21.3 per cent preferred chatting, 2.1 per cent said they especially enjoyed making friends, 5.6 per cent reported enjoying trolling (p 98).

In the second study, the researchers found that sadism, psychopathy and Machiavellianism scores were positively connected to a self-reported enjoyment of trolling. Narcissism was not linked to trolling enjoyment but was instead linked with enjoying debating issues online. GAIT scores were strongly associated with commenters' trolling enjoyment, and positively associated with scores of all Dark Tetrad and especially strongly with sadism (p 100).

They found that Internet trolls displayed high levels of the Dark Tetrad traits and in particular scored high on sadism. The researchers stated:

It was sadism, however, that had the most robust associations with trolling of any of the personality measures, including those of the Big Five. In fact, the associations between sadism and GAIT scores were so strong that it might be said that online trolls are prototypical everyday sadists (p 101).

Trolls are uninterested in open communication

In the Buckels, Trapnell & Paulhus study the researchers stated 'people troll because they enjoy doing it' (p 101). They point out that both sadists and trolls gain pleasure from hurting others and, in particular, seeing their distress. This is why the old Internet saying 'don't feed the trolls' is most relevant.

One way to stop a troll in his or her tracks is to not engage with them. Trolls get great pleasure from a person who screams at them (uses all caps) or insults them. Trolls are unsuccessful if the potential victim identifies them as a troll or if their efforts are ignored. If you don't engage with ('feed') a troll, they fail.

Sadists gain pleasure, even sexual pleasure, from harming others physically or emotionally. As the researchers put it: 'Sadists just want to have fun… and the Internet is their playground!' (p 101). If you remove yourself from the communication process, they fail. You can, for example, put the troll on your blocked or banned list.

The Internet is an anonymous environment where people can say and do things they would never contemplate in face-to-face communication. This anonymity can lead to *deindividuation*, a concept in social psychology where it is suggested people are blocked from awareness of themselves as distinct individuals and can behave impulsively and in an anti-social way (Zimbardo, 1970). Jonathan Bishop from the European Parliament has suggested that definitions of deindividuation appear to be 'perfect descriptions' of trolls (Bishop, 2013: p 29).

Deindividuation in groups has not been fully proven, and the effect can be both positive and negative. For example, it has also been shown that deindividuation can lead to increased pro-social behaviour. Further, the possible impact of deindividuation in online groups has not been adequately researched though it may be an interesting area of further study.

It would appear that sadistic people seek out others to hurt on the Internet by trolling. The findings of the Buckels, Trapnell & Paulhus study also suggest that antisocial individuals use technology more than others because it facilitates their goals (p 98). However, this is an area that requires more research.

It's important not to confuse trolling with cyberbullying, flaming, hate or other forms of online anti-social behaviour. Each of these requires study and solutions. In relation to cyberbullying of children, in particular, the child being bullied needs to talk to someone and get help. A good starting point in the UK is the Childline website (*see* below).

The 2014 study by Buckels, Trapnell & Paulhus sheds light on why trollers act the way they do. This research has demonstrated that trolling appears to be an online manifestation of everyday sadism. Sadistic people derive pleasure from behaviours that hurt others, and will go to great lengths to make someone else suffer. You do not need to go to great lengths to stop them; just don't feed the trolls.

So what are the big takeaways here?

- In this study, we saw that 5.6 per cent of people reported enjoying trolling, and that trolls do what they do because they are sadistic and gain pleasure from harming others.
- Trolls are not interested in direct and open communication.
- If you don't engage with a troll, they fail. Trolls will go to great lengths to make someone else suffer.
- You do not need to go to great lengths to stop them; just don't feed the trolls.

Source

Buckels, E. E., Trapnell, P. D. & Paulhus, D. L. (2014), 'Trolls just want to have fun', *Personality & Individual Differences*, Vol. 67 pp 97–102

References

Bishop, J. (2013), 'The effect of de-individuation of the Internet Troller on Criminal Procedure implementation: An interview with a Hater', *International Journal of Cyber Criminology*, Vol. 7 Issue 1 pp 28–48

Buckels, E. E., Jones, D. N. & Paulhus, D. L. (2013), 'Behavioral Confirmation of Everyday Sadism', *Psychological Science*, Vol. 24 pp 2201–9

Buckels, E. E., Trapnell, P. D. & Paulhus, D. L. (2014), 'Trolls just want to have fun', *Personality & Individual Differences*, Vol. 67 pp 97–102

John, O. P. & Srivastava, S., 'The Big Five Trait Taxonomy: History, Measurement, and Theoretical Perspectives'. In Pervin, L. A. & John, O. P. (Eds.) (1999), *Handbook of Personality: Theory and research* (2nd ed.). New York: Guilford Press

Jonason, P. K., Jones, A. & Lyons, M. (2013), 'Creatures of the night: Chronotypes and the Dark Triad traits', *Personality and Individual Differences*, Vol. 55 Issue 5 pp 538–41

O'Meara, A., Davies, J. & Hammond, S. (2011), 'The psychometric properties and utility of the Short Sadistic Impulse Scale (SSIS), *Psychological Assessment*, Vol. 23 Issue 2 pp 523–31

Oxford Dictionaries. (2015). Definition of word 'troll': http://www.oxforddictionaries.com/definition/english/troll (Accessed 12/2/15)

Paulhus, D. L. & Jones, D. N. (2015), 'Measuring dark personalities via questionnaire'. In Boyle, G. J., Saklofske, D. H. & Matthews, G. (Eds.) (2015), *Measures of Personality and Social Psychological Constructs*. San Diego, CA: Academic Press

Urban Dictionary (2015). Definition of word 'troll': http://www.urbandictionary.com/define.php?term=trolling (Accessed 10/2/15)

Zimbardo, P. G., 'The human choice: Individuation, reason, and order versus deindividuation, impulse, and chaos'. In Arnold, W. J. & Levine, D. (Eds.) (1970), *Nebraska symposium on Motivation 1969*. Lincoln, NE: University of Nebraska Press Vol. 17 pp 237–307

See also

Chapter 37 – Social media communication

Chapter 39 – Selfies: a new form of communication

Chapter 40 – Swearing, cursing and communication

Further reading

Bishop, J. (2014), 'Representations of "trolls" in mass media communication: A review of media-texts and moral panics relating to "internet trolling"', *International Journal of Web Based Communities*, Vol. 10 Issue 1 pp 7–24

Hardaker, C. (2013), '"Uh.....not to be nitpicky,,,,,but...the past tense of drag is dragged, not drug.": an overview of trolling strategies', *Journal of Language Aggression and Conflict*, Vol. 1 Issue 1 57–86

McCreery, M. P., Krach, S. K., Schrader, P. G. & Boone, R. (2012), 'Defining the virtual self: Personality, behavior, and the psychology of embodiment', *Computers in Human Behavior*, Vol. 28 pp 976–83

Younus, A., Qureshi, M. A., Saeed, M., Touheed, N., O'Riordan, C. & Pasi, G. (2014), 'Election Trolling: Analyzing Sentiment in Tweets during Pakistan Elections 2013', *Proceedings of the Companion Publication of the 23rd International Conference on World Wide Web Companion*: pp 411–12

Website: Childline: http://www.childline.org.uk/Explore/Bullying/Pages/online-bullying.aspx

Website: Amazon Mechanical Turk: http://www.mturk.com

39 SELFIES: A NEW FORM OF COMMUNICATION

I'd seen the same phenomenon when I was touring the Colosseum in Rome last month. So many people were fighting for space to take selfies with their long sticks – what some have called the 'Narcissistick' – that it looked like a reprise of the gladiatorial battles the place once hosted.
David Carr, The New York Times, 4 January 2015

On 27 January 2015 three friends attempted to take a selfie in front of a moving train in India – all three were killed (*The Times of India*, 2015). The US National Transportation Safety Board reported that distraction caused by taking selfies is likely to blame for a plane crash that killed a pilot and his passenger in Colorado on 31 May 2014 (*The Independent*, 2015).

In 2013 the *Oxford Dictionaries* announced that their word of the year was 'selfie', which they defined as 'A photograph that one has taken of oneself, typically one taken with a smartphone or webcam and shared via social media'. The origins of word can be traced to an Australian lad, who in 2002 posted on an Internet forum:

'Um, drunk at a mates 21st, I tripped ofer [sic] and landed lip first (with front teeth coming a very close second) on a set of steps. I had a hole about 1cm long right through my bottom lip. And sorry about the focus, it was a selfie.' ABC Online [forum posting] 13/9/02

Selfies have become ubiquitous: religious leaders, celebrities, politicians and even royalty are posting selfies on social media. However, selfies are a particular way of 'self-fashioning' oneself (Tifentale, 2014) and may communicate more about the person posting their image than merely their latest hairstyle or the celebrity they met in the supermarket.

Selfies as a modern form of communication have received limited scientific research. However, one pioneering study was published in 2015 by Jesse Fox and Margaret Rooney from Ohio State University. The researchers conducted an online study of 1,000 men's selfie behaviour during March 2014.

The results were published in the journal *Personality and Individual Differences* and attempted to assess personality trait predictors of social network site (SNS) use and the posting and editing of selfies (Fox & Rooney, 2015). They examined the so-called *Dark Triad* of personalities and a measure of *self-objectification* as predictors of social media behaviour and selfie use.

The *Dark Triad* of personalities refers to three closely related yet independent personality traits that researchers suggest trigger a host of undesirable and malicious anti-social behaviours, including aggression, callousness and impulsivity (Jonason, Jones & Lyons, 2013). These three traits are *Machiavellianism* (manipulation, cynicism), *narcissism* (egocentrism, excessive self-love) and *psychopathy* (lack of empathy, impulsivity).

Narcissism is a fixation on the self, believing the world revolves around you. Self-objectification is viewing yourself from the outside, as through the eyes of others. Objectification theory suggests that primarily girls and women develop their view of their physical selves from observations of others (Roberts & Fredrickson, 1997). Self-objectification can lead to adverse psychological outcomes such as such as shame, depression and eating disorders. Much of the research dealing with self-objectification has been conducted on women, though Fox & Rooney are exploring it in relation to men.

From the original sample of 1,000 men, 200 were removed from the study as they did not meet the criteria or because of technical difficulties. The resulting 800 men came from a number of cultural backgrounds, were aged 18 to 40, and were a 'nationally representative sample of US men' (Fox & Rooney, 2015).

The researchers used two sets of tests to measure the partici-pants' self-objectification and their scores on the Dark Triad.

The Self-Objectification Questionnaire (SOQ) was used to verify trait-level self-objectification (Noll & Fredrickson, 1998) and the Dark Triad was measured using a 12-item instrument known as the Dirty Dozen (DD) (Jonason & Webster, 2010).

Fox & Rooney found that self-objectification and narcissism predicted the time spent on Social Networking Sites (SNSs) such as Facebook, Twitter, Instagram, Tumblr and Pinterest. The average total time the participants spent each day on SNSs was found to be just under 79 minutes, though a few participants spent up to 16 hours a day online (p 162).

The researchers also found narcissism and psychopathy predicted the number of selfies posted (between zero and 30 in the past week). This compared with zero and 75 photos posted in total. The average number of selfies posted was 0.56.

Narcissism, psychopathy, time spent on SNSs and number of other photos posted were correlated with the number of selfies posted (p 163). After these variables have been ruled out by using control groups, narcissism and psychopathy predicted the number of selfies posted, partially supporting the researchers' original hypothesis.

Participants reported that they had used cropping, filters and Photoshop or other editing software to edit the selfies they posted. Narcissism and self-objectification predicted the editing of selfies that were posted. The researchers also found that psychopathy and Machiavellianism were not significant predictors (p 163).

What selfies say about us

One significant contribution of this study is that it illustrated that self-objectification is associated with the time men spend on SNSs and that this self-objectification was found to predict the frequency with which they edited selfies (p 164). Although previous research has identified similar relationships for adolescent girls who use SNSs (Meier & Gray, 2013), these findings indicate self-objectification is also a significant issue for men.

Self-objectification represents both a cultural as well as a communication problem; one in which people may be primarily valued for their appearance. The posting of selfies, often digitally enhanced, conforming with a mass-media representation of 'attractiveness' and beauty, can be damaging to both men and women. And in some people it can lead to body image issues, eating disorders, unnecessary plastic surgery and a devaluing of the self.

The Fox & Rooney study also provides the first clear scientific evidence that measures of narcissism are associated with posting and editing selfies on SNSs. The researchers also concluded that the fact that narcissists also edit selfies more often is consistent with the underlying insecurity related to narcissism (p 164).

Of course the Fox & Rooney study, like all studies, has limitations. For example, the sample only consisted of US men and only selected those between the ages of 18 and 40. Given that selfie posting may be higher in the under-18s, it would be very interesting to see the research conducted on both men and women from that group and those from other cultural backgrounds.

Selfiecity is a research project led by Professor Lev Manovich from the City University of New York. This project sampled 140,000 selfies from five global cities posted on Instagram in one week in October 2013. These were: Bangkok, Berlin, Moscow, New York and Sao Paulo (Tifentale, 2014). Three Mechanical Turk workers selected 640 selfies for each city.

The results of the Selfiecity project tell us a lot about selfies as a form of communication today. For example, the researchers reported that only approximately 4 per cent of all photographs published during that week in October were selfies. Further, they found that it was mainly young adults who posted selfies on Instagram (mean age 23.7 years).

While the Fox & Rooney study has focused on the negative aspects of selfie posting, it is also important to look at the positive aspects. Selfies are a way for people to communicate their creativity and individuality. It is a way of connecting visually with others while delivering your message.

Most selfies are harmless expressions of joy, excitement or a desire to share a moment in time. While they may be regarded as narcissistic, they also present a chance to participate in the zeitgeist, the spirit of the time. Without a doubt, selfies are a significant paradigm shift in the way that people communicate images of self.

So what are the big takeaways here?

- **The research found that men who scored higher in narcissism and psychopathy tests reported posting selfies more frequently.**
- **Further, narcissists and individuals high in self-objectification edited photos of themselves at a higher rate.**
- **Selfies are part of modern communication patterns.** While the study focused on the negative aspects of selfie posting, it is also important to note the positive.
- **Selfies are a way for people to express their creativity, a way of connecting visually with others, communicating what (and who) is important to you.**

Source

Fox, J. & Rooney, M. C. (2015), 'The Dark Triad and trait self-objectification as predictors of men's use and self-presentation behaviors on social networking sites', *Personality and Individual Differences*, Vol. 76 pp 161–5

References

Carr, D., 'Selfies on a Stick, and the Social-Content Challenge for the Media', *The New York Times*, 4 January 2015: http://nyti.ms/1F6FcOk

Fox, J. & Rooney, M. C. (2015), 'The Dark Triad and trait self-objectification as predictors of men's use and self-presentation behaviors on social networking sites', *Personality and Individual Differences*, Vol. 76 pp 161–5

Hooton, C., 'Fatal Denver plane crash was likely caused by pilot taking selfie, say investigators', *The Independent*, 10 February 2015: http://www.independent.co.uk/news/world/americas/fatal-denver-plane-crash-was-likely-caused-by-pilot-taking-selfies-say-investigators-10021185.html

Jonason, P. K., Jones, A. & Lyons, M. (2013), 'Creatures of the night: Chronotypes and the Dark Triad traits', *Personality and Individual Differences*, Vol. 55 Issue 5 pp 538–41

Jonason, P. K. & Webster, G. D. (2010), 'The Dirty Dozen: A Concise Measure of the Dark Triad', *Psychological Assessment*, Vol. 22 No. 2 pp 420–32

Meier, E. P. & Gray, J. (2013), 'Facebook photo activity associated with body image disturbance in adolescent girls', *Cyberpsychology, Behavior, & Social Networking*, Vol. 17 pp 199–206

Mishra, I., 'Selfie in front of running train costs three college-goers their life', *The Times of India*, 27 January 2015: http://timesofindia.indiatimes.com/india/Selfie-in-front-of-running-train-costs-three-college-goers-their-life/articleshow/46025185.cms

Noll, S. M. & Fredrickson, B. L. (1998), 'A mediational model linking self-objectification, body shame, and disordered eating', *Psychology of Women Quarterly*, Vol. 22 Issue 4 pp 623–36

Roberts, T.-A. & Fredrickson, B. L. (1997), 'Objectification Theory: Toward Understanding Women's Lived Experiences and Mental Health Risks', *Psychology of Women Quarterly*, Vol. 21 Issue 2 pp 173–206

Tifentale, A. (2014), 'The Selfie: Making sense of the "Masturbation of Self-Image" and the "Virtual Mini-Me"'. Selfiecity.net

See also

Further reading

Bergman, S. M., Fearrington, M. E., Davenport, S. W. & Bergman, J. Z. (2011), 'Millennials, narcissism, and social networking: What narcissists do on social network sites and why', *Personality & Individual Differences*, Vol. 50 Issue 5 pp 706–11

Buckels, E. E., Trapnell, P. D. & Paulhus, D. L. (2014), 'Trolls just want to have fun', *Personality & Individual Differences*, Vol. 67 pp 97–102

Jones, D. N. & Paulhus, D. L. (2014), 'Introducing the Short Dark Triad (SD3): A brief measure of dark personality traits', *Assessment*, Vol. 21 Issue 1 pp 28–41

McAndrew, F. T. & Jeong, H. S. (2012), 'Who does what on Facebook? Age, sex, and relationship status as predictors of Facebook use', *Computers in Human Behavior*, Vol. 28 pp 2359–65

Tiggemann, M. & Kuring, J. K. (2004), 'The Role of Body Objectification in Disordered Eating and Depressed Mood', *British Journal of Clinical Psychology*, Vol. 43 Issue pp 299–311

Twenge, J. M. & Campbell, W. K. (2009), *The Narcissism Epidemic: Living in the Age of Entitlement*. New York: Free Press

Website: YouTube Video: The Oxford Dictionaries Word of the Year 2013: https://www.youtube.com/watch?v=Gj7nnws8Zo8&feature=youtu.be

Website: Amazon Mechanical Turk: http://www.mturk.com

40 SWEARING, CURSING AND COMMUNICATION

The foolish and wicked practice of profane cursing and swearing is a vice so mean and low that every person of sense and character detests and despises it.

George Washington, US president, extract from the Orderly Book of the army under command of Washington *(3 August 1770)*

Warning: This chapter may contain words that are offensive to some people.

The English language scholar Melissa Mohr explains in her book, *Holy Sh*t: A Brief History of Swearing*, that swearing can be traced back to at least Roman times and argues that swearing is a powerful tool for bonding, for expressing emotion and even for coping with pain (Mohr, 2013). In a review of Mohr's book, Colin Burrow states 'our routine bad language instantly says something about who we are and where we are from' (Burrow, 2013).

Swearing (UK) and cursing/cussing (USA) can upset some people and delight others. Some of the most popular swear words of today have been in use for more than a thousand years. However, when the head judge on a UK ballroom-celebrity dancing show *appeared* to swear on air, it made the front page of the daily papers, was on TV news and generated an on-air apology from a co-host.

However, the UK TV regulator Ofcom has reported that the number of complaints lodged about expletives has dropped considerably in recent times, particularly among the over-65s. Ofcom says that in 2008, 78 per cent of over-65s believed there was too much swearing on television, compared with 61 per cent today. For 16-to-34-year-olds these figures have also dropped from 36 per cent (2008) to 25 per cent (2012) (Ofcom, 2013).

Swearing can be described in three general categories. These are:

- Sexual terms (fuck, prick, screw, etc.)
- Bodily fluids (shit, poo, piss, etc.)
- Religious words (hell, Jesus Christ, God, etc.)

There is a possible fourth category, racial insults (jock, spic, paki, etc.). However, these are rather different from 'standard' swear words and many people who freely use words from categories 1 to 3, would *never* use those in category four. Racial insults are also often used with a level of hate and prejudice that is not commonly present in the words from categories 1 to 3.

Some people firmly believe that people swear because they are illiterate or of low-class, even given that people of higher classes swear more (Mohr, 2013). People also state that swearing inhibits communication and is poor communication. Others claim that obscene words are no big deal.

There is very little research on who swears, why people swear or the effects of swearing. This may be because the subject is a type of taboo for communication researchers. Even writing down words such as 'fuck' or 'shit' may be of concern to some social scientists.

There has been some research conducted on brain damage, Gilles de la Tourette syndrome (GTS), and other neurological disorders that can cause an increase in swearing behaviour (*see* Van Lancker & Cummings, 1999). Timothy Jay, a psychologist at the Massachusetts College of Liberal Arts, has also written extensively on swearing in the general population (Jay, 2008; 2009a; 2009b).

Over the past 30 years, Jay has recorded 10,000 people swearing in public and found that approximately ten swear words have remained in constant use for more than two decades. These words account for 80 per cent of all public swearing (Jay, 2009a p 155). These were: 'fuck', 'shit', 'hell', 'damn', 'goddamn', 'Jesus Christ', 'ass', 'oh my god', 'bitch' and 'sucks' (p 156).

In one of the only cross-cultural studies, researchers in the Netherlands studied swearing behaviour in Dutch female students. They found that subjects (n = 72) swore quite regularly (on average three times per day) and that the most frequently used swear word was 'shit' (Rassin & Muris, 2005).

So people seem to swear a lot, and it may even be on the increase, but does swearing harm others? Well, again we turn to Jay for the empirical answer to this question. He states that:

In summary, the answer to the question, 'Do offensive words harm people?' appears to be 'Yes, maybe, and no; it depends... 'Evidence of harm is present in harassment, discrimination, and OTC cases, but it is indeterminate in verbal abuse research. There is no evidence of harm from fleeting expletives or from conversational or cathartic swearing. Public swearing research reveals that swearing is a common conversational practice resulting in no obvious harm (Jay, 2009: p 93).

Researchers from the School of Psychology at Keele University in the UK have conducted two interesting studies into swearing as a response to pain (Stephens, Atkins & Kingston, 2009; Stephens & Umland, 2011).

In the first study, the researchers had 67 students immerse their hands in icy water and measured pain perception and heart rate during the procedure. This was then repeated, and students were asked to use a swear word versus a neutral word. Swearing resulted in increased pain tolerance, increased heart rate and decreased perceived pain compared with not swearing. The researchers concluded that under certain conditions, swearing produces a 'hypoalgesic effect', that is, a decreased sensitivity to pain (Stephens et al, 2009).

The researchers suggested that swearing may have induced the 'fight or flight response' and that swearing nullified the link between fear of pain and pain perception (Stephens et al, 2009: p 1060). The research team was awarded the Ig® Nobel Peace Prize in 2010 for this study. These satirical awards are given 'For achievements that first make people laugh then make them think' (IR, 2004).

Swearing and communication

Further research by Stephens and his colleague Claudia Umland was published in 2011, where they looked at whether the amount someone swore impacted on their pain tolerance. The researchers found that daily swearing frequency had a significant effect on the effectiveness of swearing as 'people who rarely use such words place a higher emotional value on them'. They found an acclimatization to swearing reduced pain tolerance arising from the emotional release that comes from swearing (Stephens & Umland, 2011).

So swearing seems to have a positive impact on pain, but only if you don't swear all the time. It is a cheap and non-addictive method of pain relief that should be explored further. Swearing also seems to have other positive benefits.

Timothy Jay suggests that attempts to restrict swearing are misguided and that we do not often hear about the positive and desirable effects of swearing (2009b). He suggests that the positive benefits of swearing include:

- Promoting social cohesion with friends
- Producing childhood and adult humour
- Catharsis and emotional release
- Using self-deprecation and irony to produce harmony (Jay, 2009b: p 89)

Of course, what is considered a swear word and what is not can be confusing. Take the Irish word 'feck' (or 'fecken'). This is a tempered alternative to the word 'fuck', but is not considered a swear word in Ireland. Used in advertising (Magners Cider); TV shows (*Father Ted*); by politicians; and almost all Irish people will tell you 'it's not a swear word'.

There does not seem to be any empirical research to support the claim that those who swear are less literate than those who do. In fact, it may be that the upper classes and those with higher education qualifications swear even more. Many people choose to swear as it produces a positive effect on communication or because it allows people to communicate their feelings of anger or frustration.

In one study, researchers Cory Scherer and Brad Sagarin from Northern Illinois University (USA) examined the effects of swearing on persuasion in a speech. Participants listened to one of the three versions of a speech where the word 'damn' appeared either at the beginning, end or nowhere. The results showed that swearing at the beginning or end of the speech significantly increased the persuasiveness of the speech and the perceived intensity of the speaker. Obscenity had no effect on speaker credibility (Scherer & Sagarin, 2006: p 145).

This is not to suggest that swearing causes no harm. In discrimination, sexual harassment, racial harassment, bullying or hate speech, it is obvious that words in these cases can hurt and have weakened communication. However, most swearing doesn't fit this category.

One final thing. If you'd hoped to get some new curse words from reading this chapter, and are not satisfied, you could get a copy of *Viz* magazine's *Roger's Profanisaurus* (2010), a lexicon of more than 10,000 swear words.

So what are the big takeaways here?

- **Approximately ten swear words have remained in constant use for more than 20 years** and account for 80 per cent of all public swearing according to research by Timothy Jay.
- **Attempts to restrict swearing may be ill-advised,** and we should take note of the positive and desirable effects of swearing.

- **It is incorrect to jump to the conclusion that swearing (cursing) inhibits communication.** In some circumstances it may, but in others it may even enhance communication.

Source

Jay, T. (2009), 'The Utility and Ubiquity of Taboo Words', *Perspectives on Psychological Science*, Vol. 4 No. 2 pp 153–61

References

Burrow, C. (2013), 'Frog's Knickers', *London Review of Books*, Vol. 35 No. 18 pp 25–7

Improbable Research Website (IR): http://www.improbable.com/ig/winners/

Jay, T. & Janschewitz, K. (2008), 'The pragmatics of swearing', *Journal of Politeness Research*, Vol. 4 Issue 2 pp 267–88

Jay, T. (2009a), 'The Utility and Ubiquity of Taboo Words', *Perspectives on Psychological Science*, Vol. 4 No. 2 pp 153–61

Jay, T. (2009b), 'Do Offensive Words Harm People?' *Psychology, Public Policy, and Law*, Vol. 15 No. 2 pp 81–101

Mohr, M. (2013), *Holy Sh*t: A Brief History of Swearing*. New York: OUP

Ofcom (2013), 'UK audience attitudes to the broadcast media', 7 May 2013

Pinker, S. (2007), *The Stuff of Thought*. London: Allen Lane

Rassin, E. & Muris, P. (2005), 'Why do women swear? An exploration of reasons for and perceived efficacy of swearing in Dutch female students', *Personality and Individual Differences*, Vol. 38 Issue 7 pp 1669–74

Scherer, C. R. & Sagarin, D. J. (2006), 'Indecent influence: The positive effects of obscenity on persuasion', *Social Influence*, Vol. 1 No. 2 pp 138–46

Stephens R., Atkins, J. & Kingston A. (2009), 'Swearing as a response to pain', *NeuroReport*, Vol. 20 Issue 12 pp 1056–60

Stephens, R. & Umland, C. (2011), 'Swearing as a response to pain – effect of daily swearing frequency', *Journal of Pain*, Vol. 12 Issue 12 pp 1274–81

Van Lancker, D. & Cummings, J. L. (1999), 'Expletives: Neurolinguistic and neurobehavioral perspectives on swearing', *Brain Research Reviews*, Vol. 31 pp 83–104

George Washington, Extract from the Orderly Book of the army under command of Washington, dated at Head Quarters, in the city of New York (3 August 1770); reported in *American Masonic Register and Literary Companion*, Vol. 1 (1829)

See also

Chapter 25 – Educational credentials and the racism of intelligence

Chapter 35 – Using big words doesn't make you look smarter

Chapter 38 – Online communication: why do people troll?

Further reading

Bayard, D. & Krishnayya, S. (2001), 'Gender, expletive use, and context: Male and female expletive use in structured and unstructured conversation among New Zealand university students', *Women and Language*, Vol. 24 pp 1–15

Pinker, S. (2007), *The Stuff of Thought: Language as a Window into Human Nature*. New York: Viking

Roger's Profanisaurus: The Magna Farta. (2010). *Viz*: Richard Dennis Publications

Van Lancker, D. & Cummings, J. L. (1999), 'Expletives: Neurolinguistic and neurobehavioral perspectives on swearing', *Brain Research Reviews*, Vol. 31 pp 83–104

LIST OF RESEARCH STUDIES

1. Mehrabian, A. (1971), *Silent Messages*. Belmont: Wadsworth
2. Hyde, J. S. (2005), 'The Gender Similarities Hypothesis', *American Psychologist*, Vol. 60 Issue 6 pp 581–92
3. Osborn, A. F. (1953), *Applied Imagination: Principles and Procedures of Creative Thinking*. New York: Charles Scribner's Sons
4. Halevy, R., Shalvi, S. & Verschuere, B. (2014), 'Being Honest About Dishonesty: Correlating Self-Reports and Actual Lying', *Human Communication Research*, Vol. 40 Issue 1 pp 54–72
5. Neter, E. & Ben-Shakhar, G. (1989), 'The Predictive Validity of Graphological Influences: A Meta-Analytic Approach', *Personality and Individual Differences*, Vol. 10 Issue 7 pp 737–45
6. Maslow, A. H. (1943), 'A Theory of Human Motivation', *Psychological Review*, Vol. 50 Issue 4 pp 370–96
7. Matthews, G., Roberts, R. D. & Zeidner, M. (2004), 'Seven myths about emotional intelligence', *Psychological Inquiry*, Vol. 15 No. 3 pp 179–96
8. Greenwald, A. G., Spangenberg, E. R., Pratkanis, A. R. & Eskenazi, J. (1991), 'Doubleblind tests of subliminal self-help audiotapes', *Psychological Science*, Vol. 2 No. 2 pp 119–22
9. Mehl, M. R., Vazire, S., Ramírez-Esparza, N., Slatcher, R. B. & Pennebaker, J. W. (2007), 'Are Women Really More Talkative Than Men?', *Science*, Vol. 317 (5834) p 82
10. Witkowski, T. (2010), 'Thirty-Five Years of Research on Neuro-Linguistic Programming. NLP Research Data Base. State of the Art or Pseudoscientific Decoration?', *Polish Psychological Bulletin*, Vol. 41 Issue 2 pp 58–66
11. Sihvonen R., Paavola M., Malmivaara A., Itälä A., Joukainen, A., Nurmi H., Kalske J., Järvinen T. L. & Finnish Degenerative Meniscal Lesion Study (FIDELITY) Group. (2013), 'Arthroscopic Partial Meniscectomy versus Sham Surgery for a Degenerative Meniscal Tear', *The New England Journal of Medicine*, Vol. 369 No. 26 pp 2515–24

12. Egan, G. (1986), *The Skilled Helper: A Systematic Approach to Effective Helping* (3rd ed.). Pacific Grove, CA: Brooks/Cole. Chapter Three: Attending and Listening

13. Rogers, C. R. & Farson, R. E., 'Active Listening' (1957). In Newman, R. G., Danziger, M. A. & Cohen, M. (Eds.) (1987), *Communicating in Business Today*. Washington, D.C.: Heath and Company

14. Tufte, E. (2006), *The Cognitive Style of PowerPoint: Pitching Out Corrupts Within* (2nd ed.). Connecticut: Graphics Press

15. Hall, E. T. (1968), 'Proxemics', *Current Anthropology*, Vol. 9 No. 2–3 pp 83–108

16. van Baaren, R. B., Holland, R. W., Steenaert, B. & van Knippenberg, A. (2003), 'Mimicry for money: Behavioural consequences of imitation', *Journal of Experimental Social Psychology*, Vol. 39 pp 393–8

17. Jackson, T. W., Dawson, R. & Wilson, D. (2002), 'Case Study: Evaluating the effect of email interruptions within the workplace. In: Conference on Empirical Assessment in Software Engineering (EASE), Keele University, pp 3–7

18. McElroy, J. C., Summers, J. K. & Moore, K. (2014), 'The effect of facial piercing on perceptions of job applicants', *Organizational Behavior and Human Decision Processes*, Vol. 125 Issue 1 pp 26–38

19. Weger, H., Castle, G. R., Emmett, M. C. (2010), 'Active Listening in Peer Interviews: The Influence of Message Paraphrasing on Perceptions of Listening Skills', *International Journal of Listening*, Vol. 24 Issue 1 pp 34–49

20. Asch, S. E. (1951), 'Effects of group pressure upon the modification and distortion of judgments'. In Guetzkow, H. (Ed.) (1951), *Groups, Leadership and Men*. Pittsburgh, PA: Carnegie Press

21. Milgram, S. (1963), 'Behavioral study of obedience', *The Journal of Abnormal and Social Psychology*, Vol. 67 Issue 4 pp 371–8

22. *Philip G. Zimbardo Papers* (1953–2004). [SC0750] Department of Special Collections and University Archives, Stanford University Libraries, Stanford, California http://searchworks.stanford.edu/view/6022627

23. Janis, I. L. (1971), 'Groupthink', *Psychology Today*, November, 43–6, 74–6

24. Forer, B. R. (1949), 'The Fallacy of Personal Validation: a Classroom Demonstration of Gullibility', *Journal of Abnormal and Social Psychology*, Vol. 44 Issue 1 pp 118–23

25. Talk given at a Colloquium of the MRAP, UNESCO, May 1978, published in Cahiers: Droit et liberté (Races, sociétés et aptitudes: apports et limites de la science) (1978), Vol. 382 pp 67–71. Reprinted in English in: Bourdieu, P. (1993), *Sociology in Question*. London: Sage

26. Hofstede, G. (1980), *Culture's Consequences: International Differences in Work-Related Values*. Beverly Hills: Sage Publications

27. Eades, D. (1996), 'Legal recognition of cultural differences in Communication: the case of Robyn Kina', *Language & Communication*, Vol. 16 Issue 3 pp 215–27

28. Nakane, I. (2006), 'Silence and politeness in intercultural communication in university seminars', *Journal of Pragmatics*, Vol. 38 Issue 11 pp 1811–35

29. Ekman, P. & Friesen, W. V. (1971), 'Constants Across Cultures in the Face and Emotion', *Journal of Personality and Social Psychology*, Vol. 17 Issue 2 pp 124–9

30. Plant, E. A., Devine, P. G., Cox, W. T., Columb, C., Miller, S. L., Goplen, J. & Peruche, B. M. (2009), 'The Obama effect: Decreasing implicit prejudice and stereotyping', *Journal of Experimental Social Psychology*, Vol. 45 pp 961–4

31. Jessen, S. & Grossmann, T. (2014), 'Unconscious discrimination of social cues from eye whites in infants', *Proceedings of the National Academy of Sciences of the United States of America*, Vol. 111, No. 45 pp 16208–13

32. McCabe, D. P. & Castel, A. D. (2008), 'Seeing is believing: The effect of brain images on judgments of scientific reasoning', *Cognition*, Vol. 107 Issue 1 pp 343–52

33. Sweller, J. (1988), 'Cognitive Load During Problem Solving: Effects on Learning', *Cognitive Science*, Vol. 12 Issue 2 pp 257–85

34. Kidd, D. C. & Castano, E. (2013), 'Reading Literary Fiction Improves Theory of Mind', *Science*, Vol. 342 No. 6156 pp 377–80

35. Oppenheimer, D. M. (2006), 'Consequences of Erudite Vernacular Utilized Irrespective of Necessity: Problems with Using Long Words Needlessly', *Applied Cognitive Psychology*, Vol. 20 Issue 2 pp 139–56

36. Lanaj, K., Johnson, R. E. & Barnes, C. M. (2014), 'Beginning the workday yet already depleted? Consequences of late-night smartphone use and sleep', *Organizational Behavior and Human Decision Processes*, Vol. 124 Issue 1 pp 11–23

37. Shen, J., Brdiczka, O. & Liu, J. (2015), 'A study of Facebook behavior: What does it tell about your Neuroticism and Extraversion?', *Computers in Human Behavior*, Vol. 45 pp 32–8

38. Buckels, E. E., Trapnell, P. D. & Paulhus, D. L. (2014), 'Trolls just want to have fun', *Personality & Individual Differences*, Vol. 67 pp 97–102

39. Fox, J. & Rooney, M. C. (2015), 'The Dark Triad and trait self-objectification as predictors of men's use and self-presentation behaviors on social networking sites', *Personality and Individual Differences*, Vol. 76 pp 161–5

40. Jay, T. (2009), 'The Utility and Ubiquity of Taboo Words', *Perspectives on Psychological Science*, Vol. 4 No. 2 pp 153–61

INDEX